There's More Leaves on the Tree

Charles Lee Bilberry

authorHOUSE®

AuthorHouse™
1663 Liberty Drive
Bloomington, IN 47403
www.authorhouse.com
Phone: 1-800-839-8640

First published by AuthorHouse 09/26/2011

ISBN: 978-1-4634-0465-9 (sc)
ISBN: 978-1-4634-0464-2 (ebk)

Library of Congress Control Number: 2011908650

Printed in the United States of America

Any people depicted in stock imagery provided by Thinkstock are models, and such images are being used for illustrative purposes only. Certain stock imagery © Thinkstock.

This book is printed on acid-free paper.

(L to R – Adell Bilberry with son, Charles Lee Bilberry, Peggie Joyce Bilberry, Mother Barbara Neal Bilberry with smallest daughter Jerry Joyce Bilberry [aka Fonda Deleon]; circa 1955-1956)

Contents

Dedication

This book is dedicated to my relatives of the past, present and future. It is my wish to remember the departed relatives with utmost fondness and love. I hope to document the past and the present so that future generations will be entertained as well as educated. I want to, especially thank my mother, Barbara Neal Brown-Bilberry who departed this life on July 19, 2009. She gave me life, raised me up in the ways of the Lord and instilled in my heart the value of an education.

I would ask those of the present, and especially those of the future to continue this work of love and dedication for all to enjoy. The past can never be recovered, but it can be preserved by those of us in the present and of the future. Hopefully, this book will allow all of us to remember those who have added to the history of this family, as well as create new histories with new families.

The family members we have lost are greatly missed; and those living, it is a blessing to know. It is my hope that this book becomes a legacy; and that each of the family members reading it will be proud and worthy of its legacy. My love goes out to all those relatives of yesterday, today, and tomorrow. May the Lord bless each and every one of us!

Acknowledgement

There are a number of people I would like to thank in numerous ways. First of all, I want to thank my wife Taryn, who stood by me through all of the research paths that sometime led to dead ends. She transcribed the interviews I had with relatives and extended relatives. Taryn was at my side for the last 10 years of family reunions. I could never have accomplished this book without her encouragement and assistance. I cannot forget my deceased Aunt Luemmer Horn who believed in the unity of the family and therefore became the founder of the Bilberry-Horn Family Reunion in 1982. I give special thanks to my Aunt Loeast Watkins, who gave me the video tape recording of my father Adell Bilberry and Uncle Johnny Bilberry's retirement party. I thank Barbra J. Bilberry of Baton Rouge, Louisiana for sharing with me over the years a plethora of historic knowledge about the family. Also, I thank Rev. Dr. Jesse B. Bilberry, Jr., of Baton Rouge, Louisiana for sharing with me his remembrance of the arguments his father Jesse B. Bilberry, Sr., and my grandfather Ladell Bilberry had over the interpretation of biblical scriptures. He is the oldest living grandchild of my great grandfather Frank Bilberry. I thank Charles Henry Bilberry, Jr., for the stories he shared with me of his visits as a child to his grandparents, Frank and Emma Bilberry's home. He is the second oldest living grandchild of Frank Bilberry. I thank Deborah Reliford, the daughter of Luemmer Bilberry-Horn for interviewing her 94-year-old father, Seab Horn so that his story could be shared in this book with the rest of the family and generations to come.

I thank my son Jared Bilberry of Las Vegas, Nevada, who at the age of 14 waited patiently in the waiting area of the National Archives in Washington, D.C., while I researched my family's history. I, especially thank Nancy Winans-Garrison of Oklahoma City, Oklahoma, who contributed photographs and shared stories of her grandfather and grandmother Fred and Rosa Billberry's migration from Union Parish, Louisiana to Oklahoma. I thank Sheila Rowland of Marion, Louisiana for sending to me photos and obituaries of her great grandmother and children Anna Bilberry-Holland, the sister of my great grandfather Frank Bilberry; it has helped me immensely. I thank Joyce Bilberry-Cofer, the great granddaughter Jordan Ellis Bilberry, who migrated with his family from Union Parish, Louisiana to Arkansas; the pictures and stories of her family helped tremendously.

Also, I want to thank Linda Evans, the granddaughter of Gordie Bilberry-Burch; the obituary collection and the genealogical research that she provided on some of the black family surnames in Union Parish is a treasure. I want to thank Lyndell Wesley for the software and the information she provided to me concerning Hannah Bilberry-Nelson and Branch Nelson. Special thanks are in order for Jessie Mae Bilberry, Leola Wayne, Lucy Nell Johnson, John Earl Ellis and Louie Morgan for opening their homes up to me for an interview. Their hospitality and kindness made the interviews a joy and a pleasure. More importantly, I want to thank God for blessing me along this tedious journey. During this research sometimes the roads got rocky and the hills seemed hard to climb, but God gave me the strength to press on.

There are others who have contributed in ways less tangible, but no less important. I owe a debt of gratitude to my parents who were both living at the start of this research, but have now answered the clarion call to come home to be with the Father. Like a relay race in the sport of track, our ancestors ran the race of life the best way they could, but have now passed the baton on to us. It is now our turn to handle the baton and run the race the best we can because one day we too must pass the baton. This poem by Dr. Benjamin E. Mays of Morehouse, the former president of Morehouse College said it best:

> *I have only just a minute.*
> *Only sixty seconds in it.*
>
> *Forced upon me, can't refuse it.*
> *Didn't seek it, didn't choose it.*
>
> *But it's up to me*
> *to use it.*
>
> *I must suffer if I lose it.*
>
> *Give account if I abuse it.*
> •
> *Just a tiny little minute*
> *but eternity is in it.*

Finally, special thanks to my Editing Consultant, Carrie C. Johnson of BookPubCo. net for using her extraordinary knowledge in organizing the contents, and editing this book for our families. Again, thank you to all who contributed over the years!

Preface

This book focuses on the Bilberry families and their extended families in Union, Parish, Louisiana. While perusing this book you will find that the Bilberry or Billberry surname is related to many other families such as the Bridges, Benson, Ellis, Burch, Montgomery, Morgan, Honeycutt, Douglas, Roberts, Andrews, Henderson, Wayne, Archie, Armstrong, Finley, Holland, Nelson and Horn. If your ancestry includes any of these names, it's possible that you may be my paternal cousin. Also, there are variations of the surnames.

My great grandmother Emma Roberts-Bilberry would often say to her grandsons, "Boy, that's your cousin," when they would disclose to her their affection about a certain young lady in their life. It may sound far-fetched, but if you go back far enough, then you may find out that we are all cousins. Mathematically, most of us have two parents, four grandparents, eight great-grandparents, and so forth. By the time you're back ten generations, you've got 1,024 ancestors. According to an article titled "Genealogy in the Era of Genomics," Susanna C. Manrubia, Bernard Derrida and Damian H. Zanette, stated that, "In a population of 1,000 people who choose their mates randomly, 10 generations are normally enough to guarantee that any two people have some ancestor in common."

While researching my family's history, I found that there were more branches and leaves that fit on the Bilberry family tree than I originally imagined. In many cases I have included material contained in historical documents, death certificates, marriage license and obituaries. Some of the spelling and grammar in this book was left in its original state. The purpose of including this material is to support information I have provided as well as to familiarize the reader with observations from another era.

Many family histories are being lost because the leaves are falling and there is no one to tell the stories of the past. The Bible says that when Moses died the people mourned his loss. They asked among themselves: "Who will tell the story?" Later in biblical history a man name Joshua stood and said, "As for me and my house, we will serve the Lord." It is my hope that the narrative, interviews, biographies and appendices in this book will tell the story of the Bilberry's early years in Union Parish of Louisiana.

Usually the transmission of family knowledge is passed onto succeeding generations by the parents or grandparents. They are the keepers of the family story. If our parents or grandparents did not tell the story, we would lose our connection with our past. The seniors of our families can tell the whole story. Most of them have sojourned a full length of life experiences. They have made the foolish mistakes of youth, meandered the maze of marriage, faced sickness, shouldered the burden of death of loved ones, and endured hardships, all while surfing the sea of life in their golden years. The seniors of every family have a full story to tell.

Today's microwave mom cannot fully appreciate her microwave family unless she knows how far God has brought the family. When the story is told she'll soon learn that there weren't always microwaves, but there was a time when the family cooked on cast iron stoves, heated by freshly chopped wood. If she listens as the story is told, she will learn that there was a time when we didn't "shake and bake." But it was a time when she would "cook and wake" her family to a table of 15 minute grits, homemade biscuits soaked in freshly cured butter, fresh hen house eggs and cured bacon straight from the smoke house. When the family prayed over breakfast, there was no doubt that God made it all happen. The women of the family learned they were part of a long line of Christian women who remained faithful to their husbands and families and even pursued careers with success in proportion to their trust in God. That's what she will learn when the story is told.

When dad drives away in his shiny new car, he won't appreciate it fully until he knows how God has really blessed the family. When he begin to understand that God has moved the family from hitching up the mules to the wagon to loading everybody into Cadillacs, Lincolns, Toyotas, Fords and Chevrolets then he will better appreciate the work of God in his family. If he endures hard times and trouble in the world, he will gain faith in knowing that the men of the family have survived slavery, depressions, race discrimination and deprivation, with the help of God. That's what he will learn when the story is told.

The challenge of every family facing the death of a patriarch or matriarch, who was the strong one for many years, is to answer the question: "Who will tell the story?" Who will rise to be sure that if they trust in the Lord, He will bless them? Who will champion justice and speak against sinfulness in the family with strength of conviction that will both inspire faith and discourage wrong doing? Who will tell the story?

Introduction of Heritage and Generations

Initially, I perceived my research as being a direct path that would take me back to my family's origin in Africa. I had a burning desire to put my finger on the exact place where the slave traders apprehended my ancestors. I have been researching my relatives' family history since 1996 and it has opened my eyes to the doors that are being closed as family members depart this life. I learned while researching that the journey back in time was full of frustrations, pauses, disruptions and distractions. I often paused and pondered over the significance of my research. I was questioned by others and sometimes I even questioned myself as to why I continue searching!

While researching your family's history, in some strange mystical way it will take you back in time. But as you immerse from the depth of your research you come back wanting to go back for more research and more study. That is what this research has done to me. As I continued to research over the years, somehow I seemed to have developed a deep connection with family members that I never met. In some unknown way, I felt I had at least a spiritual connection with them even though I was not familiar with their character or the personality that made them who they were.

There were times in my research I only knew a person's name and sometimes their place of birth or perhaps where they died. Eventually, I would accumulate enough information where I could speak comfortably about people who are more and more being lost in the sand of time. I had developed a researcher's relationship with them by my persistence and perseverance of knowing who they are; or had been! I found myself with the ability to connect my ancestors in an orderly fashion and develop an impressive pedigree chart. I knew who followed who in the lineage and where they branched off. Yet, pedigree charts and family trees did not do justice to the research. There seemed to be something missing. There seemed to be a story that needed to be told!

My research did not occur without some challenges. In this book, I have not attempted to include an all-inclusive genealogy of the Bilberrys, who resided in Union Parish, Louisiana. One purpose was to reveal the relationship between the slave master and the slave women in my family that resulted in light-skinned or fair-skinned children who were later classified as mulatto. This being said, no way implies that all black Bilberrys of Union Parish, Louisiana were of fair complexion. Many slave women, who birth mulatto children by the white slave master, later married and birth children by black men. The other purpose was to include a collection of photographs, death certificates, marriage licenses, obituaries and other documents to support the research and to show other extended families of the Bilberrys.

Every effort has been taken to ensure the correctness of the material offered in these succeeding pages. Valid information concerning black families was often difficult to obtain or it may appeared to be vague or contradictory. As a result, errors will inevitably surface. There were inconsistencies in the spelling of names, ages and grammatical irregularities. When this occurred, the author used the original source material in his writing. Regardless of these special problems, I sensed a need to document materials on the families in this book. It is hoped that families and friends will share additional data as the history of the Bilberry family continues to evolve.

I have spent 14 years exploring the genealogy of the Bilberrys and their relatives in Union Parish, Louisiana. I immersed myself in the National Archives in Washington, D.C.; The Louisiana State Archives; Union Parish, Louisiana courthouse records and several local cemeteries. The African-American Bilberrys of Union Parish was a somewhat confusing, but an amazing genealogy. It tells a story of extraordinary people who strived to bring themselves out of a life of servitude and poverty in order to find their niche in the mainstream of America.

Also, the genealogy and stories give us an understanding of the fate of the white Bilberrys, who saw the decline and fall of the 'Old South'. The loss of the Civil War and the emancipation proclamation had politically, economically and socially left its mark on many white families. But underneath the surface of both black and white Bilberrys lies another story. It is not a story of hate, horror or bitterness, but one of redemption and reconciliation. I firmly believe that in order to heal the wounds and hurts of the past, you must embrace those things in the future, and that's what it takes to make us a healthy family. Three charts showing the heritage and generations of the Bilberrys' will follow this introduction:

Charles Lee Bilberry's Pedigree Chart

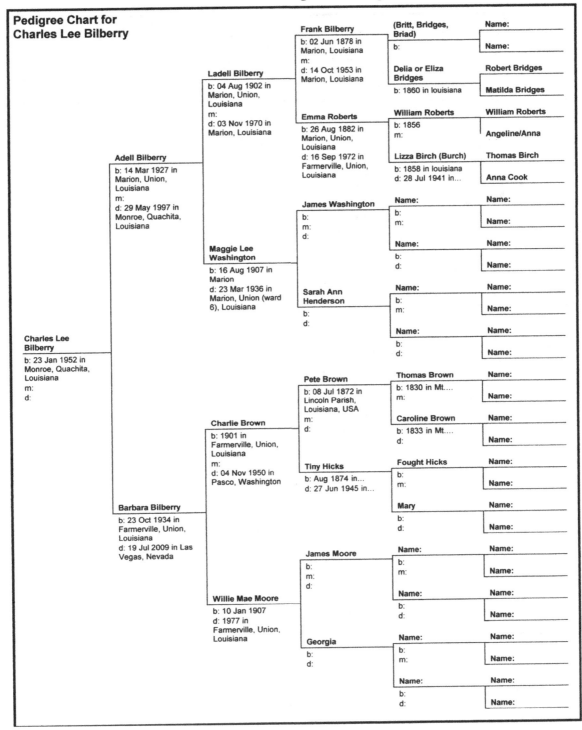

Pedigree Chart for Charles Lee Bilberry

Frank Bilberry
b: 02 Jun 1878 in Marion, Louisiana
m:
d: 14 Oct 1953 in Marion, Louisiana

(Britt, Bridges, Briad)
b:

Name:

Name:

Delia or Eliza Bridges
b: 1860 in louisiana

Robert Bridges

Matilda Bridges

Ladell Bilberry
b: 04 Aug 1902 in Marion, Union, Louisiana
m:
d: 03 Nov 1970 in Marion, Louisiana

Emma Roberts
b: 26 Aug 1882 in Marion, Union, Louisiana
d: 16 Sep 1972 in Farmerville, Union, Louisiana

William Roberts
b: 1856
m:

William Roberts

Angeline/Anna

Lizza Birch (Burch)
b: 1858 in louisiana
d: 28 Jul 1941 in...

Thomas Birch

Anna Cook

Adell Bilberry
b: 14 Mar 1927 in Marion, Union, Louisiana
m:
d: 29 May 1997 in Monroe, Quachita, Louisiana

James Washington
b:
m:
d:

Name:
b:
m:

Name:

Name:

Name:
b:
d:

Name:

Maggie Lee Washington
b: 16 Aug 1907 in Marion
d: 23 Mar 1936 in Marion, Union (ward 6), Louisiana

Sarah Ann Henderson
b:
d:

Name:
b:
m:

Name:

Name:

Name:
b:
d:

Name:

Charles Lee Bilberry
b: 23 Jan 1952 in Monroe, Quachita, Louisiana
m:
d:

Pete Brown
b: 08 Jul 1872 in Lincoln Parish, Louisiana, USA
m:
d:

Thomas Brown
b: 1830 in Mt....
m:

Name:

Name:

Caroline Brown
b: 1833 in Mt....
d:

Name:

Name:

Charlie Brown
b: 1901 in Farmerville, Union, Louisiana
m:
d: 04 Nov 1950 in Pasco, Washington

Tiny Hicks
b: Aug 1874 in...
d: 27 Jun 1945 in...

Fought Hicks
b:
m:

Name:

Name:

Mary
b:
d:

Name:

Name:

Barbara Bilberry
b: 23 Oct 1934 in Farmerville, Union, Louisiana
d: 19 Jul 2009 in Las Vegas, Nevada

James Moore
b:
m:
d:

Name:
b:
m:

Name:

Name:

Name:
b:
d:

Name:

Willie Mae Moore
b: 10 Jan 1907
d: 1977 in Farmerville, Union, Louisiana

Georgia
b:
d:

Name:
b:
m:

Name:

Name:

Name:
b:
d:

Name:

Frank Bilberry's Family Group

Family Group Sheet for Frank Bilberry

Husband:	Frank Bilberry	
Birth:	02 Jun 1878 in Marion, Louisiana	
Death:	14 Oct 1953 in Marion, Louisiana	
Father:	(Britt, Bridges, Briad)	
Mother:	Delia or Eliza Bridges	
Wife:	Emma Roberts	
Birth:	26 Aug 1882 in Marion, Union, Louisiana	
Death:	16 Sep 1972 in Farmerville, Union, Louisiana	
Father:	William Roberts	
Mother:	Lizza Birch (Burch)	
Children:		
1	Name:	Willie Frank Bilberry
M	Birth:	Jun 1901 in Marion, Union, Louisiana
	Death:	14 Jul 1940 in Farmerville, Louisiana
	Marriage:	20 Jan 1936
	Spouse:	Lettie Warren Archie
2	Name:	Ladell Bilberry
M	Birth:	04 Aug 1902 in Marion, Union, Louisiana
	Death:	03 Nov 1970 in Marion, Louisiana
	Spouse:	Corene McGough
	Other Spouses:	Maggie Lee Washington
3	Name:	Eddie (uncle Son) Bilberry
M	Birth:	20 Mar 1913 in Marion, Louisiana
	Death:	31 Mar 1997 in Monroe, Louisiana
	Marriage:	08 Nov 1941 in Farmerville, Louisiana
	Spouse:	Georgia Willie Mae (aunt Sally) Benson
4	Name:	Jesse Bernard Bilberry Sr.
M	Birth:	20 Jul 1904 in Marion, Union, Louisiana, United States
	Death:	19 Feb 1961 in Farmerville, Louisiana
	Spouse:	Joe B. Dixson
5	Name:	Charlie Henry (Bud) Bilberry
M	Birth:	27 Apr 1906 in Marion, Louisiana
	Death:	07 Nov 1979 in Flint, Michigan
	Spouse:	Dellie Dixson
6	Name:	Mary Bilberry
F	Birth:	01 Nov 1910 in Marion, Louisiana
	Death:	21 Aug 1956 in Farmerville, Louisiana
	Spouse:	Jethro Horn

Three Generations of Frank Bilberry's Descendants

Outline Descendant Report for Frank Bilberry

..... 1   Frank Bilberry b: 02 Jun 1878 in Marion, Louisiana, d: 14 Oct 1953 in Marion, Louisiana
.... 2   Willie Frank Bilberry b: Jun 1901 in Marion, Union, Louisiana, d: 14 Jul 1940 in Farmerville, Louisiana
.... 2   Ladell Bilberry Sr. b: 04 Aug 1902 in Marion, Union, Louisiana, d: 03 Nov 1970 in Marion, Louisiana
.... 3   Luemmer Bilberry b: 05 Dec 1924 in Conway, Union, Louisiana, d: 16 Mar 1989 in Provencal, Natchitoches, Louisiana, USA
.... 3   George Willie Bilberry b: 24 Mar 1926 in Conway, Union Parish, Louisiana, d: 27 Apr 1926 in Conway, Louisiana
.... 3   Adell Bilberry b: 14 Mar 1927 in Conway, Union Parish, Louisiana, d: 28 Apr 1997 in Monroe, Louisiana
.... 3   Clyde Bilberry b: 03 Dec 1928 in Conway, Union Parish, Louisiana, d: 05 Jul 1991 in Conway, Union Parish, Louisiana
.... 3   Sarah Bilberry b: 23 Feb 1930 in Conway, Union Parish, Louisiana, d: Nov 1980 in West Monroe, Louisiana
.... 3   Booker T. Bilberry b: Oct 1930 in Conway, Union Parish, Louisiana, d: Sep 1976 in Farmerville, Union, Louisiana
.... 3   Johnny Bilberry b: 27 Dec 1933 in Conway, Union Parish, Louisiana, d: 24 Nov 2003 in Farmerville, Louisiana
.... 3   Joseph Bilberry b: 21 Mar 1936 in Conway, Union, Louisiana, d: 06 Jul 1936 in Farmerville, Union, Louisiana
.... 3   Loeast Bilberry b: 10 Sep 1937 in Marion, Union, Louisiana
.... 3   Clare Bilberry b: 24 Sep 1941 in Marion, Union, Louisiana
.... 3   Clarence Bilberry b: 18 Apr 1943 in Marion, Union, Louisiana, d: 22 Nov 2004 in Kansas City, Missouri
.... 3   Herbert Bilberry b: 24 Jan 1945 in Marion, Union, Louisiana
.... 3   Ladell Bilberry Jr. b: 31 Mar 1947 in Marion, Union, Louisiana
.... 3   Emma Jean Bilberry b: 31 Aug 1949 in Marion, Union, Louisiana
.... 3   Richard Bilberry b: 27 Apr 1954 in Marion, Union, Louisiana
.... 3   Loreace Bilberry b: 02 Dec 1938 in Marion, Union, Louisiana
.... 2   Jesse Bernard Bilberry Sr. b: 20 Jul 1904 in Marion, Union, Louisiana, United States, d: 19 Feb 1961 in Farmerville, Louisiana
.... 3   Jesse Bernard Bilberry Jr. b: 12 May 1929
.... 3   Johnny Bernard Bilberry b: 10 May 1932, d: 02 Jan 1984
.... 3   Frankie Lee Bilberry b: 04 Mar 1934
.... 3   Lelia Ruth Bilberry b: 20 Aug 1936
.... 3   Ralph Waldo Emerson Jones Bilberry b: 14 Mar 1939
.... 3   Barbra Jean Bilberry b: 18 Mar 1942
.... 3   Joe Frederick Bilberry b: 26 Jun 1944
.... 3   Charles Lane Bilberry b: 11 Sep 1946
.... 3   Elaine Bilberry b: 11 Sep 1946
.... 3   Edward Landon Bilberry b: 02 Feb 1949, d: 06 Apr 2000
.... 2   Charlie Henry (Bud) Bilberry b: 27 Apr 1906 in Marion, Louisiana, d: 07 Nov 1979 in Flint, Michigan
.... 3   Charlie Henry Bilberry Jr. b: 20 May 1929 in Farmerville, La., d: A
.... 2   Mary Bilberry b: 01 Nov 1910 in Marion, Louisiana, d: 21 Aug 1956 in Farmerville, Louisiana
.... 2   Eddie (uncle Son) Bilberry b: 20 Mar 1913 in Marion, Louisiana, d: 31 Mar 1997 in Monroe, Louisiana
.... 3   Eddye L. Bilberry-Washington b: 02 Oct 1942 in Monroe, Louisiana, USA
.... 3   John W. Bilberry b: 12 Nov 1954 in Monroe, Louisiana
.... 3   Donald R. Bilberry b: 29 May 1960 in Monroe, Louisiana, USA, d: Dec 2010 in Monroe, Louisiana
.... 3   Eddie W. Bilberry b: 18 Apr 1957 in Monroe, Louisiana, USA

CHAPTER ONE

Brief History of Union Parish

Union Parish, located in the north center part of Louisiana, was established on March 13, 1839, from a portion of Ouachita Parish by an act of the legislature to create a new judicial district. It derived its name from the sentiment of the time—"liberty and union, now and forever, one and inseparable" (from a speech by Daniel Webster).

The 1860, population census shows that persons born in Louisiana were outnumbered by settlers who came from other states during the early and mid-1800. For the most part, the new arrivals were farmers, who soon discovered that the land was suitable for growing a variety of crops, such as cotton, potatoes, beans, peas, and sugar cane. From its beginning, Union Parish has remained a cotton parish. Cows, cattle, wild horses, swine, and sheep for wool were in abundance.

Natural gas, lumbering, and manufacturing of wood products have contributed to the economy of the parish for many decades; these natural resources account today for a major portion of the monetary worth of the parish, including other agricultural sources. Also, Union Parish is a center for growing and distributing watermelons. The Farmerville, Louisiana Jaycees in 1963, founded the Louisiana Watermelon Festival, which is held in Farmerville, Louisiana.

Farmerville, the parish seat, was named after a prominent family of the area. William Wood Farmer, who served as lieutenant governor from 1852 to 1853; he died in New Orleans of yellow-fever on October 29, 1854. His remains were moved to the Farmerville Cemetery on January 15, 1855.[1]

John Honeycutt, Sr., arrived in the Ouachita Valley region with his family between 1790 and 1795, which was the earliest permanent European settlement and now known as Union Parish. He obtained the first known Spanish land grant for property that later fell into Union Parish. Honeycutt's land lay along Bayou D'Arbonne Lake. On October 14, 1797, he sold his land to Zadoc Harman, a man of African descent, who had formerly lived in North Carolina (Ouachita Parish Conveyance Book Z, Folio 46, Deed 68. Also see, Ouachita Parish Deeds, John Hunnicut [sic] in chapter ten. Although, the specific location of the land that the Spain granted to Honeycutt is unknown, it was probably near the property that his son John Honeycutt, Jr., purchased from the United States government

1

in 1826, when it finally opened the first land office in Monroe, Louisiana. John Honeycutt, Jr., was among the very first purchasers to appear at the Ouachita Land Office in Monroe that year; he bought 80 acres (320,000 m²) near Bayou D'Arbonne Lake in present-day Union Parish, located just a mile below the present-day Lake D'Arbonne Dam.[2]

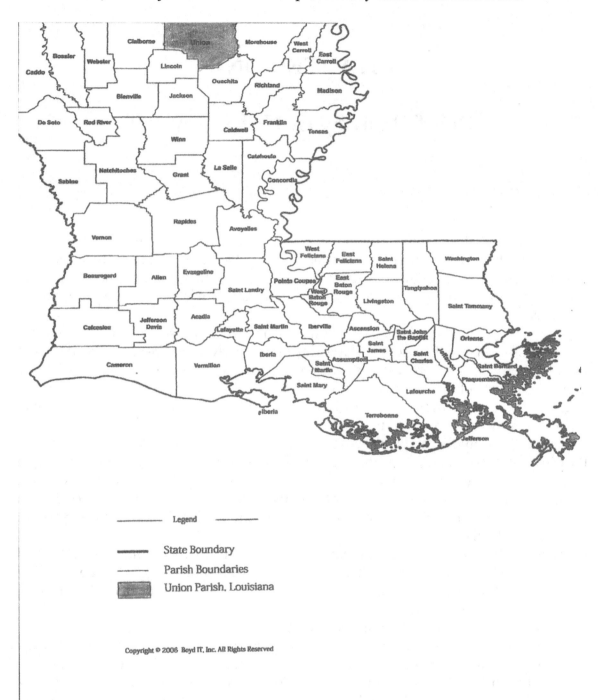

State of Louisiana Map
(Permission given by "Arphax Publishing Company")

Farmerville, Louisiana Annual Watermelon Festival

Lake D'Arbonne State Park Entrance
Courtesy of Taryn D. Bilberry, July 2010

Lake D'Arbonne State Park fishing pier
Courtesy of Taryn D. Bilberry, July 2010

CHAPTER TWO

My Visit to the Old Home Place

We headed south on the lonely Sweet Lilly Road. Uncle Johnny and I had just left the Sweet Lilly Baptist Church Cemetery located about eight miles southwest of Marion, Louisiana. We went there to visit my father's gravesite and to see the new headstone that my younger sister Fonda (aka Jerry Joyce Bilberry) had purchased. We both had agreed that the workers did an excellent job installing it. There aren't any houses in the area where the church is located. The nearby open fields that seemed to go on forever during my youth have now grown into a thick pine forest.

The pavement finally ran out as we bumped along creating a tail wind of dust on the rutted gravel road. We got to another dirt road that had a street sign that said Burch Road. The area seemed familiar; as I remembered my father, Adell Bilberry and mother, Barbara Neal Brown married and lived at the corner of Burch Road and the road that led to my grandfather's place. My older sister Peggie and I were their children at this home. As we continued down the old road, it reminded me of my mother saying that she never liked living back here in the woods. She was 18 years old and had enough of the farm life. Later, when I became an adult, she disclosed to me her secret of escaping the country style of living. There was an old bell that dangled outside of their house that the families could ring in case of emergency. One day my mother rang the bell as loud as she could to alert someone that she had an emergency. My father's sister, Aunt Loeast, came running from my grandfather's farm, which was about a quarter of a mile away to find my mother terrified. My mother said, "I saw a 'haint' (a Southern slang term for haunt; it also means ghost) near my baby boy." Aunt Loeast perused the house, but did not find anything that appeared ghostly to her. She calmed my mother down and went back to my grandfather's house and informed the family of what had happened. Relatives that knew my mother felt she had lost her mind. Many family members believed that she was following in her own mother's footsteps. My mother's mother was sent to the state psychiatric hospital for attempting to take her life with a butcher knife, but back then it was called an "insane asylum", located in Pineville, Louisiana. Her mother was incarcerated there for 23 years. I remember my family going to visit her in the early 1960's. My mother was always excited to go and see her. My father had only a few visits with her in the past and he was equally excited. His mother-in-law was almost a stranger to him. After completing the necessary paperwork for visitors, my father pulled his car up to the hospital; we were led to a courtyard where we sat down at one of the gazebos and waited for her to come out. A nurse escorted her out where I observed a bag in her hand and expressions of joy on her face.

"How ya'll doing," the nurse said to us as we stood up to greet them. "Willie Mae, your daughter, her husband and kids are here to see you. I'm going to leave you here with them and I'll come back in a little bit to see how ya'll are doing okay." As the nurse turned away to leave, my mother with tears bubbling from her eyes immediately gave Big Mama a long awaited hug and kissed on her cheek. She really missed her mother. Big Mama was the name my mother taught us to call her. She was the only parent left to raise my mother and her four brothers after her husband Charlie Brown left them when they were small children. Some have said that while working as a carpenter on one of the chemical plants in Sterlington, Louisiana, he accidently killed a white man who was harassing him because he was jealous of his craftsman skills as a carpenter. He left the state, moved to Pasco, Washington where he lived for the rest of his life. My mother had to be raised by her grandparent, aunts and uncles on her father's side. It wasn't easy for her and her four brothers. They were passed around from grandparents, uncles to aunts like a new toy that had gotten old; eventually you don't want it anymore. My mother didn't finish high school. She went as far as the eighth grade. She met my father, who only went as far as the fifth grade himself, but more importantly, she liked him and he had a job. They decided to be husband and wife and married in 1951.

"Hello son," Big Mama said to my father as they both hugged each other with gladness. "You 'chull'uns' have sure grown up" as she reached down, hugged and kissed us one by one. She sat down at the gazebo and carried on a normal conversation. She acted very normal except for the times where she would look with quietness into the distance when there were pauses in the conversation. "What do you have in the bag mama, my mother politely ask her mother?" She replied while reaching in the bag revealing her gifts, "Oh just a few little things I made for you and the 'chull'uns'. This is for you girls!" It was a handmade Raggedy Ann doll she had made herself. "And this is for you," as she handed over to me a monkey made from a pair of thick gray socks. "And this is for you son," speaking to my mother and father. It was several beautiful crocheted doilies used as mats for placing on furniture. We were there for about two hours and our time had ended. My mother hated to depart because she knew it would be at least another year or two before she would make the 130 mile drive back to Pineville, Louisiana. On our way back to Marion, Louisiana, she would talk with my father about her brief years with her mother.

It really hurt her to see Big Mama in the sanitarium. She had been admitted there by her uncles' as being suicidal, but no one attempted to get her out when she got better. As we continue to drive through the piney hills of North Louisiana, my mother vowed to get her out of that place. Around the year 1965, she made good on that vow. Big Mama was released to go and live a normal life, with normal people in a normal place. Her brother-in-law, Shelton Brown built a small home behind his house in Farmerville, Louisiana for her to live in. People were still skeptical about her new sanity. Some of her relatives even gave her a new name. They called her aunt "Two Way," meaning that she has two sides to her personality, sane and insane. My mother despised the names they called her mom. She remained kind, but would kindly ask that they would not address her mother that way. Big

Mama was self-supporting and lived by herself. She was later moved to a nursing home in Farmerville, Louisiana where she died in 1977, of complication from diabetes.

I had flashback moments of my youth as we drove further into the thick pine and oak lined road; the tree branches began to reach out and touch the body of Uncle Johnny's black 1987 Dodge Ram pickup truck; the branches left their scratch marks in the thick dust that covered it. "They've cut some timber on Papa Frank's old place," he remarked as though some special landmark had been removed. Papa Frank was the old patriarch of my family. He was born in 1878 in the Ward Six area of Union Parish and was a man of mulatto complexion, much like many of the Bilberrys in my family.

According to oral testimonies from family members, his father was a white man that lived in the area as well. He had many sisters, half-sisters, brothers and half-brothers. Some of his sisters and brothers were sired by the same white father and some by a black man. Frank Bilberry married Emma Roberts on September 2, 1900.[3] They had six children from this union, Willie Frank, Ladell, Jesse Bernard, Charlie, Mary and Eddie. He purchased 120 acres of land from Otis L. Tugwell on January 17, 1918. [4]

Frank Bilberry and Emma Bilberry on their 50th wedding anniversary with children; L to R – Mary Bilberry, Ladell Bilberry, Sr., Frank Bilberry, Emma Bilberry, Eddie Bilberry, Sr., Jesse B. Bilberry, Sr., and Charles Henry Bilberry, Sr., (inset) circa 1950. Note: Frank and Emma Bilberry's oldest son Willie Frank died in 1940.

Courtesy of Georgia Willie Mae Bilberry and Charles Henry Bilberry, Jr.

State of Louisiana- Parish of Union.

BE IT KNOWN, That this day, before me Emmett J. Lee- - - - - - - - -
Clerk and Ex-Officio Recorder and Notary Public in and for said Parish,
duly commissioned and sworn, came and appeared Otis L. Tugwell, a
married man, having been once married, whose wife is Mrs. Ossie Tugwell
(nee Clark) who is living with him undivorced,

a resident of Union Parish, La., who declared that he- - - - - does
by these presents grant, bargain, sell, convey and deliver, with full
guarantee of title, and with complete transfer and subrogation of all
rights and actions of warranty against all former proprietors of the
property herein conveyed unto Frank Billberry, a married man, having
been once married, whose wife is Mrs. Emma Billberry (nee Roberts) who
is living with him undivorced,

the following described property situated in   Union   Parish, La.,
to-wit:

The SE¼ of NE¼ and the E½ of SE¼ Section 28 in Township 22 North,
Range One (1) East, Louisiana Meridian, containing 120 acres more or
less, with all improvements situated thereon and thereunto belonging,
less and except all oil, gas, coal and all other mineral rights thereon
which rights are hereby expressly reserved to this vender.

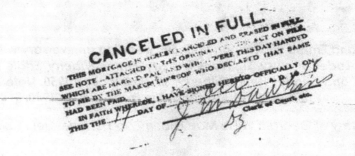

CANCELED IN FULL

THIS MORTGAGE IS HEREBY CANCELED AND ERASED IN FULL
SEE NOTE ATTACHED PAID AND WITH THE ACT ON FILE
WHICH ARE MARKED PAID AND WERE THIS DAY HANDED
TO ME BY THE MAKER HEREOF WHO DECLARED THAT SAME
HAD BEEN PAID.
IN FAITH WHEREOF, I HAVE SIGNED HERETO OFFICIALLY ON
THIS THE 17 DAY OF   A.D. 19 56
                                        Clerk of Court, etc.

*Frank Bilberry purchase 120 acres of land from Otis Tugwell in Ward Six between Marion,
Louisiana and Conway, Louisiana*

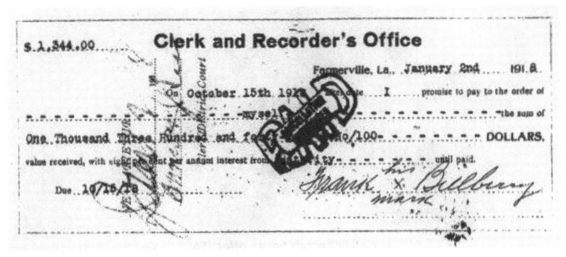

Frank Bilberry recorded receipt for land purchased for $1344.00 from Otis Tugwell

His older sons Jesse B. Bilberry, Sr., and Ladell Bilberry, Sr., later bought land adjacent to their father as they became adults.

We got out of the truck and I could see faint traces of foot tracks that led off the dirt road into the woods. Uncle Johnny stepped from the edge of the road into the tree laden forest and began to elbow himself sideways through underbrush and grass. I followed along with anticipation of what it was that he was seeking.

He confirmed: "This is dad's old place he said. This is where the property begins as he pointed to a recently planted wood stake survey marker in the ground. "I wanted you to know where the property line was; just in case I'm not around anymore." Uncle Johnny had taken over the duty of paying the taxes on the property from my father Adell Bilberry since his death from lung carcinoma in 1997. My father and his other brothers and sisters had agreed to periodically have timber cut from the 20 acre parcel in order to pay the yearly taxes on it. These are pictures of Ladell Bilberry's last homes.

Ladell Bilberry's old home prior to 1965

Ladell Bilberry's home after 1965
Courtesy of Loeast Watkins Courtesy of Loeast Watkins

I could see in the distance a structure silhouetted among the dark forest among the trees, bushes, and branches. It was something made from human hands. An old porch poked out from the front of the structure. Uncle Johnny pressed his way through the dense underbrush, warning me of snakes as he continued toward the structure. He was always afraid of snakes. D'Arbonne Lake in Farmerville, Louisiana was his favorite fishing waters. However, if the snakes were in abundance at his favorite fishing spot, he would leave and find another fishing spot regardless of how good the fish were biting. We made our way past a thick briar patched area; and immediately the structure was upon us. It was my grandfather's, Ladell Bilberry's last home before he died in 1970. Uncle Johnny was next to the last child of eight children my grandfather had with his first wife Maggie Washington. They had married on January 24, 1924.[5]

He was 21 and she was 19. Their first child George Willie Bilberry died soon after birth, living only one month and three days. My father Adell Bilberry told me years ago that his mother loved to fish. She loved to take her favorite cane fishing pole with her and fish the D'Loutre River and its tributaries near her home. It was a great place to go fishing and it was within walking distance. However, in March of 1936, where the coldness of winter began to give way to showers of the spring, she became sick after giving birth to their son Joseph. She died after his birth at the age of 28 years old.[6] My grandfather now had seven children that he had to raise himself. His children Luemmer, Adell, Clyde, Sarah, Booker T., Johnny and Joseph were too young to do for themselves. Joseph was later raised by his grandfather and grandmother, Frank and Emma Bilberry. The economic situation of the Great Depression made things even harder for him. He was a farmer and an active church member at Sweet Lilly Primitive Baptist Church, where he was the church clerk, a position he held for 10 years. During the earlier years, Sweet Lilly was the black Bilberry's family church. Numerous other families and extended families attended there as well. The church was organized from the Liberty Hill Primitive Baptist Church (White) under the supervision of Elder Henry Brooks, Deacon Enoch Albrittion, and Deacon King Simms. Joe Benson, Sr., (Black) sold two acres of land to construct the church in 1905. [7]

In 1881, the church chose its first pastor, Elder Mason Charles; Deacons: Elisha Smith, Joe Benson; clerk, Sumly McGee. Elder Mason Charles served until 1884, after which Elder R. W. Thrower was called as pastor and served there until his death in 1936, a total of 52 years. Under his administration, Sumly McGee, Normia McGee, Anderson Benson and Frank Bilberry were ordained as deacons and Monroe Finley as clerk. [8]

In 1936, Elder Minor Thrower was called to the church as pastor and served until his death in 1942. Under his administration, two ministers were ordained, Elder Jesse Bernard Bilberry, Sr., and his brother Ladell Bilberry. After the death of Elder Minor Thrower, Elder Jesse Bernard Bilberry, Sr., was chosen as pastor and served until 1947. He resigned and Elder L. R. Thrower from El Dorado, Arkansas was chosen as pastor. Under Jesse Bernard Bilberry's administration, Lee Roberts, David Benson, and John Evans were ordained as deacons. Joe Benson was made clerk. Elder L. R. Thrower served as pastor until 1950. In 1950, Elder B. J. Hayes was chosen as pastor and served until his death. Elder L.V. Thrower was called as pastor. Under his administration, Johnny Bilberry, George Tate, and Almer Roberts were ordained as deacons and Johnnie Thompson was elected church clerk. Edna Nabors was elected as assistant clerk, and Sarah Ellis was elected as church treasurer.[9]

On October 3, 1936, Ladell Bilberry united in wedlock with the lovely Corene McGough.[10] He was 34 years old and she was 22. Corene was from the Antioch Community near Truxno, Louisiana. Her father George McGough, Sr., was deceased, but her mother Cornelia was willing to let her go to become one with her new found love. I remember her as being very soft spoken and a nice grandmother. We called her, "Mother Corene." Together they had eight children, Loeast, Loreace, Clare, Clarence, Herbert, Ladell, Jr., Emma, and Richard. Grandpa Ladell became pastor of the Antioch Primitive Baptist Church in Provencal, Louisiana (near Natchitoches, Louisiana) around 1953. This church was over 100 miles away from his home; but that was the way it was in the Primitive Baptist denomination where churches were scattered and preachers were few. The few did a lot of traveling; and many of those churches that had to share the traveling preachers met only once a month, sometimes called "once-a-month-churches." The main reason for meeting only once a month was because "that's how it's always been." Tradition dies hard with the Primitive Baptists; perhaps that's why they call themselves "hard-shells."

Preachers traveled, not by car or plane, but by horseback, wagon, or walking—often very long distances. When these road-weary servants reached their appointed destination, they boarded with members of the church. Otherwise, the preacher slept wherever he could. A closely related reason is that Primitive Baptists are very careful to maintain their differences from other Baptists. Most hard shells Baptist (as they are sometime called) don't celebrate those things that they have in common with other churches. Instead, they go to great lengths to emphasize differences. Major uproars are caused when it's even hinted at that someone may start a Sunday morning Bible study (don't dare call it a Sunday school class!), or that communion might take place without foot washing, or that a church might support a missionary. To meet every weekend would be too much of a move toward other Baptists. But, now those churches have dwindled, and most of the pastors and preachers have died (and not been replaced). Is it time for a change? Probably not because they've been doing it this way for decades! Why change now? [11]

Sweet Lilly Primitive Baptist Church; Photo Taken July 2010
Courtesy of Taryn Denise Bilberry

As I reminisced about the churches and my family, I said to Uncle Johnny: "The place seems so quiet and still." The home-place that used to fill the air with sounds of roosters crowing, turkeys gobbling, and ducks quacking no longer exist. It was almost like I went through time and return to a place that I once knew and you start looking for signs of how things use to be. The roof had fallen in on the old house and the widows were all shattered. Nature has now reclaimed much of it. Yet, I seemed to have drawn strength from the house and its memories. It was the place where my great grandfather, grandfather and father lived and worked.

We decided to head back to the road after Uncle Johnny had finished showing me all of the property lines. We drove to his house in Farmerville, Louisiana where my rental car was parked. A few days later I returned to the area and drove down the road looking for my grandfather's old home. I wondered back and forth through the woods, but was never able to find the old house.

CHAPTER THREE

The End of Jim Crow Education: My Educational Journey

From Farmerville I headed north toward Marion, Louisiana, the self-proclaimed, "Timber Capitol [sic] of the South." It is a town of approximately 800 people with 54 percent of them being African American. Marion was the place where I was reared up as a child. It's one of the oldest towns in Union Parish; and it was settled by pioneers from Alabama. It was named after Marion County, Alabama, and the old home community of some of the first settlers in Union Parish. These new settlers worked their way across what is now known as the Alabama Landing, located on the Ouachita River just east of Marion, Louisiana. These settlers made their way west near the present site of Marion as early as 1830. Prior to 1945, black children attended several different elementary schools in Union Parish. Some of the names of these schools were as follow: Woodlawn Baptist Church School, Milliard Hill Baptist Church School, Gum Springs Baptist Church School, Lane Chapel School, Zion Hill Baptist School, Jerusalem Church of Christ School, Carl Hall Elementary School, Pleasant Grove Elementary School, Shiloh Elementary School, County Line Elementary School, Centerline Elementary School and Springhill Elementary School. Around 1945, a school for Negro children in the community was constructed near present day Mount Union Baptist Church. This school was later expanded into what became known as "Marion Industrial High School" on the site of present day Oliver Community Center. The school's football team won the 1957 State Championship. After integration in 1968; all children in the Marion area began attending present day Marion High School. [12]

I started the first grade at Marion Industrial High School. The school was the product of the Plessy vs. Ferguson case in 1896. In 1892, a 30-year old shoemaker named Homer Plessy was arrested for sitting in a car for only white people on the East Louisiana Railroad. He had refused to move to a black car. Even though he was mostly white, seven-eighths white and only one-eighth black, he was put in jail. The Louisiana law stated that if you had any black ancestors, you were considered black. Because of this, Plessy was required to sit in the "colored" or "black" car.

In court, Plessy argued that the law violated the Thirteenth and Fourteenth Amendments of the Constitution. The Thirteenth Amendment made slavery illegal in the United States. The Fourteenth Amendment states that all persons born in the United States are citizens of the United States and of the state where they live. It also says that no state can deny citizens of the United States equal protection of the laws. Plessy argued that the Louisiana law violated these amendments because on the train blacks and whites could be separate, if it was equal, but it wasn't. The white cars were nicer and cleaner than the black cars. Judge John Howard Ferguson had recently ruled the law "unconstitutional on trains that traveled through many states," but in this case, Judge Ferguson ruled that Plessy was guilty, because the state had the right to regulate railroad companies that run only in the state. The court said Mr. Plessy was found guilty, because the Louisiana law did not violate the Thirteenth and Fourteenth Amendments. They claimed that Plessy wasn't forced to be a slave and he wasn't being treated unequally, just separately. [13]

The Court held that a state could require racial segregation in public facilities if the facilities offered were equal lodging for the two races. The court's requirement became known as the "separate but equal" doctrine. Segregation in schools had, in fact, been illegal since 1954, when the Supreme Court issued a unanimous landmark decision in the case of Brown vs. Board of Education of Topeka. In 1955, the courts decided to implement the decision, declaring that schools must be integrated "with all deliberate speed." The ambiguous language of the court's decision left the door open to many forms of delaying tactics at the state and local levels. Union Parish School Board was one of the many school districts in the south that took advantage of the law's vagueness. At this point in the south, you had dual laws working concurrently; the older "separate but equal of 1896" and the newer Brown vs. Board of Education of 1954. However, few black students dared to attend the all-white schools. It seemed that the tacit or unwritten law of Jim Crow was still prevailing over the written laws of the courts. For blacks, it was summed up like this---"you knew your place and you just stayed in it."[14] Marion Industrial High School didn't last very long. The Union Parish School Board decided to build two separate, but equal schools in Union Parish for black children or "colored" as we were referred too. One school would be in the east area of the parish and the other would be in the west. The schools were thusly named Eastside High School in Farmerville, Louisiana and Westside High School in Lillie, Louisiana. In 1959, Marion Industrial High tenure as a school ended. Eastside High School was responsible for providing me an education for the next 10 1/2 years.

Belated Graduation Ceremony at Marion High School in 1992
Former principal George Herman Smith awards Donny Reeves his commemorative
diploma 22 years later. Below, Emmitt Burch, Jr., cries before receiving his diploma 22
years after he finished high school at Marion. Marion High School chose to cancel the
commencement that year – the first commencement exercise after a court-ordered
integration. [15]

Emmitt Burch Shed tears during the Graduation Ceremony

Charles Bilberry and Jerry Traylor looks over news reports about their belated graduation from high school in Marion, Louisiana after being interviewed by a Las Vegas news reporter [16]

My educational journey took another turn in 1969. As stated earlier, schools in Union Parish were integrated in 1968, but only a token few blacks children elected to go to the all-white schools. Three of the children that went to Marion High School lived down the street from my family. Unfortunately, their home was fire-bomb later that year. One night while asleep, a cross was burned in front of my parents' house at the location where we caught the bus to go to Eastside High School each day. My father shot it down with his shotgun while we slept that night. We saw the remnants of what was left of the cross lying on the side of the street. I didn't have very many racial confrontations with the white kids except for when I was sixteen years old. I had two jobs at that age; catching chickens at night after school and delivering groceries for Kennedy's Grocery Store to local homes on Saturdays. One afternoon I was driving the van to pick up all of the chicken catchers. We were all high school students. It was a job where I made four dollars each day for doing about four hours of work. The owner paid me an extra dollar to pick up the chicken catchers at their homes. While driving to pick up the last chicken catcher, a car with four white teenagers playfully swerved into my lane as I approached it. I playfully swerved back at them and proceeded to pick up my next rider Bill Fields. The car turned around and followed me to Bill's house. I stopped at his house and he proceeded to come out to get in the van. The white guy driving the car was Mike, the son of a local timber contactor

16

in town. He got out of his car with a 22 caliber rifle, approached me and said, "why were you swerving at me back there? Don't you know I'll blow your brains out?" I said, "You swerved at me first." He was stuttering, huffing and puffing while he continued to talk about what he would physically do to me; shouting expletives at me as I shouted some back at him. For some odd reason I wasn't scared of him or the gun. I said to him: "Why don't you put the gun down and we can settle this right now?" I didn't think he wanted to fight. But at that moment I felt as strong as a Brahma bull. He jumped back in his car and sped off while peeling rubber from his tires; he was mad and so was I. I didn't think much about the confrontation anymore for the rest of the week. I went to work at my grocery delivering job on Saturday, got off from work and that night I was shooting pool and playing pin ball machines with my friends. Sunday morning, my father asked me about the incident. It never came to my mind that I should have told him about it. He asked me what had happened and I explained the incident to him. He mentioned that his friend Felbert Andrews told him about it. Felbert worked as a butcher in the Kennedy Grocery Store and he overheard the white ladies in the store talking about it. He thought my father needed to know about it. My father said to me in a semi-irate tone, "Next time something like this happens, you make sure you tell me. I may not be able to do anything, but I'll jump him about it." I've always respected my father for teaching me the manly things over the years such as working on cars, garden work, mowing lawns and other outdoor chores. At that point I had a new respect for him. He showed me that he was a man who wouldn't bow down to anybody when it came to the safety of his family. I haven't given much thought about that incident over the years. Race relations were very tense at that time. Both Mike and I were teenagers venting our frustration over the changing social structure of the Deep South. Since then I've forgiven him for his actions and I hope he has forgiven me for mine.

In December of 1969 our principal, Mr. O. B. Adams announced that we would no longer be attending the Eastside High School. We were all astonished and surprised. In its 10 years of existence, the school had become the center of black community life through sports, drama and cultural events. The loss of the school shocked the black community. It was the best kept secret of the decade!

The holiday day break seemed to have gone by as quick as it came. Secondary school students in Union Parish, Louisiana were about to embark upon a new tradition. The Union Parish School Board had decided to disperse over seven hundred students from grade one through twelve, among other white schools in Union Parish. Black and white students were about to attend the school in their respective neighborhoods together for the first time. Initially, the second semester at the new school, there were no incidents or major problem. Some white parents got together and utilized a building in Marion, Louisiana for an all-white private school prior to the start of the new semester; the school was a lot a smaller but it served the purpose for what it was intended. Academically, I was only required to attend three classes. We played dominoes and cards for our physical education class; but that was an accepted practice for those of us that were seniors. The semester came to a conclusion when it was announced that there would not be a senior prom or graduation. Socially, Union Parish had not matured to full integration so fast. I had attended a prom as a junior and also as a sophomore where I was an usher for the class of 1968. Cancelling the prom was not a catastrophe for me; but to not have a graduation was ridiculous. What was even more absurd was the reason behind the cancellation. There was the problem with the marching order. The traditional processional was to march down the aisle starting with the highest grade point average students to the lowest. Most white parents did not want their kids marching behind a black kid even if their kid was a student with a grade point average of a grade "D"! Also, there was the problem of who would be the valedictorian. My classmate, Jerry Traylor had the highest grade point average for the students that attended the all-black Eastside High School. The all-white Marion High School had a student that represented the highest grade point average for them. The Union Parish School Board could not find a resolution to these issues so they made a decision to cancel it.

Black families collaborated and decided to have a separate graduation for the black kids in a local church. But threats of bombing the church ran rampant and that idea was squashed. So, there we were black and white seniors who finished the long journey of completing high school. It was a journey that many black parents were proud of because it was a fulfillment of something they never achieved. I remember a statement made by Dr. Felicia Campbell, a guest lecturer, in a multicultural education class I took at the University of Nevada at Las Vegas. She was speaking about the struggles that women have in society. She spoke of having to work twice as hard to get half as far. The statement that became fastened in my mind is when she said: "Sometimes the battle is so bitter because the stakes are so small." It was much like that during my final days at Marion High School. A group of my classmates found out that the high school diplomas were ready to be pick up in the principals' office. We made the short walk to his office, received our diploma with a congratulations and a handshake from the principal, Mr. George Herman Smith. I felt that Mr. Smith made that moment as dignified as he could for us that day. It was all that he could do.

Segregation was a more complicated phenomenon than blacks on one side and whites on the other. The separate, but equal rules were as unreasonable as the system of segregation itself. You could have separate schools, bathrooms and buses, but blacks can cook in white restaurants and raise little white children. Nevertheless, those of us who lived during the time of a segregated South knew where the boundaries lay. We knew what lines could be crossed and who could cross them. I was amazed at how my parents and other parents of the community were so respectful and cordial to white people as the "white only" signs finally disappeared. They had a much harder time with segregation than I. One would probably expect bitterness, disrespect or retaliation towards white people; but God knows what people He could put in certain places at a certain times because He knew that they could handle the burden.

Three days after I received my diploma I left Marion, Louisiana to live with my older sister in Las Vegas, Nevada for a better opportunity. My younger sister, Jerry Joyce Bilberry who in later years changed her name to Fonda Deleon decided she did not want to be left behind. So, she too sought a better opportunity out west. A few years later, my father's employer, Thad Kennedy of Kennedy Contracting, asked my father why I didn't stay in Marion, Louisiana. He told my father that he thought that I would have made a good chain saw man for cutting timber. My father said to him that the only time he wanted to see a chain saw in his son's hand was to sell one to someone else. Like my mother, I also made a vow that if I went to college I was going to march in the graduation ceremony regardless of how old I was. Upon arriving in Las Vegas, I worked as a dishwasher at a local casino for 14 months; worked at a chemical plant in Henderson, Nevada for almost five years and worked at the Nevada Test Site for various engineering firms. I was going to school part-time concurrently while working. It wasn't easy in the "Entertainment Capital of the World." I could have easily gotten caught up and perhaps lost in the pleasures of a 24 hour city; but I was determined to further my education and be the best that I could be in this life. In 1980, I was hired as an engineering inspector for the Las Vegas Valley Water District eventually retiring 30 years later as an engineering inspection supervisor. Fifteen of those years I worked and went to school at night.

God blessed me to see the vows that I made when leaving Louisiana in 1970, come to fruition. I received undergraduate degrees from the College of Southern Nevada, University of Nevada at Las Vegas, and Bethany University, Santa Cruz; a graduate degree from Fuller Theological Seminary, and a post graduate degree from Louisiana Baptist Theological Seminary, Shreveport, Louisiana.

At each of the graduations, many of my fellow classmates gave reasons for not wanting to march in the ceremony, such as being too old. But I dressed in the cap and gown at each graduation. I had a deeper reason and I had a vow to keep. Ironically, God granted me the opportunity to go back in 1992, to be a participant in the Marion High School 22nd year belated graduation ceremony, less than two months after the Rodney King verdict that sparked racial unrest and rioting across the nation. Through it all, I harbor no ill feelings of not graduating in 1970, because in the South at that time "Jim Crow" was just the way of life.

I've returned to Marion, Louisiana many times since 1970. When I left this town, there were signs posted on the restrooms that said "colored and white." It's not like that anymore. Time has a way of changing things. People seem to respect each other now. In Marion as in other southern towns, Jim Crow laws are only a bad memory.

CHAPTER FOUR

Daddy's Smoking Caught up with Him

Let's get a transistor radio, is what my sisters and I would say to my father after counting almost a thousand redemption coupons he had collected from his numerous cartons of Raleigh cigarettes he bought each month. It was fun for us to count these coupons because daddy would let us get whatever we wanted from the items listed in the catalog. He had switched from smoking Pall Mall to Raleigh cigarettes because he felt he was getting something back from his purchases.

On April of 1997, I received a call from my mother that my father had passed away. The years of smoking had taken their toll on his lungs. He had stopped smoking about 15 years prior to his death, but the residual damage had now manifested itself. He lost his battle with lung cancer eight months after being diagnosed. Daddy was raised up during the hardship of the Great Depression. It was a time where the gap between the "haves" and the "have-nots" was widening. Unemployment rose from a shocking 5 million in 1930, to an almost unbelievable thirteen million by the end of 1932. It was rural America that would suffer the greatest. Children left school to support their families. Daddy's childhood was much like that; he was the third oldest child of Ladell and Maggie Bilberry. His older brother, George Willie, died as an infant. Daddy had to stop attending school in the 5th grade in order to help raise crops on the family farm. When daddy died in 1997, at the age of 70 years old, he had acquired some outward signs of success in life; a house; a new truck; a boat; some land; money in the bank and children that were successful in their careers in Las Vegas, Nevada and Santa Barbara, California.

Daddy worked as a loader operator for a logging contractor, T.L Kennedy Contractors in Marion, Louisiana. Such work would not account for much these days, but it made a living for his family. He worked for this logging contractor for 46 years, retiring at the age of 63. The mass of the black people in my home town cleaned houses or held similar laborious positions.

Daddy's death elevated my memories of him. I would often go back home and visit with him and my mother; suddenly fishing and hunting outings became important because now they were all that I had to remember of him. Conversations we shared in person or on the phone became final events. When relatives visited he was quick to have a big fish fry or barbeque for them. I think he enjoyed doing it as much as they enjoyed eating it. He would go out of his way to make you feel at home. He had a benevolent character. A lot of people attended his funeral. Family and friends sat shoulder-to-shoulder leaving only enough room for latecomers to stand in the small, but quaint Sweet Lilly Primitive Baptist Church. Uncles, aunts, cousins and friends sat upright with their eyes on the pulpit and tears flowing down their cheeks. They were crying not because they were weak, but because they had lost a man they had looked up to for so long. I grieved for my cousins who had lost their uncle; and I cried for my mother who had lost her help mate. Sometimes my parents fought like other parents. They fought over money; my father's coming home late at night; my mother wearing short pants; my mother's stubbornness. The weekends would sometimes be hell at home because my father would come home so late at night. When that happened, we kids spent our weekend in fear of mama's temper. Even a minor request to go out and play with the kids down the street may bring out the wrath in mama. We knew that her wrath was really not directed at us, but to our father. We just had to endure until the cloud passed over.

Despite the cracks in their relationship, their marriage never shattered. When I look at pictures that they have taken over the years, I see a love that survived forty six years, as if it was cultivated by the years of feeding and watering their relationship. I see the dedication that would keep my mother sitting in his hospital room for weeks as my father slowly succumbed to the cancer that had taken over his lungs. I see her pride as she would often brag of her forty six years of marriage to my father. They agreed on a marriage vow that stated that they would be together until death, and they kept that vow.

I cried for both of my sisters and I cried for myself. I missed my father. I wanted to go hunting and fishing with him one more time. I wanted him to share family history with me one more time. But daddy did like all of us must do; he answered the call to come home to his final resting place. He was a good and loving father; he was my hero. Funerals are sad way to get families together.

My Aunt Luemmer Bilberry-Horn decided that it was time to do something about that and she organized the first Horn-Bilberry family reunion in 1982. Like many family reunions, our family reunion started at the old family home site, a public park and private homes that was held in Louisiana where the family's history started. Traditionally, it begins on Friday where we meet, greet, wear t-shirts and renew our acquaintances. Saturday was usually a busy day. After breakfast, we began by having everyone pose for a family portrait. The remainder of the day was spent on activities done together (zoo, amusement park, shopping) or something on your own. Saturday night we have a banquet with plenty of food; we blessed the food for everyone to enjoy. On Sunday we attended a church service in the city where we are at; or conduct a worship service ourselves. I attended my first Horn-Bilberry family reunion in Kansas City, Kansas in July 1992. I was elated to see all of my relatives and sadden that I had missed the previous five. It was a blessing for families to be able to pause to exchange memories and stories about our heritage.

Our ancestors' sacrifices are one of the main reasons why families convene for family reunions, so that we can share stories and pass our history from one generation to the next. Our children need to know the story, the struggle, and the price that was paid for their liberty. Families like Frank and Emma Bilberry, Calvin and Lola Horn worked hard for almost nothing trying to make a better life for their families. They knew that these challenges wouldn't last always. They put their pennies and nickels together and put them in a common pot and they built community schools, colleges and universities. They knew that there will come a time when one of their children or grandchildren will attend one of these schools, graduate and get paid for what they know and not so much for what they can do.

Many have passed on since the family reunion began in 1982. We must continue to raise-up new organizers and leaders; to bring-up and implement new ideas in order to continue this legacy. Harvey Horn son of Seab Horn, Sr., developed a website, Bayoufamilytreasure.com for the Horn-Bilberry Family Reunion. This website provides the family members an opportunity to share pictures, acknowledge birthdays, get information on the upcoming family reunion, and look at past family reunion photographs. Harvey and his lovely wife Carolyn live in Magnolia, Mississippi and they are commended for a job well done.

Luemmer Bilberry-Horn (Dec. 5, 1924-Mar. 6, 1989)
Wife of Seab Horn Sr., and founder of the Horn-Bilberry Reunion.

Bilberry-Horn Family Reunion Oklahoma City, Oklahoma – July 2010
Courtesy of Harvey Horn

CHAPTER FIVE

Researching Family History:
Many Branches, Several Leaves, and Two Colors

Researching family history can bring you face-to-face with uncomfortable truths. You may uncover that your family is racially mixed through an era in life where white men enjoyed almost unquestioned supremacy over black women. Over the years I have asked many people about the connection between the black Bilberrys and the white Bilberrys. I have even asked the question why the surname was sometimes spelled Bilberry (with one L) and Billberry (with two L's). No one seems to know or want to talk about it. It is not uncommon to find this type of variation in spelling of surnames when researching your family history. For me, there is no shame in discovering the truth; I don't pass judgment, I just accept my kinfolks, whoever. Many white people believed that if the slave owner had children by their slave women, it degraded the slave owner and not the slave.

My goal in this research was to discover the father and mother of my great grandfather Frank Bilberry. To accomplish that, I needed the name of white people. I needed the name that linked my black ancestors with the white Bilberrys that resided in Union Parish. According to the 1870 U.S. Census, there were only eleven Bilberrys counted in Union Parish. [17] It was the first census that black people were counted in after being emancipated. There were not any black Bilberrys counted in that census—all of them were listed as being white. Two of them were in the Ward One area and the other nine were in the Ward Six area. It was not until the 1880 U.S. Census that African American Bilberrys were counted in Union Parish Census. The majority of both black and white Bilberrys were found in Ward Six area. [18]

When a slave owner died, a court appointed appraiser made an inventory of the owner's property, including the slaves. The property and the slaves' first name were listed in the appraisal and how much money the property and each slave were worth. In Union Parish, estate administrations were found in successions, rather than in probates as in some of the other parishes. A lot of information can be found in these documents if you are willing to dedicate some time and patience for doing the research.

My first real experience in researching my family's history was at the Las Vegas Regional Family History Center in Las Vegas, Nevada. It is a research center owned and operated by the Church of Latter Day Saints. I walked in with hopes of finding exactly what I needed about my family's history. I thought it would take possibly two or three years to gather the data that I needed. But, to my utter amazement, I am still looking for information 14 years later.

As I walked into the Regional Family History Center, the older white-haired gentleman asked me: "Have you visited with us before?" I could tell by the look in his eyes that he already knew my answer. He continued with questions: "Let me give you a tour of our facility; this will get you started and if you have any questions just come up to the counter and see me." After a brief tour of the facility; I immediately went over to the microfilm area and started searching the 1880 Census. The United States census is a decennial census mandated by the United States constitution. The population of the United States is enumerated every 10 years and the results are used to allocate congressional seats, electoral votes, and government funding programs. Also, some states and local jurisdictions conduct local census. [19] The census discloses another story; it reveals the community where people lives; the kind of jobs they had and what states people were born in; the birth state of their parents and much more. The United States census releases this information after 72 years has passed. Unfortunately, the 1890 Census was destroyed in 1921, during a fire in the basement of the commerce building in Washington, D.C. This is a great loss since it leaves a twenty year gap of information. As previously stated, my great grandfather Frank Bilberry was born in 1878. I was attempting to find out the name of his mother and father. I searched the 1880 Census for all of the Bilberrys in Union Parish Louisiana, but could not find Frank Bilberry. Since the 1890 U.S. Census were destroyed; Frank Bilberry first shows up in the 1900 U.S. Census at 21 years of age, working as a servant for Alcandor Ewing and Ada Ewing. This census list his mother and father's birthplace as Louisiana. [20]

Much of the information that I have collected over the years has been by way of conversation through telephone or in person. Their testimonies about Frank Bilberry and Emma Bilberry gave me a sense of accomplishment. I felt that I was able to catch hold of something valuable from the receding tide of the past. I came to realized that as each day passed by in the lives of the older generation, irretrievable history was slipping away with each moment.

On August 30, 1997, I had a short phone conversation with my great grandfather's nephew Paul Bilberry. He is the son of Lawrence Bilberry, my great grandfather's brother. He was 75 years old at the time of our conversation. "Hello cousin Paul. This is Charles Bilberry, the son of Adell and Barbara Neal Bilberry of Marion, Louisiana." "Yeah, I know who are. How you're doing, he replied?" I stated that I was doing fine and said: "Cousin Paul, I would like to ask you a few questions about Uncle Lawrence's mother, father, brothers and sisters." He said: "I don't know much, but I'll tell you what I can remember. You know the old folks back then didn't talk too much about that." I said: "I know it's been a long time, but do the best you can and tell me what you know." At that moment I started my series of questions: Do you know who the mother and father of Uncle Lawrence, I politely asked? " Well I heard him mention the name Narsis as his mother, that's all I've heard him say about his mother." What about his father? Did he ever mention the name of his father? "No, all I know is that he was a white man and he did mention the name Britt or Bridges Bilberry." I asked with politeness again; did Uncle Lawrence have any other brothers and sisters beside Papa Frank? He said: "I can't remember them all, but I heard him say he had a brother name Ed. He named my brother Ed after his brother.

He had another brother name Jordan or Horton. He had some sisters too; Annie, lived in Crossett, Arkansas. His sister, Anna, lived in Monroe, Louisiana; she married Mason Holland. They used to live around here (meaning Marion and Farmerville, Louisiana area), but they moved to Monroe, Louisiana later on in life. He had another sister name Mamie (Mary) Bohannon." Upon researching this in the 1900 U.S. Census, I found out that Mamie Armstrong married Will Bohannon. [21]

Mamie's mother name was Narsis. She was married to Fred Armstrong. [22] According to the 1900 U.S Census Lawrence Bilberry was a servant living nearby in the household of William T. Smith. William T. Smith's occupation was listed as a minister. Later research revealed that he was a pastor of the Meridian Missionary Baptist Church near Marion, Louisiana. Willis Andrews, a nearby neighbor of Lawrence Bilberry stated to me in a telephone conversation in November 2010, that Lawrence Bilberry would called Fred Armstrong, Uncle Fred. When the census was taken in 1910, for Ward Six of Union Parish, Fred Armstrong was married to a lady name Sallie. They had been married for four years. This was the second marriage for both of them. Horton Armstrong, the brother of Lawrence Bilberry mentioned previously is enumerated as one of the children living in their household. Other children listed were Eva, Percy and Edna. On December 19, 1923, Horton Armstrong, Mamie Armstrong-Bohannon, and Edna Armstrong-Ward deeded sixty acres of land to Lawrence Bilberry. [23]

As I continued my conversation with my great grandfather's nephew Paul Bilberry, I asked: Did you know a lady name Angeline Douglas? "Yeah, I knew her; she was a half-sister to Uncle Frank." Did Uncle Lawrence work any other place other than his farm? "Yeah, he worked at Crow and Netters Saw Mill for a while." We said goodbye to each other and our conversation ended there.

Cemetery research can be very rewarding when it comes to finding information regarding your ancestors. You can find an overwhelming amount of information once you began your search. Also, it can be very frustrating, when you don't have answers to questions that usually pop up in your mind while you are at the gravesites. There are several cemeteries in Union Parish, Louisiana. Many of the churches have family cemeteries. Over the years I have focused my research on the Sweet Lilly Primitive Baptist Church, Antioch AME Church, Springhill Baptist Church and Meridian Baptist Church. These churches were chosen because of the abundance of my ancestors that were buried there. There are some that are buried in other cemeteries, such as the Farmerville City Cemetery; but there are few of my ancestors' gravesites. I visited the Sweet Lilly Primitive Baptist Church Cemetery. It is an all-African American cemetery and congregation. It was clean and had been recently mowed. Most of the visible stones were in good condition. It was quite impressive considering this little cemetery is stuck so far back in the woods. There is a chain link fence around the entire cemetery. During my last visit there in July 2010, I noticed that they were expanding the cemetery to the east of the existing one. Many Bilberry gravesites are located there as well as relatives (Roberts, Benson, Finley, Montgomery, and others). This is the cemetery where my father, grandfather and great grandfather are buried.

Charlie Sidney Roberts (Sept. 25, 1911-Jan. 25, 1996) Son of Jerry William Lee Roberts

Ashby Finley (Dec. 18, 1905)
(Dec. 18, 1905-July 1981)
Son of Monroe Finley

Son of Will and Liza Roberts Jerry Williams Lee Roberts (1875-?) Lee Roberts acted as the undertaker on many family members' deaths(see death certificates in Appendix A)

**Algie and Addie Roberts-Payne; Addie (April 8, 1909-June 14, 1991)
is the daughter of Jerry Williams Lee and Ollie Roberts**

The Antioch African Methodist Episcopal Church Cemetery is located about one mile southeast of the Antioch AME Church, which is about four miles southeast of Truxno, Louisiana. I visited the cemetery on a hot and humid day in July 2000. It was the kind of weather that can really discourage you from going outside and doing anything. Although, the weeds and grass were high, I was able to survey the cemetery. If you are serious about researching your family history, you will plod through cemeteries in pouring rain, scorching heat, and disregarding poison ivy just to take a picture of a headstone that may or may not be there. The Bilberry's located here were all descendants of Lawrence Bilberry. I found his gravesite and it has a picture of him embedded in his headstone. Lawrence Bilberry was the half brother of my great grandfather Frank Bilberry. They had the same white father but a different mother. Some of Papa Frank's maternal aunts, Lura and Sallie Bridges are buried in this cemetery. Lura and Sallie were twins. Lawrence donated one acre of land for the building of Antioch AME Church.

Just northeast of Truxno, Louisiana is the Springhill Cemetery. This cemetery is located west of Oakland, Louisiana approximately 10 miles north of Marion, Louisiana. In the mid to late 1800's the area was known as Crossroads, where two roads intersected each other. Initially, there were two Springhill Baptist Churches at the site; a white church and a black church. The white church was moved closer to Oakland, Louisiana in later years.

Lawrence Bilberry brother of Frank Bilberry and the son of Narsis Armstrong and Britt. Lawrence owned a land patent in 1913

Paul Bilberry son of Lawrence Bilberry (Oct. 8, 1921-April 11, 2005)

LAWRENCE BILBERRY
OCT. 19, 1883
OCT. 8, 1965

Lawrence Bilberry Headstone at Antioch AME Cemetery in Truxno, Louisiana

I noticed that both the white and black cemeteries were on one large plot of land, but separated by an interior wire fence. I found only one black Bilberry buried at the African American portion of the cemetery, George Bilberry, son of Lawrence and Lou Bilberry. There were no Bilberrys found in the white portion of the cemetery.

The Meridian Baptist Church building and cemetery is located in Union Parish, Louisiana. It is approximately six miles southwest of Marion, Louisiana. The church minutes records both white settlers and a few slaves in attendance in this congregation prior to the Civil War. I was reading some of the minutes from the Meridian Baptist Church and I noticed that the few slaves that were members or candidates for baptism were called "servants."[24] The slave owners firmly believed that blacks were ordained to slavery by God. The slavery of the past few centuries was often based exclusively on skin color. In the United States, many black people were considered slaves because of their nationality; many slave owners truly believed black people to be inferior human beings. First, it is possible that certain moderate forms of "servitude"—for example, indentured (voluntary) servitude—were considered morally beneficial before God under certain circumstances in the Old Testament. Examples of this are seen in voluntary indenture in order to earn a living or to learn a trade. Also, it may have included the indenture of a criminal in order for the offender to render restitution. But in none of these kinds of cases would the so-called slave be viewed as a mere piece of property without human rights. Nor would the time of servitude be constituted as a life term of bondage. Therefore it is clear that some forms of servitude practiced in biblical times bear little resemblance to the tyrannical types of slavery found in many parts of the ancient and modern world.

Two separate cemeteries are located at the church grounds. The largest and younger cemetery is located next to the church and the older and smaller one is across the road from the church. There were not any Bilberrys found in the smaller cemetery. Much like the Springhill Baptist Church the two cemeteries here were primarily segregated. The smaller and older cemetery is African American slaves and descendants of slaves with the exception of a few slave owners that are buried there. The following white Bilberrys were found at this site. Elza B. Bilberry, Jr., George W. Bilberry, James M. Bilberry, Louisa Bilberry and Mary J. Bilberry (all names located on a headstone spire). Mary J. Bilberry is the wife of Elza B. Bilberry, Sr. The other Bilberrys noted on the headstone inscription are their children. One other white Bilberry, Mahala Bilberry, is buried at this cemetery. She is the sister of Elza B. Bilberry, Sr.; Elisha Brashier, the husband of Mahala Bilberry is buried here as well. Mahala married a second time to Miller Bledsoe Edwards. The people buried at the all-white cemetery were heirs of a dead dynasty. They were descendants of men and women who had ruled over this part of Union Parish like pharaohs ruled over Egypt. [25]

Headstone of Mary Jane Honeycutt-Bilberry at Meridian Baptist Church Cemetery. She was E. B. Bilberry's first of three wives. Mary Jane was the daughter of John Honeycutt, Sr.

Headstone of Elza B. Bilberry, Jr., and George Bilberry at Meridian Baptist Church Cemetery; sons of E. B. Bilberry and Mary Jane Honeycutt-Bilberry

The classification of slave owners varied according to the size of the plantations and the number of slaves owned. The first classification was the "planter elite." They were slave owners that held more than twenty slaves. The second classification were the "small planters" that held ten to 19 slaves. The third classification was the "yeomen farmer," that held nine slaves or fewer." [26] Elza B. Bilberry was a slave owners in Union Parish. The 1860 Slave Inhabitants Schedule list Elza B. Bilberry as holding six slaves; four females and two males. Mary Feazel-Honeycutt the mother-in-law of Elza B. Bilberry, Sr., also owned slaves through the death of her husband John Honeycutt. She inherited seven slaves; four males and three females. Women often inherited slaves at the death of their husband or father through court proceedings known as successions. Upon the death of Mary Feazel-Honeycutt confusion arose between the heirs of her estate. A lawsuit was filed in the Hunt County, Texas Courthouse in an attempt to correct the John Honeycutt, Sr., and Mary Feazel-Honeycutt Estate. Alfred Honeycutt was interrogated in court concerning the lawsuit.

Mary's property was left to her succeeding heirs—Britten Honeycutt, Sarah Willhite (wife of John Honeycutt, Jr., and son of John and Mary Feazel-Honeycutt who had previously died), Alfred Honeycutt and Elza B. Bilberry, Sr., husband of Mary Jane Honeycutt (deceased and the daughter of John and Mary Feazel-Honeycutt). The slaves that are named in the interrogation of Alfred Honeycutt delineate dividing of the slaves to family members and the household goods. Alfred Honeycutt was interrogated in court concerning the lawsuit. [27]

```
ESTATE OF MRS. MARY HONEYCUTT, DECEASED.

APPLICATION FOR THE ADMINISTRATION:  Filed October 24, 1864.

To the Honorable the Judge of the Eleventh Judicial District Court in and for the Parish of
Louisiana.

The petition of Alfred Honeycutt a resident of the Parish of Union State of Louisiana res-
pectfully represents that Mrs. Mary Honeycutt late of said Parish of Union departed this
life in said Parish, intestate, March 1863.  That she left a small property consisting of
negroes and some personal property and her children Elizabeth Wilhite (represented by her
minor heirs) Austin Honeycutt, John Honeycutt, Button Honeycutt, Mary Jones the wife of E.
Bilberry & your petitioner that the property cannot will be divided in kind and that a sale
at the present time may not be advisable needing an Administration of the same necessary
until there be a change in the times for the better.

Wherefore he prays that this his application be advertised according to Law and after the
legal delays that petitioner be appointed Administrator of said Estate of Mary Honeycutt
Decd. on his taking the oath and giving the bond required by law.  For an inventory of sa
Estate to be made and for all further orders and decrees necessary in the premises and for
general relief etc.

                                              Jno. L. Barrett, Atty.


STATE OF LOUISIANA  )
                    )
PARISH OF UNION     )

Before me the undersigned authority personally came Alfred Honeycutt who being by me duly
sworn deposes that he has not at any time since the twenty sixth day of January eighteen
hundred and sixty one taken an oath to support the government or the constitution of the
United States nor in any manner made a declaration of allegiance to the United States nor
given any information or support aid or confort to the United States or to the soldiers
officers or armies thereof nor been engaged either directly or indirectly as an agent for
others or on his own account in carrying on any trade or traffic for purposes of gain with
the citizens soldiers or government of the United States or with any other person so that
the United States has been benefitted thereby during the war waged against the Confederate
States by the United States.  And that he is not a citizen or resident of the United Stat
So help him God!

                                              Alfred Honeycutt
```

Alfred Honeycutt's application for administration of Mary Feazel-Honeycutt's Estate
Page 1

The premises considered it is ordered that the within application for Administration be advertised according to law.

It is further ordered that Wm. C. Smith Parish Recorder etc. make an inventory and appraisment of all the property belonging to the Estate of Mary Honeycutt, Decd. and due return thereof make to this office.

Done and signed in office on this 24th. day of October A. D. 1864.

Thos. C. Lewis, Clerk.

ADMINISTRATOR'S BOND: Filed _____.

STATE OF LOUISIANA)
)
PARISH OF UNION   )

Know all men by these presents that we Alfred Honeycutt as principal and as his securities are held and firmly bound unto Honl. W. B. Egan Judge of the 11th. Judl. Dist. Court in and for Union Parish State of Louisiana for the time being or to his successors in office in the just and full sum of _____ dollars to the true and faithful payment whereof well and truly to be made we bind ourselves our heirs, assigns administrators and legal representatives firmly by these presents.

Dated at Farmerville, La. on this day of _____ A. D. 1864.

The conditions of the above obligation is such that whereas the above bounden Alfred Honeycutt has been duly and legally appointed Administrator of the Estate of Mary Honeycutt decd. and he has taken the oath prescribed by Law.

Now therefore if the said Alfred Honeycutt shall well and faithfully perform all the duties incumbent on him as Administrator aforesaid and shall render to the Judge of said Court a true and faithful account of all his acts and doings in his said Administration capacity and shall whenever legally required so to do pay over all sums of money and deliver all the property of whatever nature received belonging to the said Estate to the proper person or persons to receive the same, then and in that case the above obligation to be null and void, otherwise to remain in full force and virtue against the principal and his said securities.

Done, signed and acknowledged before me on the day and date above written.

OATH & LETTERS OF ADMINISTRATOR: Filed_____.

STATE OF LOUISIANA)
) 11th. JUDICIAL DISTRICT COURT.
PARISH OF UNION   )

I, Alfred Honeycutt do solemnly swear that I will faithfully and impartially perform all the duties incumbent on me as Administrator of the Estate of Mary Honeycutt, Decd. according to the best of my knowledge and ability. So help me God!

Sworn to & subscribed before me on this)
          day of   A. D. 1864.   )

STATE OF LOUISIANA)
) 11th. JUDICIAL DISTRICT COURT.
PARISH OF UNION   )

Whereas Alfred Honeycutt has been duly and legally appointed and confirmed as Administrator of the Estate of Mary Honeycutt decd. and he has given bond with good security and has taken the oath prescribed by law.

Now therefore the said Alfred Honeycutt is hereby duly and legally authorized and empowered to do and perform all the acts appertaining to said appointment according to law.

Given under my hand and seal of said Court on this the _____ day of _____ A. D. 1864.

(Seal)

LETTERS OF ADMINISTRATOR: Filed _____.

STATE OF LOUISIANA)
) 11th. KUDICIAL DISTRICT COURT.
PARISH OF UNION   )

Whereas Alfred Honeycutt has been duly and legally appointed and confirmed as Administrator of the Estate of Mary Honeycutt decd. and he has given bond with good security and has taken the oath prescribed by law.

Now therefore the said Alfred Honeycutt is hereby duly and legally authorized and empowered

Alfred Honeycutt appointed administrator of Mary Feazel-Honeycutt's Estate
Page 2

Int 3 — If you answer that John E. Green made the deed to John Hunnicutt to some lands in Hunt County Texas to whom was the deed delivered - was said deed ever delivered to John Honeycutt of Hunt County, Texas or to any person for him — if so when and to whom?

Int 4 — When did your father die? Is your mother living or dead — if she is dead, when and where did she die?

Int 5 — If you make any answers to the matter enquired of in direct Int. 15 state whether you make said answers of your own personal knowledge or from what others have told you - Is not all you know about said matters derived from what you have heard from others say and tell you?

Int 5½ — did your father own any negroes at the time of his death. If he ever came to or visited Texas, did he bring his negroes with him?

Int 6 — If you made any answers to the matters enquired of in direct Int. 16, state whether you made said answers from your own personal knowledge or from what others have told you? Is not all you know about the matter derived from what others have told you?

Int. 7 — If you make any answer to direct Int. 18, give your means of knowledge - state time, place and give the names of those who were present?

Int. 8 — When did your mother die and how many negroes belonged to the estate of John Hunnicutt Sr. and your mother at the time of her death? and what land belonged to said estate at that time in Louisiana?

Int 9 — Was not your fathers and mothers estate that was in Louisiana, be paral, divided and partitioned among all the heirs of John Hunnicutt Sr. and your mother except John Hunnicutt Jr. of Hunt County Texas in the year 1864 and in that partition did not Brittain Hunnicutt get a negro named Ellis, Austin Hunnicutt a negro named Jordan, Willhite a negro named Jack, Alfred Hunnicutt a negro named York and Bilberry a negro named Sinda and her three children and did not Bilberry get all the household and kitchen furniture?

Int 10 — Was not the land in Hunt County Texas in that division, set apart to your brother John Hunnicutt, Jr. — Was he present at the time it was made — did he know anything about it?

Int.11 — Specially to Alfred Hunnicutt — Did you not write to your brother John Hunnicutt Jr. from Marshall, Texas in June or July 1864 that said partition had been made and the Hunt County Lands were his, and did you not write a letter to Mrs. Sarah A. Hunnicutt the widow of your brother John Hunnicutt Jr., Dec. 10, 1865 in which letter you stated that you left a deed with Hardin Hart for the land sued for in this case, for John Hunnicutt Jr's part and that the land was hers, Mrs. Sarah A. Hunnicutts, and that you left the deed with said Hart as your brother John had wrote you to send him the deed?

Int 12 — Did John Honeycutt Jr. ever get anything from his fathers or mothers estate except the land sued for?

Int 13 — If you answer that there was a division of your fathers and mothers estate, was said division or a memorandum of it in writing or was it a verbal division?

Jones & Cushman Attys for Defts.
Filed July 7th 1885

Page from transcript of District Ct. File 1898 Hunt Co, Tx - Interrogations to Alfred Honeycutt filed 7 July 1885 -- Answer in file

Hunt County, Texas interrogation of Alfred Honeycutt about settlement of his parent's Union Parish Estate
Courtesy of Grace Nezworski

White slave owners often fathered children with their slave women. One slave that was suspected to be sired by E. B. Bilberry and documented through a primary source is Jordan Bilberry. Jordan was born in Conway, Louisiana – Union Parish, in 1857. It is a small village near southwest Marion, Louisiana. He died February 14, 1915; his "certificate of death" indicates his mother name as Martha Gilbert and his father as Elzie [sic] B. Billberry.[28] Oral history quoted through conversations with descendants of Jordan E. Billberry confirms him as the father as well. As previously stated some former slaves' as well as mulatto children of former slaves' owners selected the slave owner's surname. I believe this is true of Jordan Billberry and my great grandfather Frank Bilberry. Jordan married Amanda Durden in Union Parish, Louisiana. The 1880 U.S. Census of Ward Six in Union Parish, Louisiana list Jordan with his wife Mandy (Amanda), and sons John, Ade (Adell) and Domien. Jordan later married Mattie Carson on September 10, 1891.[29] He moved his family from Louisiana to the town of Chidester, Arkansas – Ouachita County and lived there until his death in 1915.[30] One of his sons, Adell Billberry married Annie Ross, who was from Arkansas. They lived and reared a family in Arkansas, but later moved the Stockton, California area where children and grandchildren have relocated.

Adell (Abe) Billberry (Dec. 15, 1877-Jan. 8, 1953) son of Jordan Billberry

**Annie Ross-Bilberry,
wife of Adell (Abe) Billberry**
Courtesy of Joyce Billberry-Cofer

Jordan Ellis Bilberry, son of Adell (Abe) Billberry

Jordan Ellis Billberry, Sr., headstone in Chidester, Arkansas

Courtesy of Joyce Billberry-Cofer

Lineree Billberry son of Adell (Abe) Billberry and wife Elizabeth

Minner Billberry, son of Adell (Abe) Billberry

Courtesy of Joyce Bilberry-Cofer

The issues were debatable of whether or not slave women were forced into sexual relations with their masters or if they were actually involved in long-term relations with them. Issues that were known were that white men often sought after relationships with slave women. If the relationships were not consensual, then Martha Gilbert's slave status rendered her powerless much like other slave women.

Another man that was emancipated and registered in the first voter's registration in Union Parish after the Civil War was York Morgan. York was born circa 1820, according to the 1870 U.S. Census for Union Parish, Louisiana. [31] York was the property of slave owner A. J. Morgan. A. J. Morgan deeded a set of Negroes to John Honeycutt, Jr., on November 6, 1816.[32] The Negroes were as follow:

SLAVES BELONGING TO A. J. MORGAN DEEDED TO JOHN HONEYCUTT, JR., NOVEMBER 6, 1816		
RACE	NAME	AGE
Negro boy	York	3
Negro girl	Fortune	5

Also, living in the household with York in 1870, was his wife Lucinda (Sinda); She was possibly the slave woman that was mentioned in the "Interrogation Transcript of Alfred Honeycutt" in Hunt County, Texas. Sinda and her three children were given to E. B. (Britton) Bilberry in the succession of Mary Feazel-Honeycutt's Estate in 1864. E. B. (Elsa) first wife was Mary Jane Honeycutt, the daughter of Mary Feazel-Honeycutt; he lived next to the York and Sinda's home according to the 1870 U.S. Census. Others that resided in their household were Jack Morgan, Harrison Morgan, York Morgan, Hanah Morgan, Sam Morgan, Milton Morgan, Puss Morgan and Jane Taylor. The family's oral history passed down over the years has stated that E. B. Bilberry sired an illegitimate child named Puss with Sinda. Hanah used the Bilberry surname also and was probably fathered by E.B. Bilberry as well. Puss' real name was Bellzora Bilberry, but she later changed her name to Georgia Ann Bilberry because she did not like the name Bellzora [33] (see Marriage License Collection in Appendix B). Hannah and Jack carried the surname Bilberry in succeeding years; Jack later married Francis Jones and Hannah married Branch Nelson.

Lucinda (Sinda)Morgan, wife of York Morgan (circa 1827-?)

Georgia Ann Bilberry-Ellis, aka Aunt Puss
and Bellzora Bilberry (Dec. 9, 1866-Jan. 22, 1958)
Courtesy of John Earl Ellis Courtesy of John Earl Ellis

Sam Morgan (1862 --?), Vosier Morgan and wife Sarah Montgomery-Morgan.-Sam is the son of Lucinda Morgan. Sam owned a land patent in 1892. His last known residence was in El Dorado, Arkansas

John Hiram Morgan (May 12, 1885-Nov. 1977) and wife Idell Miller-Morgan. John is the son of Sam Morgan

Courtesy of Louie Morgan Courtesy of Louie Morgan

The 1900 U.S. Census of Ward Six in Union Parish, Louisiana indicates that Branch Nelson had a new wife. Her name was Fanny and they had been married for two years. Also, enumerated in his household was Milton Morgan (servant), the brother of Sam Morgan. Sam and his wife Sarah were close neighbors of Branch and Fanny Nelson; and Elzy and Cynthia Bilberry. Living in the household with Sam and Sarah were their children Mary, John, Mell, Willis, Sindy, Ollie, Caroline, Girty, Vosier and Sam's mother Lucinda. Furthermore, the census counted William Henry Bilberry as a servant in the household with Elzy and Cynthia Bilberry. William is the son of Jack and Frances Bilberry.

Robert and Tildy (Matilda) Bridges were close neighbors as well. By this time their children had left home and made lives of their own. Several grandchildren, Anna, Linsey, Edwin and Dolly were living in the household with them. John Bright, son of Martha Turner headed a household in the neighborhood as well. Counted with him in the 1900 U.S. Census was his wife Mattie, daughter Mandy and two servants, James Bilberry and Guy Bilberry. Several of these people were related in some manner.[34] Most of them or their parents had a current or former connection with Elzy B. Bilberry and/or the John Honeycutt family.

		The name of every person whose place of abode on the first day of June, 1870, was in this family.	Age	Sex	Color	Profession, Occupation, or Trade of each person, male or female.	Value of Real Estate	Value of Personal Estate	Place of Birth, naming State or Territory of U. S.; or the Country, if of foreign birth.								Whether deaf and dumb, blind, insane, or idiotic.	
1	2	3	4	5	6	7	8	9	10	11	12	13	14	15	16	17	18	19
1	108 108	Fuller Dallas	25¾		m	Farm Labor		25	Tennessee									✓
2		" Hester	27	F	B	Farm Labor			Alabama									
3		Harper Ned	23	m	B	Farm Labor			Alabama									
4		" Charles	9	m	B				Louisiana									
5		" Jacob	1	m	B				Louisiana									
6	109 109	Buckley John	34	m	W	Farmer	360	300	Tennessee									✓
7		" Josephine	27	F	W	House Keeper			Georgia									
8		" Eugene A	6	m	W				Louisiana									
9		" John O	2	m	W				Alabama									
10	110 110	McKinney Eliza	35	F	W	House Keeper			Alabama									
11		" Joseph	19	m	W	Farm Labor			Arkansas									
12		" Mary	15	F	W				Arkansas					✓				
13		" Eliza B.	8	F	W				Arkansas					✓				
14	111 111	Bilberry Elza B	43	m	W	Farmer	360	200	Alabama									✓
15		" Cintha P	27	F	W	House Keeper			Alabama									
16		" Elizabeth M	17	F	W				Louisiana									
17		" Elza B	14	m	W	Farm Labor			Louisiana					✓				
18		" George W	12	m	W				Louisiana					✓				
19		" Lela G	10	F	W				Louisiana					✓				
20		" John M	5	m	W				Louisiana									
21	112 112	Smith Mary S	6	F	W				Louisiana									
22	113 113	Morgan York	50	m	B	Farm Labor		75	Virginia									✓
23		" Lucinda	40	F	B	House Keeper			Mississippi									
24		" Jack	23	m	B	Farm Labor			Louisiana									✓
25		" Harrison	17	m	B	Farm Labor			Louisiana									
26		" York	15	m	B	Farm Labor			Louisiana									
27		" Hanah	12	F	B	Farm Labor			Louisiana									
28		" Sam	10	m	B				Louisiana									
29		" Milton	8	m	B				Louisiana									
30		" Puss	4	F	B				Louisiana									
31	114 114	Taylor Jane	16	F	m	Farm Labor			Louisiana									

1870 U.S. Census, Union Parish, Louisiana Ward One, Union Cross Road. Note that York and Lucinda Morgan lived next to Lucinda's former slaveholder, Elsa B. Bilberry.

1880 U.S. Census, Union Parish, Louisiana Ward Six; Jack Bilberry and Francis Bilberry's Family and Dely (Delia) Bridges shown in the household of Robert and Matilda Bridges

1900 U.S. Census, Union Parish, Louisiana Ward Six: Note: Sam Morgan's Name Appears Prior to Sarah Morgan on Previous Page; also Branch Nelson, Elzy B. Bilberry, Ed Bridges-Thompson and Dolly Bridges-Thompson, John Bright, James Bilberry and Guy Bilberry

President Abraham Lincoln issued the Emancipation Proclamation that freed slaves held in Confederate territory on January 1, 1863. Louisiana was one of the states that were not affected by the order because parts of the state were already under the control of the Union. The signing of the proclamation meant freedom for the slaves, but for "tens of thousands, emancipation meant the freedom to die of starvation and illness." Emancipation came at a high price.[35] Many wandered the countryside with no place to go and no means of economic support for themselves and their families.

After the ending of the Civil War in 1865, Congress adopted the Thirteenth, Fourteenth, and Fifteenth Amendments to the Constitution of the United States, which freed the slaves, established citizenship, and gave former slaves the right to vote; but again freedom came with a price. The enactments of laws were not enough to soften the hearts of those who viewed blacks as less than human. Liberty for slaves had not made the huge leap from a life of servitude to a status of honor and respect. The slaves were now thrust into a world that left them filled with both joy and sorrow. They experienced the joy when the strait jackets of bondage were severed. Also, they experienced the sorrow of not knowing where to go and what do. Life for former slaves became both sweet and sour.

The period from 1865 to 1877, was commonly referred to as Reconstruction, but former slaves faced opposition on every front as they sought to exercise their rights as freedmen. By the late 1860s, the racial climate in North Louisiana and other parts of the South had become extremely violent. Ultimately blacks had no power or representation; they were frequently beaten and murdered in the years following the war for trying to exercise the few political rights available to them.[36]

On March 3, 1865, Congress established the Bureau of Refugees, Freedmen, and Abandoned Lands, commonly known as the Freedmen's Bureau, which was intended to address all of the concerns of the refugees and freedmen, who lived within the states during Reconstruction. It was to be in service for only one year but, on July 16, 1866, Congress extended the life of the bureau despite the veto by President Andrew Johnson. The bureau's main purposes were to establish schools, to help the freedmen to resettle, to provide food and medical care, to manage abandoned or confiscated property, to ensure justice for the freedmen, and to regulate labor. In many cases, it also provided aid for destitute whites.

The bureau opened 4000 free schools, including several colleges, and educated 250,000 African-Americans. By 1870, 21% of African-American population could read. Although the bureau was successful in some of its educational goals, it failed in its goal to help the freedmen to resettle. While the bureau gave 850,000 acres to the freedmen, President Andrew Johnson revoked the land and gave it to the Confederate landowners, instead. Consequently, the bureau focused upon employment and encouraged the freedmen to work on plantations. However, problems arose when the freedmen became sharecroppers and tenant farmers.

Even though there were many problems, the Freedmen's Bureau did help the newly freed African-Americans to get the rights that they had been denied. These included the right to an education, the right to due process, the right to the practice of religion, and the right to contract.[37]

Blacks had been freed legally, but it was far from the kind of freedom expected and outlined in the amendments to the Constitution. They wanted an opportunity to vote and to participate in the political process; if this were permitted, it would give them a sense of being a "somebody" in a world in which they were considered a "nobody." In 1867, many black males registered to vote in Union Parish. The records were the first list of Union Parish's black males after slavery ended in 1866, with the 14th Amendment to the Constitution. The former slaves were indicated by the "C" after their names (for "Colored"). In order to vote and regain their rights as citizens, all male Southerners had to register by swearing an oath to the United States and renouncing allegiance to the Confederate States of America. Some of the black men mentioned in this book that resided in Union Parish's that took the oath and registered to vote are listed below. Most southern counties (parishes in Louisiana) made such a record.[38]

BLACK MEN REGISTERED TO VOTE IN UNION PARISH AFTER SLAVERY ENDED IN 1866		
PAGE	**NAME**	**C→ COLORED**
24.	Thos. Birch	C
167.	William Roberts	C
360.	Joseph Benson	C
812.	Jack Bilberry	C
813.	York Morgan	C
1459.	Reubin Wallace	C
1468.	Sandy Waine (Wayne)	C
1597.	Sandy Waine, Sr., (Wayne)	C
1599.	Henry Ellis	C

***NOTE**: The list was filed on September 6, 1867. Women could not vote until 1920. The number to left of the name is the order in which they registered. There were a total of 1624 registered black and white male voters.*

The 1898 Union Parish, Louisiana "Grandfather Clause" Voter Registration Records transcribed by Union Parish, Louisiana transcribers indicates approximately two hundred eighty two white men registering to vote according to the terms delineated under the 1898 Louisiana Constitution. The timing of the registration probably was one of the reasons why so few men registered to vote—they had less than three months to register from the time the new Constitution was ratified. The "Grandfather Clause" was enacted by seven southern states during and after the Reconstruction Era to prevent freedmen from voting. The clause, designed to negate the 15th Amendment to the U.S. Constitution, which allowed black men to vote, significantly reduced African-Americans' political participation well into the 20th Century. Starting in Louisiana in 1898, and working its way into laws and constitutions in seven other states by 1910, the "Grandfather Clause" stated that all men or lineal descendants of men, who were voters before 1867, did not have to meet the educational, property, or tax requirements for voting then in existence. This effectively allowed all white males to vote while denying the franchise to black men and other men of color. The "Grandfather Clause", with its voting denial, became the centerpiece of a much larger system of discrimination and racial segregation. The "Grandfather Clause" applied to all men—black or white. The wall created by it had holes in it for poor whites. If you were white and could not read or write, you were allowed to vote through the holes of having "good character." If you were black and your ancestor did not vote in the previous election or you did not pass the literacy test or any other test that was given, then you were not allowed to vote.[39]

The story is told of a black teacher, a graduate of Harvard, who presented to a Mississippi registrar that he could read the state constitution and several books. The registrar came up with a passage in Latin, which the teacher read; and a passage in Greek, which the teacher read, and a passage in French, German and Spanish, all of which the teacher read. Finally, the registrar held up a page of Chinese characters and asked, 'what does this mean?" The teacher replied: "it means you don't want me to vote." These tactics were extremely effective against black voters. In 1896, for example, there were 130,000 registered black voters in Louisiana. Black voters were the majority in twenty-six parishes. In 1900, two years after adoption of a state constitution with a "Grandfather Clause," there were only 5,320 blacks eligible to vote.[40] By 1904 the number of black registered voters had dwindled to 1300.

The National Association for the Advancement of Colored People (NAACP), newly formed in 1909, mounted the first legal challenge to the "Grandfather Clause". It filed suit in the Guinn vs. United States; a case which reached the U.S. Supreme Court in 1915. The Court ruled that "Grandfather Clause" in Maryland and Oklahoma were null and void because they violated the Fifteenth Amendment to the U.S. Constitution.[41]

Former slave descendant such as Frank and Emma Bilberry wanted nothing more than the rights, which would give them the opportunity to live in dignity. They only wanted to have the rights that had been bestowed upon them by their Creator; life, liberty and the pursuit of happiness.

When Emma Roberts married Frank Bilberry on September 2, 1900, she wanted the opportunity to be all she could be as a woman in this society. Much like other woman of her time, she was not a stranger to farm work. She was born a free person in 1882 near Farmerville, in Union Parish, Louisiana. She was the daughter of Will Roberts and Eliza Burch-Roberts.[42] The 1900 Census list her soon to be husband, Frank Bilberry, working as a servant for Alcandor and Ada Ewing. The 1910 U.S. Census for Union Parish lists her as a farm laborer on their home farm. Emma and Frank had four children living and one that died—Willie, and three living—Ladelle, Jesse B. and Charlie. Also, Angeline, Papa Franks' half-sister resided in the household; she was twenty one years old at that time. My research shows Angeline living in the household with Robert and Hattie Bridges based on the 1900 U.S. Census of Ward Six in Union Parish, Louisiana. Angeline later married Isaac (Ike) Douglas.[43] Frank and Emma had two other children by 1917— Eddie and Mary; all of their children lived to be adults. By the time of the 1920 Census for Union Parish, the entire family was listed as mulatto for the color of race.

Angeline Bilberry-Douglas (1894-?)
half-sister of Frank Bilberry

L to R-sitting -Emma Bilberry, Ada Ewing, Jeanette Cleveland, and Estelle Ewing-Evans, standing-L to R-Lucille Ewing-Wayne, Trudie Ewing-Billberry, Odessa Ewing-Mitchell, and Beleter Ewing-Carter. Note: Trudie Ewing-Bilberry was married to Jessie Bilberry. Jessie Bilberry was the son of Frances Bilberry and Jack Bilberry.
Courtesy of Charles Henry Bilberry, Jr.

Also, Emma (aka Mama Emma) served her community in other meaningful ways. In addition to her duties as a housewife and farm laborer, she often practiced midwifery by helping women bring their babies into the world. On other occasions, Mama Emma served as a medicine woman because of her knowledge of the medicinal value of certain roots, leaves and herbs. I remember my parents visiting with her as a child and in the 1960s. The strong scent of eucalyptus, mullein, pine needles, and cow-chip tea would permeate the atmosphere upon entering. She used these herbs to treat illnesses such as colds, flu and pneumonia. She knew the medicinal value of sulfur and salves for treating or warding off infections. Mama Emma's parents, Will and Eliza Roberts had other children—Daniel, Clinton, Littleton, Charlie, and Lee. Stella Jackson and Allise Richards lived with them as well as their grandson Robert Benson according to the 1910 U.S. Census. Robert Benson was the husband of Bessie Benson. Georgia Willie Mae Benson was one of their daughters; she married Eddie Bilberry in 1941.[44]

L to R-sitting – Georgia Taylor -Wayne, Bessie Benson (May 9, 1893-October 1990), Beulah Lee, Mady Benson, and standing – Bettie Ann Davis, Willie B. Wayne, James Lewis. Joann and Barbara are daughters of Mady Benson.
Courtesy of Georgia Willie Mae Bilberry-Benson

Georgia Willie Mae Benson-Bilberry Daughter of Robert and Bessie Benson
Courtesy of Georgia Willie Mae Bilberry-Benson

Frank Bilberry with Horse

By the 1930 U.S. Census, Eliza Roberts was shown living in the household with her daughter and son-in-law, Emma and Frank Bilberry. Eliza's husband, Will Roberts had died a decade earlier at the age of 63 from complications associated with pneumonia.[45] Frank Bilberry was still a general farmer with three children, Willie Frank, Eddie and Mary residing in his household. Like numerous other Americans, they were struggling to survive the Great Depression. They lived off the land; the crops and their livestock they raised and harvested provided nourishment for themselves. Willie Frank, the oldest child, married Lettie Warren Archie on January 20, 1936.[46] Four years later on July 14, 1940, Willie Frank died at the age of 39 from coronary failure. His father, Frank Bilberry's name was listed on the death certificate as Jesse Frank Bilberry. It was interesting to see that Frank Bilberry was listed as Joe Frank Bilberry on his marriage license with Emma Roberts.[47] He went on to name one of his own sons Jesse Bernard Bilberry, Sr., and a grandson was named Joseph Bilberry.

Eliza Roberts died of heart failure the next year at the age of 91. Frank Bilberry succumbed to the years of chronic nephritis and arteriosclerosis and died on October 14, 1953. His wife Emma would live to see two more decades beyond the life they shared. Frank and Emma's daughter Mary married Jethro Horn; they became homeowners in Farmerville, Louisiana where she had a small store. She died at the age of 46 on August 21, 1956, from pulmonary edema (see Death Certificate Collection in Appendix A). Eddie Bilberry lived for another 41 years. He served the country in World War II; married Georgia Willie Mae Benson and they became homeowners in Monroe, Louisiana; he retired from years of employment at the Holiday Inn. He departed this life March 31, 1997, at the age of 84 years old.[48] Frank and Emma's older children had moved away from home by 1930. As previously mentioned Ladell Bilberry married Maggie Washington. He purchased land near his grandfather, Frank and started a farm. Maggie died at the age of 28 on March 23, 1936, from pneumonia.

Frank Bilberry (1878-October 14, 1953) son of Eliza (Delia) Bridges and Britt

Lizza Burch-Roberts mother of Emma Roberts.
Courtesy of Charles Henry Bilberry, Jr.

Ladell then married Corene McGough and continued farming.[49] He died November

3, 1970 from heart complications. Emma Bilberry, the matriarch of my Bilberry family, had administered help to many who were sick and suffering from illnesses. She passed away on September 12, 1972; she was 90 years old.[50] Also, Jesse Bernard Bilberry, Sr., purchased land near his father Frank and was a general farmer as well. He graduated from Southern University and did further study at Tuskegee Institute and Grambling University. He became the principal of Union Parish Colored School in Farmerville, Louisiana and was married to Joe B. Dixson; Jesse Bernard Bilberry died on February 19, 1961.[51]

Ladell Bilberry and Maggie Washington-Bilberry

Jesse B. Bilberry, Sr., and Joe B. Dixson-Bilberry)

Corene McGough-Bilberry; Second wife of Ladell Bilberry (November 17, 1915-October 31, 1984)

Charles Henry Bilberry, Sr., and Dellie Dixson-Bilberry

Courtesy of Charles Henry Bilberry, Jr.

Georgia Willie Mae Benson-Bilberry   Eddie Bilberry, Sr., (March 20, 1913--March 31, 1997)

Mary Bilberry-Horn (November 1, 1910-August 21, 1956) First wife of Jethro Horn

Jethro Horn (April 26, 1912-November 13, 2002 (aka Uncle Jay)

As previously mentioned, Jesse Bernard Bilberry, Sr. was a pastor of Sweet Lilly Primitive Baptist Church. In the earlier years, Sweet Lilly was considered the family church. Charlie Bilberry married Dellie Dixson, Joe B. Dixson's sister in Vaugine, Arkansas (near Pine Bluff, Arkansas). They lived there a few years and then moved to Flint, Michigan; Charlie Bilberry died on November 7, 1979, at the age of 73.[52]

For 14 years I've tried to find the evidence that would validate my great grandfather, Frank Bilberry's white father. Many relatives have said that Frank Bilberry was the illegitimate son of a white man name Britt Bilberry (Elzy Britton Bilberry) of Union Parish, Louisiana with Frank's mother, Delia or Eliza Bridges. Delia was the daughter of Robert and Matilda Bridges according to the 1880 U.S. Census of Union Parish, Louisiana. Their other children were William, Lura, Sally, Fanny, Anna, Robert, Jr., Rastus and Andrew. Britt probably sired two other daughters with Delia named Annie and probably Anna Holland.[53] Delia married Anderson Thompson where she had another son and daughter name Ed Thompson and Dollie Thompson-Mayfield. Ed Thompson and Dollie Thompson-Mayfield was Frank Bilberry's half-brother and half-sister—same mother, but different father.[54] Dolly and Ed were full sister and brother. Mary Lee Warren, a 90 year old granddaughter of Lura Bridges stated to me that Matilda Bridges, the mother of Delia Bridges was beaten by her slave master before giving birth to twin daughters Lura and Sally Bridges. The reason for such beating was never revealed to her by her grandmother Lura. Sally Bridges married George Washington; she died in West Monroe, Louisiana. Sallie and Lura are buried at Antioch Cemetery in Truxno, Louisiana. William (Bill) Bridges is buried at Fellowship Cemetery in Spearsville, Louisiana. On one of the many conversations I had with Mary Lee Warren, she mentioned that Frank Bilberry would call her grandmother Lura, "Aunt Lura" and Sally, "Aunt Sally." Delia was the sister of Lura and Sally (Sarah) Bridges. Therefore, Delia is probably Frank Bilberry's mother.

Frank Bilberry's father was Britt Bilberry according to a testimony given to me by phone and in person by Barbra Bilberry, granddaughter of Frank and Emma Bilberry. Barbra would often visit her grandmother and discuss the family's history with her. Her grandmother would often say to her that Papa Frank's dad's name was like that of the poker player Bret in the television western "Maverick" that was shown from 1957 to 1962.[55]

It is ironic that Britten Honeycutt the brother-in-law of Elsey B. Bilberry owned land next to both Lawrence Bilberry and Frank Bilberry according to the Land Patent Map in Appendix C and Frank Bilberry's land purchase from Otis Tugwell. As mentioned earlier from the oral testimony of Paul Bilberry, Frank also had a brother name Lawrence Bilberry. Paul had said that his father's mother was Narsis and the father was Britt or Bridges Bilberry.[56]

Ed Thompson (Mar. 15, 1892--May 1972)
Half-brother of Frank Bilberry

Courtesy of Lucy Nell Johnson

Anna Bilberry-Holland and Husband
Mason Holland Sister of Frank Bilberry

Courtesy of Sheila Rowland

According to the 1900 U.S. Census, Narsis married Fred Armstrong; he was a farmer born in 1840, and his father's birthplace was listed Alabama. I read and reread thousands of names in U.S. Census lists, slaveholders' records, successions, conveyances, and land patents, but most of those led to dead ends. There were no "white people" with the name Bridges Bilberry or Briad Bilberry (Lawrence Bilberry's death certificate and Frank Bilberry's death certificate are found in Appendix A). Often, I felt that I was chasing a phantom man through the maze of my research. It became a consuming struggle for me to try and penetrate the past. I felt that one day I would be able to grasp my great grandfathers' white fathers' name from a document that had been hidden for years. At some point, my research became fruitless. Books, pictures, death certificates, marriage licenses began to fill our office at home. My computer desktop was stacked with articles from the internet and the local Latter Day Saints' family history library. My wife understood my quest even though the office was often a total mess. At times, there appeared to be nothing left for me to find; all that is left is my insane urge to keep looking. Insane because I had no idea what I was looking to find! Is it a picture, a will, a deed or maybe an oral history testimony? The only way to find out is to keep looking and piecing together the fragments of information that I have.

Dollie Mayfield (December 25, 1895--July 12, 1991) Half-sister of Frank Bilberry; full sister of Ed Thompson

Clara Holland-Waters (September 1929-?) Daughter of Anna Bilberry-Holland

I found out later that perseverance pay dividends because E. B. Bilberry's middle name was "Britton." Everyone called him Britt Bilberry. Many people named their children after his name such as Elzy Billberry Robinson; the son of John Bishop Robinson and Frances Bilberry-Robinson. Frances was E. B. Bilberry's sister. John and Frances were faithful members of Meridian Missionary Baptist Church. J.W.B. Roberson and Mollie Wallace-Robinson named their son Elzy Britton Roberson. Elzy died at the age of 32 and was buried in Haile, Louisiana in Union Parish.

CHAPTER SIX

Mama's Death

A few years ago there was a movie about a man that was characterized by his simplicity, honesty, and integrity. This man's name was Forrest Gump. As I watched the movie, I laughed when Forrest laughed. I cheered when Forrest Gump ran with the football to score a number of touchdowns. I choked up when Forrest lost his best friend in the Vietnam War. My toes began to tap when I heard the music of my youth from the 1960's and the 1970's. Along with everybody else that was in the movie that day I cried as Forrest sat down and grieved and moaned the loss of his mother. But what captivated me the most was that even though Forrest Gump only had an IQ of 75 and was severely limited in his mental capacity; by using the wisdom of his mother Forrest became a better person. One of Forrest Gump's favorite lines in the movie was, "mama said."

At my mother's funeral, I stood before the audience and shared with all in attendance, some of the wisdom that my mother instilled in me. Like Forrest Gump, I talked about the things that mama said. As I reflect back on those words that I spoke at my mother's funeral on July 24, 2009. I cannot help but to recall the events that led to her demise. Mama always told me that she wanted to live into her 90's; but little did she know that she too would die of cancer just like my father. She stayed with him in the hospital room in Monroe, Louisiana while he battled his sickness for weeks at a time. They had a small cot for her to sleep on during her stay. She went home only to do the things that were necessary such as paying bills and wash clothing. She would only be gone from his bedside for two or three days. In her earlier years, she cleaned homes for the local white people that lived in the area. Every now and then she would chop and pick cotton. She did these things in order to have her own money. Later in her life, she worked as a nursing assistant for eleven years at Marion Nursing Home in Marion, Louisiana and Lakeview Nursing Home in Farmerville. She stopped working in order to take care of my father during his illness. I had asked her years ago if daddy passed away, where, she would want to live at! She quickly replied that she would sell every damn thing and come to Las Vegas, Nevada! She had visited Las Vegas on numerous occasions where two of her children Peggie and Charles (the author); a grandson Jared and a brother, Clifton Brown resided. My sister, Fonda Deleon moved from Las Vegas and lived in various parts of Southern California for the past twenty five years.

Daddy passed away, but my mother changed her mind about coming to Las Vegas,

Nevada. She had mentioned to me of all that my father and she had accumulated over the past 44 years and the friends and memories were too great to walk away from. Five months later, I received a call from my mother that she was ready to come to Las Vegas. She mention to me that it was too hard to maintain the two acres of land that had a vegetable garden, trees , flowers and shrubs that seem to grow out of control over night. On October 23, 1997, she decided to sell her home with everything in it except personal possessions and move to her new place of abode in Las Vegas.

Mama fell in love with her new apartment home. She loved the fifty-five and older age requirement for residents of the apartments and the free shuttles to local stores, banks and casinos, even though she did not gamble. She really loved living in Las Vegas and the conveniences it offered. She enjoyed having Christmas and Thanksgiving dinner with family, going to church and the parties they offered for seniors at her apartment complex. She never wanted to marry again. She often said to me, "I'll date a nice man, but most of them that I know are too old and broke down to do anything." She was blessed to live in the city with her children and grandson for thirteen years. But God gives us all an appointed time to live and an appointed time to die.

I watched her and took care of her each day from the time she was diagnosed with this dreaded disease. She would shrink and her skin withered as her muscles died cell by cell. Two days before her death, I was at her bedside where she was in an almost comatose state. I held her hand and called her name. She recognized my voice and squeezed my hand as if to say that everything was going to be all right. At that moment I knew that she had accepted her fate, to be absent from the body, but present in the Lord.

My youngest sister Fonda decided not to come to our mother's funeral. Upon my mother's request, she had come to visit her about a month before she passed. My mother wanted us all to be there together just to talk to us. My sister's decision ended hopes I had for a complete family memorial service with my mother's three children and one grandson. Instead, I accepted her absence with much disappointment. Sometimes we aren't the type of people that would put everything aside to gather together at important occasion such as this.

Both of my parents are now deceased. We can no longer delude ourselves into thinking that this life would stretch into eternal life; we too will die one day! In life, we often find out that the higher we climbed the "ladder of success," the farther we remove ourselves from our roots. We remove ourselves from those who matter most to us when we were little children.

CHAPTER SEVEN

What They Knew: Oral History Interviews

Oral history is the facts, traditions, and stories passed from one generation to the next by word of mouth. It is recording and sharing interviews of people about their past memories. When studying oral history, one discovers early in the process that seldom does one person serve as the repository of all of the family's history. Quite often, many individuals with a little information here and there help put pieces of the story together. The following oral history transcripts are the result of tape-recorded interviews from July 31, 2010, through December 31, 2010. *The interviews were conducted by the author of this book, Charles Lee Bilberry.*

Interview with Jessie Mae Bilberry – July 31, 2010 – 12:10 pm – Truxno, Louisiana

Jessie Mae Andrews-Bilberry, is the husband of Paul Bilberry, who is deceased; Jessie provided, this author with vital information about Lawrence Bilberry, the brother of Frank Bilberry.

Jessie Mae Bilberry

Charles:	How long have you been living in this house?
Jessie:	Since 1942.
Charles:	Did you have a nickname?
Jessie:	I had a lot of nicknames. Some called me Molly. I can't think of another one right now, but I had several nicknames. Okay, just use that one.
Charles:	When were you born?
Jessie:	February 22, 1927.
Charles:	What are your parents' full names?
Jessie:	My father's name was Winzer Andrews, they called him Doc. My mother's name was Gertie Andrews; Gertie Warren Andrews.
Charles:	What cemetery are they buried at.
Jessie:	Out at Antioch AME.
Charles:	Your grandparents?
Jessie:	Yeah, they are out there too.
Charles:	What are their names?
Jessie:	Sarah was my grandmother. Dennis was my grandfather.
Charles:	Is there anything you remember about your family on the Andrews side? I am going to stick to the Andrews side right now; anything that's unique to you? They lived in this area here too? Or did they live somewhere else?
Jessie:	They did live in this area for a while, before I was born, then they went to other different places. I had an uncle that lived in Chicago. I had an aunt that lived in Texas. The others I guess were right around here. Some of them passed when I was small.
Charles:	What do you know about the Douglas'? Did you know very many Douglas'? Ike Douglas, Angeline Douglas?
Jessie:	Yeah, I know them. I know Arnet Douglas. That's about all I know. I knew about some of their children. The older people, that's the oldest that I know about.
Charles:	What kind of lady was Angeline Douglas? How did she look?
Jessie:	Well, she was kind of low; heavy set, dark skinned. As far as I know; she was a real nice person.
Charles:	What do you know about the Bilberrys? Frank and Lawrence! I think you might have heard of Anna Bilberry? She was Mason Holland's wife!
Jessie:	Well, that's all I knew about her; she was Lawrence's sister. They didn't live around here. I didn't know too much about them.
Charles:	What did you know about Frank Bilberry and Mama Emma?
Jessie:	Papa Frank? I was never around Uncle Frank very much, but Aunt Emma! Aunt Emma was a midwife. She was with me when all of my children were born, except the last two, I believe. Even though she didn't do the midwife when I went to the hospital, she was at the hospital with me when all my kids; all but two. She stayed with me, almost like another mother. She was with me with the first one. Sometimes she had to stay a day or two, but she stayed there until the kids were born. As far as I know about her, she was just a good person.
Charles:	She did a little doctoring too.
Jessie:	Oh yeah. Yeah she did.
Charles:	She took care of a lot of people as far as when they were sick. She was like a little community doctor.

Jessie:	Yes, you could ask her things and she could pretty well tell you what you need to do; what kind of medication; the home remedies!
Charles:	Get some sassafras roots and stuff like that and boil it and drink it.
Jessie:	Yeah, make some tea out of it and all like that; mullein and pine tar and all that kind of stuff.
Charles:	Yeah, I remember daddy taking about boiling some hog hoofs to make some tea, boil it, sweeten it, and drink it. It was supposed to get rid of a fever or something. I don't remember what he was trying to do, but it made you feel better.
Jessie:	I don't remember what it was for, but it helped whatever you had; it surely did.
Charles:	What about Papa Frank? You said you weren't around him much?
Jessie:	I wasn't around him a whole lot.
Charles:	Did he ever visit Uncle Lawrence?
Jessie:	I'm sure he did, but I don't remember.
Charles:	What did people tend to think about them being half white?
Jessie:	Well didn't anybody think that way. They didn't talk about it.
Charles:	Everybody just said, "well, you know he's half white."
Jessie:	Yeah, you could tell they were mixed though. I don't guess nobody had no problem with it cause my family was mixed with the Andrews; the white Andrews. You don't find too many that are not mixed up with somebody, you know.
Charles:	Now in your family, did you know any of the white Andrews that you were mixed with?
Jessie:	Well, they had let me see! Paul Andrews, but I can't think of the other one that they said was really on down the line, but the elder one that was really mixed! I can't remember his name right now, but they were mixed up with the Andrews all right.
Charles:	I remember talking to your husband Paul the last time I was here. He was telling me that Uncle Lawrence's mother's name was Narsis.
Jessie:	Yeah, that's what they called her. I don't remember her nickname, but I heard him say that. She was gone before my time.
Charles:	Also, he mentioned that Lawrence's father was a white man and his name was Bridges Bilberry or Britt Bilberry.
Jessie:	Britt, I heard that too! It was before my time, but I did hear that.
Charles:	Yeah, and it looks like most of the white Bilberrys tend to have moved out of the area.
Jessie:	Well some of them did.
Charles:	Do you know some of the white Bilberrys that were still here?
Jessie:	No, I didn't know, but I guess all of them were gone.
Charles:	They got out of here. Looks like by 1920 all of them were gone.
Jessie:	That was a little bit before my time.
Charles:	Right. Did you know a lady by the name of Rachel Thompson?
Jessie:	I heard of her. I didn't know her. I remember the name, but don't know anything about the person.
Charles:	Now she stayed with Angeline Bilberry-Douglas and according to the U.S.

	Census it listed Rachel Thompson as her aunt. I'm trying to find out—who Angeline's mother was too.

Jessie: Well I don't know. Georgia Ann didn't know?

Charles: No, I talked to Georgia Ann this morning and she said, "I don't know anything!" I don't think she wanted to talk, but that's okay. She don't know me and probably wasn't as comfortable talking to me about it, but she had told me, even ten years ago she said she didn't know and so I didn't want her to have to make something up if she didn't know. I don't think she would have done that anyway. But she was a Bilberry and I've been looking at the census and seems like I've seen Angeline's surname written down as Bridges. Did you know any Bridges around here?

Jessie: No, I didn't.

Charles: A guy named Jessie Bridges? There were lots of Bridges. It looks like the Bilberrys, Frank and Lawrence had the same white father, but different mothers. Like Paul's mother was Narsis, but Papa Frank's mother from what I gather; her name was Delilah, Eliza or Delia Bridges. It appear that the white man went and had kids by different black women, but some of their half brothers and sisters were sired by a black man because the black women eventually married a black man. Then there was a lady named Dolly Mayfield. Her maiden name was Bridges. She then took on the surname Thompson, because her mother Delia Bridges birth her and a son, Ed Thompson by a man name Anderson Thompson. She was Papa Frank's half-sister.

Jessie: Okay, I gave you the wrong date from when we began living here. We moved here in1964.

Charles: Oh, 1964.

Jessie: Right, we were staying not too far from here, but we moved here in 1964.

Charles: And where did you live before.

Jessie: Not far from here, right over across in Farmerville. I don't remember what I told you.

Charles: You said 1942.

Jessie: Okay, we married in 1942 and we moved here in 1964.

Charles: How were times at that time?

Jessie: Well, not too well! Paul went in the service. We married in June and he went in the service not long after that and he was in the service for three years.

Charles: Yeah, I saw his discharge papers. He was an artillery gunner.

Jessie: Well, you know. It wasn't too good. It could have been worse, but it could have been a whole lot better, you know. Everybody was on the same basis; black folks I'm talking about. You know they were just drafting people then. You didn't volunteer. They drafted you in the service.

Charles: What was it like as far as the living among the whites here in this area, the Smith's and the Cobbs and all of them that lived in this area. Blacks, you stay over there; and if white, you stay over here? Did they try to get along and help you out?

Jessie: Well you know the blacks were always separated. Whites didn't live in this area. No closer than up to Truxno up there. Way back, there was one white family that stayed right up here. I imagine you heard tell of the Brashiers? Well you know they lived right up there, but I didn't know anything about them because I hardly saw them. We have been by ourselves the whole time.

Charles: Yeah, I was looking at the census and I see at the age of 16 years old, Lawrence Bilberry was living with William T. Smith. He was a minister at Meridian Baptist Church. A lot of the Smiths belonged to Meridian Baptist Church.

Jessie: Oh Yeah, they was living down in that area.

Charles: Lawrence stayed with them at the age of 16 years old.

Jessie: Yeah, I heard that too.

Charles: You heard that he stayed with them?

Jessie: I heard he did. You didn't hear too much about old people way back because they didn't talk too much. When they go to talking about things like that, you got out. Not like the kids now! You can go to talking and they got to be right where you're at. But older people back there then, when they got ready to talk about stuff like that, you got out and went to playing, you know. So, I didn't know anything about that.

Charles: Yeah, he supposedly stayed with them. He was like a boarder and servant. He worked for them and I assumed he lived there too. The denomination you belong to is AME (African Methodist Episcopal) right?

Jessie: Right.

Charles: How long have you been AME?

Jessie: All my life.

Charles: And your husband Paul?

Jessie: Same thing.

Charles: And Uncle Lawrence?

Jessie: Same thing.

Charles: So he's been AME since the two of you've been here right? Did you know anybody that was black that went to Meridian Baptist Church?

Jessie: No, not that I know.

Charles: Years ago, slaves went there. I found this in the Meridian Baptist Church minutes. Also, I noticed that they have two cemeteries; a black cemetery and a white cemetery with a road dividing the two. I noticed there were a lot of Ellis', Douglas's buried there, and Burch's buried there. On the white side, there were a lot of Smiths, Cobbs, and Slades. The church closed down. Did you remember when it was an active church with people going to it? I think it closed in the early 1970's.

Jessie: No, that was before my time.

Charles: Okay.

Jessie: Because when we moved from out there, I heard my mother say that Mr. Lawrence was a trustee, yeah, I believe he was. They had some kind of little trial or something and I remember her say that she was pregnant with me. They put off the court date. I don't what it was about now, until after I was born. Now that was before my time when we moved from out there.

Charles: You talking about Antioch?

Jessie: I think you talking about the old church that burned down. When they moved from out there Mr. Lawrence gave them an acre of land here where the church is now. You got that in your records too?

Charles: No, but I'm getting it now. So he gave an acre of land?

Jessie:	An acre of land here where the Antioch AME Church is now. The white Church is the AME Church. The brick church is full Gospel, I believe. Did you see the name on it?
Charles:	The one right up here somewhere?
Jessie:	The name is in front of the brick church. It belongs to the white people over here.
Charles:	That's a historical thing to remember? That's good.
Charles:	You got any old obituaries or photos of family members from way, way back in the day? I think I've already looked at your photo album before.
Jessie:	Yeah, you did. The granddaughter got that now. She wanted to take it and do her some pictures.
Charles:	She heard I was coming and wanted to get them before I got here!
Jessie:	She lives in Baton Rouge, Louisiana and she begged me to take the book. She promised that she would not lose it. I told her that she better not lose any pictures. She put them in a bag and took them.
Charles:	Annie Bilberry was Frank and Lawrence Bilberry's sister. You mentioned to me on a previous visit that she lived in Crossett, Arkansas. How did she look by the way?
Jessie:	She looked like a white woman.
Charles:	Another white woman.
Jessie:	Real light skinned.
Charles:	Was she a heavy set lady or skinny.
Jessie:	Well, I just saw her a time or two. She was tall, medium built.
Charles:	Did she have good hair? Black hair?
Jessie:	Yeah, she had white folks' hair; well you know it wasn't exactly straight. Well, you know when you mixed up, it's kind of wavy or whatever.
Charles:	What kind of personality did she have?
Jessie:	I was not around her enough to know anything about her because she was sick.
Charles:	She was sick?
Jessie:	Yeah, at the time, she was sick
Charles:	Do you know if she died there?
Jessie:	As far as I know, she was there when she passed. I don't remember anything about any of them going to her funeral. They might have gone, but I don't remember.
Charles:	Do you know if she had any kids?
Jessie:	Well, I thought she had a daughter. But what I was telling you, somebody said that was the other lady, Miss Anna. That's the one that lived in Monroe right?
Charles:	Right, and she had a daughter named Ella. Did you know Ella Lowe?
Jessie:	Yeah, I heard of her, but I thought Miss Annie had a daughter; I can't prove it because I don't know nobody I can ask, but I thought she had a daughter.
Charles:	When I look at the census record, I see where Annie Bilberry married and she lived up around Junction City area. That's where she ended up living and she married General Wallace. You said you remembered him.
Jessie:	Yeah, I remember him.

Charles:	He was an older fellow at that time. Did you ever see him?
Jessie:	Yeah, I saw him plenty of times.
Charles:	What did he look like?
Jessie:	Well, he was a little low man and he walked kind of bent. He was a real neat man. When he dressed up and I remember he had a white suit. When he dressed up and got on his good looking shoes and everything, I don't care how muddy the road was; General could walk and didn't get any mud on his shoes. He was kind of peculiar to my knowledge. You know, young people back then paid attention to people like that. He didn't ever have that much to do with children as far as I can remember; but I can remember him. I can almost picture him now.
Charles:	When you saw him, did he come to see relatives? Did he have people that lived in this area?
Jessie:	You know Miss Letha was his sister.
Charles:	Right, Letha Archie.
Jessie:	He didn't do a whole lot, but I don't know. You know, I always thought we called him uncle. He would come around sometimes, but I don't guess he wasn't any kin to us. But all the old people at that time, you had to call them an aunt or uncle.
Charles:	Right, whether they were kin to you or not. Do you know if he was married at that time? You just saw him by himself most of the time.
Jessie:	Well, at that time, he wasn't married. I don't know anything about no wife. He might have been married, but I didn't know.
Charles:	I see in the U.S Census where, they mentioned that he was widowed. If this is the same lady that I'm thinking about, they put on the census that she was a widow, but yet I have their marriage record. I talked to Benny Archie the other day and of course he is at our class of 1970 reunion. He said he has a picture of Letha, his grandmother. Hopefully I can get a picture of her too! I noticed that General Wallace and Letha Archie parents' name were Rueben Wallace (father) and Crecy Wallace (mother). General Wallace was twelve years older than Miss Letha. Is there anything else that you think that might be worth sharing in this story when I write this book? I'm supposed to talk to Rodell Burch too and get a little information from him. His mother was Hannah Burch. I'm sure you know her too.
Jessie:	Yeah, I remember Hannah.
Charles:	I'm supposed to talk to John Ellis. His father was Claude Ellis, I think. There were some Nelsons in this area too. Branch Nelson?
Jessie:	I never did know anything about him.
Charles:	Also, there were some Morgans in this area, John Morgan, lived up in Oakland, Louisiana didn't, he?
\Jessie:	The older ones are all dead.
Charles:	I think you told me that his mother, Sam Morgan married Sarah Montgomery.
Jessie:	Her name was Sarah, but I didn't know what she was.
Charles:	You told me one of the sons lives up there now. I'm supposed to see him too. He's got pictures too. You are my first interview. You're the one that knows me the most anyway other than John Earl Ellis.

65

Jessie: Maybe you'll get more information from them than you did me.

Charles: I've gotten information from you over the years since 1997. I started my first Bilberry-Horn family reunion book then. I think I sent you a copy of it.

Interview ended. Looked at family reunion books.

Interview with Lucy Nell Johnson – August 1, 2010 – Farmerville, Louisiana

Lucy Nell Johnson is a retired school teacher in the Union Parish School District. She continued to work part-time as a teacher with the District.

Lucy Nell Johnson
Courtesy of Lucy Nell Johnson

Charles: We are in the home of Lucy Nell and T. J Johnson. Lucy Nell is going to give us a little history. Lucy Nell, please state your name for the record; what is your full name?

Lucy Nell: Lucy Nell Finley-Johnson.

Charles: Did you ever have any nicknames?

Lucy Nell: No, everybody calls me Nell.

Charles: When were you born?

Lucy Nell: September 23, 1931.

Charles: What are your parents' full names?

Lucy Nell: My mother was Lucy Kemp-Finley. My father's name is Wise Finley.

Charles: You had mentioned to me when I talked to you on the phone that Ashby Finley was Wise's brother.

Lucy Nell: That's right. That was my uncle.

Charles: What were your grandparents' names? Did you know who they were?

Lucy Nell: Yes, my grandmother was Martha Moses-Finley. That's my father's mother. My grandfather's name was Monroe Finley. Now my mother's mother was Fronie Kemp-Thompson. My grandfather was Dan Kemp, but later after he passed away, my grandmother married my step-grandfather, Mr. Ed Thompson. I believe that was in 1955 or 1956.

Charles: What kind of a man was Ed Thompson? What kind of personality did he have?

Lucy Nell: He was a great person. He accepted us just as if we were his real grandchildren and we couldn't really tell the difference. It was as if we were his real grandchildren; he had one favorite out of us, which was my sister's son Dan Edward. Dan was named after him and his name was Dan Edward Lewis. That was his favorite out of all of us, but he was a great person. He was a religious person and the evening he passed away, he was on his way to church. He was driving to church and passed away as he was coming down the hill from his house. Yes, he was driving and the car rolled over. He and my grandmother were in the car and the car rolled over in a ditch; they backed up in a ditch. That's where they had to stay until the coroner could get there because we couldn't get her out of the car either until the coroner got there.

Charles: Did she pass away too?

Lucy Nell: No, I mean not then, she lived a long time. She even moved up here with us and she stayed here with us ten years.

Charles: He passed away from the accident.

Lucy Nell: He had a heart attack. He didn't pass away from the accident. He had a massive heart attack.

Charles: Later on?

Lucy Nell: No that evening.

Charles: Oh, that same evening?

Lucy Nell: The evening he was driving to church. He was on his way to church. He was on his way to prayer meeting; and he had the heart attack as he was driving to church. They were just blessed that the car rolled back in a ditch and that's where it stayed until the coroner could get there and get him out.

Charles: How was Ed Thompson related to Dolly Mayfield?

Lucy Nell: Miss Dolly was his sister.

Charles: They had the same mother and father?

Lucy Nell: I really don't know. All I remember was her name Dolly Mayfield and she lived in Washington. She stayed in Washington; I remember that much. My grandmother used to converse with her when she lived in Washington after Ed passed away.

Charles: Did you ever see her?

Lucy Nell: No, I never did.

Charles: Do you have a picture of her?

Lucy Nell: No, I don't have a picture of her.

Charles: Did you know any Bridges?

Lucy Nell: The only Bridges I know is Wilber Bridges.

Charles: There were supposed to be some Bridges that are related to Ed Thompson and Dolly Mayfield. They were supposed to have stayed with Robert and Matilda Bridges. What I found in the census records so far, it looks like Ed and Dolly's mother was Delia Bridges. I'm trying to make that connection. I just wanted to see if you knew anything about the Bridges.

Lucy Nell: No, I only know Wilber Bridges and Wilber's sister-in-law lives next door over here.

Charles: From what I understand too, it seems as though Ed Thompson and Frank Bilberry were brothers? Like half-brothers.

Lucy Nell: Right, they were half-brothers.

Charles: Did he ever talk about Papa Frank?

Lucy Nell: He really did. He loved his people and that was brother Frank.

Charles: Did they ever visit each other?

Lucy Nell: I don't really know. I do know that his children, the grandchildren would ask about him when I would see them. Most of the time Barbra would ask about Uncle Ed.

Charles: Also, she knows about Dolly. She mentioned that they have a picture of her somewhere. It could be with one of the older girls like Lena Ruth or one of the other sisters.

Lucy Nell: I used to work with Barbra.

Charles: Were you raised up in that Ward Six area at any time?

Lucy Nell: Never was; I lived over here all my life.

Charles: Your Uncle Ashby, what role did he play over at Sweet Lilly Church? Was he a deacon over there?

Lucy Nell: He was a deacon.

Charles: What church do you belong to here in Farmerville?

Lucy Nell: Zion Hill Missionary Baptist Church.

Charles: Were you always at Zion Hill?

Lucy Nell: No, I used to belong to Triumph Church down the street, but later I joined with Zion Hill Missionary Baptist Church where Tommy Carr is my Pastor.

Charles: Senior, not junior. There was senior there right?

Lucy Nell: Junior, I mean Tommy L. Carr is the Pastor, now his father was George Allen Carr.

Charles: Triumph Church, is it still around?

Lucy Nell: Yes, right down the street.

Charles: How long has it been in existence?

Lucy Nell: It has been here all of my life. I was reared up in Triumph Church. It's a Holiness Church.

Charles: I remember when I was a kid coming up we would come from Marion to see Uncle Shelton. I knew about Blooming Grove Baptist Church. Let's see there was another church. Was it Beulah? It was right where the Green Onion Cafe used to be.

Lucy Nell: Yes, it was Beulah. Triumph Church is on this street; it's a Holiness Church; Church of God and Christ. Now the Church of God and Christ was behind Mr. Shelton's house. They had a two story building up there.

Charles: Also, on this street Jewell Bilberry lived. Did you know him?

Lucy Nell: Yes, I did.

Charles: And Laura Archie-Bilberry. What did you know about them?

Lucy Nell: Well, I know that Miss Laura was a member of Triumph Church. I don't know exactly, but I think he was a member of Center Branch Baptist Church, and she was a member of Triumph Church. I've known them all of my life.

Charles: From what people tell me, they used to own a store?

Lucy Nell: Yes, in front of their house; also that was on this street.

Charles: Little merchants. Then, I guess right up the street here was Jay Horn and Mary Horn.

Lucy Nell: They were in the same block. They had a store too!

Charles: I remember as a kid, they used to have that little gas pump where the gas went up in it glass tank. It was there for a long time, until they finally tore it down,

I guess. What were they like, I mean I know about Uncle Jay, but Aunt Mary died a lot sooner than he did. Mary Horn, what was she like?

Lucy Nell: I didn't know Miss Mary that well. I knew her, but as far as just being around her I just didn't know her that well.

Charles: Okay, let's move on to Emma Bilberry aka Mama Emma.

Lucy Nell: I knew her as Mama Emma. That's what everybody called her, Mama Emma. Also, they were in this block.

Charles: From what I hear from everybody and of course as a kid coming up too; she did a lot of doctoring on people around here.

Lucy Nell: Yeah, I understand that she delivered quite a few babies around here too. I've been told that she was a midwife.

Charles: Yes, that's what a lot of people said. I guess her husband, Papa Frank died in 1953 and she died in 1972. Did you ever go to Sweet Lilly Primitive Baptist Church?

Lucy Nell: Oh yes, I did. I used to go to Sweet Lilly. That was my family's Church.

Charles: Your roots were there!

Lucy Nell: Yes, my daddy's people that was my daddy's people over there and for a long time, that's all I really knew about, Sweet Lilly. Every meeting, I think that's the first Sunday in May we used to go to Sweet Lilly. Even when before I married my husband, his grandmother was a member there; also, we would go every first Sunday in May. We continued to visit because his grandmother was a member there and we would go and visit Sweet Lilly on first Sundays in May.

Charles: It's a once a month church?

Lucy Nell: I think so! I think it's still once a month. I remember Henry is a member, Uncle Ashby's son and I think he is a deacon.

Charles: Well, I got a couple of pictures here I want to show you. Do you know this lady, Georgia Ann? Have you heard of her?

Lucy Nell: Georgia Ann, I don't know her.

Charles: Everybody called her Aunt Puss.

Lucy Nell: Oh, I remember that name. That's why I detest nicknames; I never use nicknames.

Charles: You never know their real names.

Lucy Nell: That's right. I remember even trying to get to Aunt Puss' funeral, but the high water was up.

Charles: Tell me about that.

Lucy Nell: I just remember trying to get over to Sweet Lilly.

Charles: That's where it was at, Sweet Lilly!

Lucy Nell: It was at Sweet Lilly and I was trying to get there and the water was up over the bridge and I thought I better get myself back this way instead of trying to go.

Charles: You were trying to cross D'Loutre River bridge?

Lucy Nell: Trying to cross D'Loutre to a funeral.

Charles: So do you know anything about her? Do you remember what she was like? How did she look?

Lucy Nell: I don't just really know, but I know everybody loved Aunt Puss; I knew that much. They were always talking about Aunt Puss. I have seen her, but right now, I just can't remember how she looked. I should know because I grew up going to Sweet Lilly and she would be there. Now see that was John Earl's people too and we were trying to get to the funeral.

Charles: I am going to see John Earl tomorrow. Aunt Puss' real name was Georgia Ann. Actually, she changed her name to Georgia Ann, her real name was Belzora; and she married Lorenzo Ellis. They called him Rance Ellis. He died a lot sooner than she did. They had her funeral at Sweet Lilly, but she is buried at the cemetery at Meridian Baptist Church. This is a picture of her mother, her name was Lucinda.

Lucy Nell: Lucinda Morgan.

Charles: Yes, and Georgia Ann, Aunt Puss used the surname Morgan as a child, but her father is a Bilberry, a white guy. My goal is to try to find out who the father was and which white man! I know it was a Bilberry, but I don't know, which one. So, I'm going to try to get there. Do you know her (showing a picture)? That's my grandfather, Ladell's wife, his second wife. He had two sets of kids by two different women. The first wife died; I think she was 28 years old when she died. The last kid that she had by him, was Joseph. He had eight more kids by his second wife Corene; she was from the Truxno area and moved to Kansas City, Kansas just before her husband passed away. Now, I'm going to jog your memory here (showing pictures). You recognize that Church there? That's Sweet Lilly.

Lucy Nell: Yes, that's Sweet Lilly (looking at pictures). That's John Earl there, he went to school where I was working and then he ended up working with me; later I ended up working under him. He was the principal. Also, Mr. Bilberry was my principal. Mr. J. B. Bilberry was my first principal. I taught first grade under him. Let's see, Rich Thrower! I know the Throwers, but I don't know that one by name; I know Miss Joe B. and Mr. Bilberry and I know Mr. Frank. I know Frank Bilberry and Mama Emma and Lou Emma Horn; now I remember this name. Lou Emma lived in Natchitoches, Louisiana, I believe!

Charles: Yes, she married a Horn. She married Seab Horn and he is still living; he is 94 years old.

Lucy Nell: I remember him.

Charles: Did you ever know this guy here?

Lucy Nell: Mr. Lee Roberts, I remember him. He's Mrs. Addie Payne's father.

Charles: Her husband was Algie Payne.

Lucy Nell: I knew Almer Roberts, his son. I think Annie Mae was the granddaughter. I used to live next door to Mrs. Addie Payne; and also used to work with her. Anna Roberts, I know them; Ollie Roberts, I know him. Florine and Lorine, those are the twins, I know them; I know Flossie too! She was Mrs. Addie Payne's baby sister; I remember Floyd Roberts and Liza Roberts.

Charles: That was Mama Emma's mother. She stayed with Mama Emma and Papa Frank for a long time. Her husband died; his name as Will; I think he died in 1920. She died in the 1940's.

Lucy Nell: I knew Mr. Charlie (Roberts) and Miss Mittie Mae. I knew Miss Mittie Mae's boy, but I can't think of his name right now. I know Sterling Jones.

Charles: That's Mary Horn (showing a picture). That's how she looked; everybody tells me that she got a lot heavier than that later on.

Lucy Nell: She was kind of heavy, now I remember that part about her, that she was a little heavy. I remember Gracie Benson and Edie. We are church members now; I saw her this morning. She married the Page boy. Eboy passed away this year; I believe Aunt Versie was last year. This is my uncle (showing a picture); his grandson preached this morning, his name is Ashby too! Joe Benson, I knew him real well, he used to come and stay with us sometime. These are my people here (showing pictures), John Evans; John and Mady. All these are my people here, the Evans.

Charles: John Murray is still living right?

Lucy Nell: John Murray is still living. I think he is somewhere in Texas. I don't know about her, Sarah Ellis.

Charles: You want to know what her nickname is! It's Bama.

Lucy Nell: Okay, I know Mrs. Bama; I do remember her.

Charles: I know you know him right (showing a picture).

Lucy Nell: John Ellis.

Charles: He and Claude Ellis were brothers.

Lucy Nell: I never let my children call each other nicknames. I don't call them by their nicknames in school either. They used to tell me that they preferred to be called by nicknames, but I never liked to call them by their nicknames. Charlie Bilberry (showing a picture); I don't think I remember that one.

Charles: That was Ladell and Jessie B. Bilberry, Sr.'s brother. He moved to Michigan at an early age.

Lucy Nell: I knew Johnnie and Bernice (showing a picture) .

Charles: You probably knew Clyde Bilberry; he married Jesse Fields.

Lucy Nell: Miss Maltee might be able to tell you some things you might need to know.

Charles: Is she still living? Where does she live at?

Lucy Nell: Do you remember where your Uncle Ed Thompson used to live at?

Charles: No.

Lucy Nell: She lives off of Bernice Street (she goes on and gives directions).

Charles: Does she live by herself?

Lucy Nell: One of her boys lives with her.

Charles: She's gotta be in her nineties now?

Lucy Nell: Yes, she about 90; she can tell you something too.

Charles: She was at Sweet Lilly for years.

Lucy Nell: This is Herbert Finley (continuing to look at pictures). He was my uncle too! We had quite a few people buried at Sweet Lilly.

Charles: Yes, I've seen their gravesites at the cemetery. Well, I thought I'd let you look at this book of pictures to jog your memory a little bit. Some old faces, huh! They made the book over 30 years ago.

Lucy Nell: Yeah!

Charles: Now you told me something about having some obituaries.

Lucy Nell: I have a lot of old obituaries. Who are you looking to find?

Charles: Did you have any of the Bilberrys or Roberts. You said you did not have Ed Thompson's obituary.

Lucy Nell: I didn't have that one, but I tell you what, I'll just get them out here and you can just look at them.

Interview ended.

Interview with John Earl Ellis – August 2, 2010 – Marion, Louisiana

John Earl Ellis is a retired school teacher and principal in the Union Parish, Louisiana School District. He is the grandson of Georgia Ann Bilberry-Ellis and Lorenzo Ellis.

John Earl Ellis
Courtesy of John Earl Ellis

Charles: John Earl, you're holding one of those lofty positions here in Union Parish now, right!

John: Yes, I am a glutton for punishment. I'm on the school board; the Union Parish school board.

Charles: What district do you cover?

John: District 6; my second term started in January. No one ran against me so I didn't have to do any campaigning.

Charles: I'm going to ask you some questions now. So just sit back and relax and tell it like it is. I want to get your full name first.

John: John Earl Ellis.

Charles: Were you named after somebody?

John: I was named after my Uncle Johnny Ellis. You remember him don't you?

Charles: Yes. Did you have a nickname?

John: My nickname was "Brother."

Charles: What is your birthday?

John: March 2, 1945.

Charles: What are your parent's full names?

John: Claude Ellis and Lotie Wayne-Ellis. Do you remember my parent?

Charles: Yes. What cemetery are they buried at?

John: Meridian.

Charles: What were your parents like as far as their personalities? Is there anything unique about them?

John: My dad was a soft spoken quiet man; he was easy on the strap. My dad whipped me only one time. My mother gave me one every day, sometimes two a day or

	three a day; I can't remember. She was the disciplinarian and she kept things in order.
Charles:	Anything else you remember about your parents; anything else unique?
John:	My mother was one of the first people that were registered to vote. They had to take a test; they had to study to take the test. My mother was one of the first to pass the test and was allowed to vote. Many people didn't pass it.
Charles:	Here in Union Parish?
John:	Yes, here in Union Parish!
Charles:	That's a milestone.
John:	Yes, it was a milestone.
Charles:	She blazed the trail. I can imagine the test was not easy. Do know what year that was?
John:	No. I can vaguely remember it though.
Charles:	Who is the oldest relative that you remember as a child?
John:	Miss Georgia Ann; Aunt Puss.
Charles:	Let's back up and talk about her. You said Georgia Ann. She had some other names didn't she? Wasn't she also called Bellzora and Aunt Puss.
John:	The white people gave her the name, Aunt Puss.
Charles:	How did they come up with that name?
John:	I don't have a clue.
Charles:	You were telling me some stories about her. I understand that her father was white?
John:	Yeah! That's how we are related. Your great grandfather Frank was her nephew; her brother's son.
Charles:	Who was her brother?
John:	That I don't know.
Charles:	Could it have been her sister's son?
John:	No, because it would not have been Bilberry because she was out of wedlock. She was the only Bilberry that I know. Angeline, I don't know what they were. Was she a Bilberry?
Charles:	She was a Bilberry or Bridges. I think Papa Frank and she had the same mother. They took on the Bilberry name because of the white guy; whoever the slave master or slave master's son was at that time.
John:	No one has been able to get that guy's name.
Charles:	I looked at the death certificates of Papa Frank and grandpa Ladell. They put down his name was Bridges Bilberry or Brit Bilberry. I looked at Uncle Lawrence's; I got his death certificate. Paul Bilberry wrote down that his father's father was Bridges Bilberry and they are all saying that it was a white guy. That's who it was, but this white guy apparently had kids, evidently by different black ladies. So, they had the same white father, but a different black mother. Paul Bilberry wrote down that Lawrence Bilberry's death certificate and that Lawrence's mother's name was Narsis; that's all he wrote down. There are some people named Norsis that lived in that area. Ladell wrote down that Papa Frank's mother's name was Deoines or something similar. What I traced down to was that her name was Delia Bridges; she was a Bridges, but she married a guy named Anderson Thompson. I'm thinking that Angeline and Papa Frank had the same mother, but Angeline's father was black because her

mother, Delia married a black man. She had kids by a white guy; the same white guy impregnated another lady in Truxno named Narsis and had Uncle Lawrence. Dolly Mayfield was Papa Frank's half- sister. Everyone says that Aunt Puss looked just like a white woman. I'm gathering more information right now; I'm going to go to the courthouse tomorrow. I want to get back to Aunt Puss!

John: I think she died in 1954; I believe.

Charles: Papa Frank died in 1953. Tell me more about Aunt Puss. You told me that she didn't take any mess from anyone!

John: No! She was an outspoken lady. I guess she was protected by the white people because of who she was. She was allowed to do some things that the other black women could not do; mainly speaking what she thought. You had your Ku Klux Klan and other organizations that came about to keep black women in their place so to speak. I heard them (black people) say that they would meet. The white men would come together and get their plans together, but they never would mess with her or her boys. Other men had to leave the area, but not her boys.

Charles: What were some of the families' names that ran away?

John: Some of the Ellis', but not her boys.

Charles: What did they run them away for? Was it because they would speak out against certain things?

John: No! They were thinking that, I guess that the black men were a threat to the white women. So they didn't want them around in the area. I never really thought about why they didn't want them, but they ran them out of the area. Really intimidating, but it didn't take much to intimidate them because they were beaten, whipped and those sort of things. It wouldn't take much for me to leave!

Charles: You would comply in a minute to keep from getting hung!

John: That's right!

Charles: So Aunt Puss, they just sort of left her alone! Now I understand too and I heard this from Louie Morgan; he told me that he was talking to Rodell Burch about 2 or 3 months ago and he said that Aunt Puss nursed some of the Tugwell's kids.

John: Also, she nursed some of the Ewings.

Charles: Okay, so black people and white people.

John: Yes, sometimes they had babies at the same time.

Charles: Aunt Puss had a lot of kids too; didn't she? Any Tugwells still live in this area?

John: They're all dead.

Charles: There were a lot of Tugwells in this area. I saw their names in the U.S. Census.

John: My grandmother had 15 kids.

Charles: And she was married to Lorenzo; some people called him Rance Ellis.

John: That's right; he was a black man and real dark.

Charles: Do you remember him?

John: No, he died in 1927.

Charles: Now in the 1870 Census, they show Aunt Puss and they put her name down as

Puss too. They show her and her mother Cindy as Cindy Morgan. They call her Lucinda; they show her as being the wife of York Morgan. There was Milton Morgan, Sam Morgan, Hamilton Morgan, York Morgan, Jr., and Hannah. Hannah was a lady that married Branch Nelson. There were some Nelsons that lived in this area too.

John: Yeah, I met some of her grandchildren at an Ellis reunion in Cleveland. Karen and Wanda are the only ones I can remember. Karen had a brother named Willie. Their mother was a Nelson.

Charles: Do you remember Sam Morgan and Milton Morgan?

John: I don't remember them. I knew John Morgan. He was Louis' (Louie's) dad.

Charles: What did he look like?

John: I don't remember that well. I just remember seeing him when I was a little boy.

Charles: I'm not sure how the Morgans come in. A lot of people, I'm seeing in the census will have the mother as being say 50 years old and their first daughter or son was 40 or 45. So a lot of them, I think just took on kids as family members from perhaps other former slaves. Do you remember Gordie Burch?

John: I remember her well!

Charles: Let's talk about her. I've talked to Linda Evans and she sent me the obituary of Gordie. There was a lady at the last reunion that I went to, her name was Nancy Winans-Garrison and she is related to the Bilberrys through Gordie's side. Gordie's mother and father were Jack Bilberry and Francis Bilberry. Francis had a lot of kids, but all of them couldn't have been her kids. She was only 38 and one of her kids was 28; a lot of them, I think she just took in.

John: You remember Gordie right?

Charles: I can't remember her. I left here in 1970. I'm not sure when she died, but as a kid coming up I remember my father used to drive by here where she used to live. As we passed by my dad used to say, "that's Ed Burch's house." Of course Odessa was his wife and they all went to school under her. I guess she taught over at Center Branch Community School. Ed Burch's mother was Gordie. Gordie married a Burch, but her maiden name was Bilberry.

John: Her father's name was Jack Bilberry right?

Charles: Yes, Jack Bilberry.

John: That was my grandmother's nephew. Jack Bilberry was cousin Gordie's dad; Aunt Puss' nephew. That's why they called her Aunt Georgie.

Charles: Oh, okay. Everything is leading back to Aunt Puss. If I could just find out what her father's name was I can close this book! Good luck huh?

John: He is up at the cemetery.

Charles: Meridian? I didn't see his name up there. I haven't look at it in a long time.

John: He used to have a headstone up there, but I think it broke.

Charles: Jack died a lot sooner than his wife Francis. She died in 1938. I saw the deed of her land being transferred in my research. I saw where she bought the land. She was about to lose the land and Gordie, her daughter ended up buying it

Charles: Also, there were other families in this area such as Bensons. There were a lot of Bensons; Joe Benson was J. C. Benson. J.C lived here for years with his wife Verma. As a matter of fact, I talked to Aunt Sally (Willie Mae Bilberry) this morning. She had surgery on her hand. I'm going to go by and see her tomorrow.

76

Her mother, Aunt Bessie lived in this area too; Aunt Bessie's husband's name was Robert Benson. They had a son named Woodie Benson, who lived in this area. It was a big community at that time. There were Finley's, Montgomery's, Wallace's and Ewing's. Did you ever know a guy named General Wallace?

John: I heard of him.

Charles: He was supposed to have married a lady named Annie Bilberry. She was supposed to be another one of Papa Frank's sisters. There was Annie Bilberry and there was Anna Bilberry; they were his sisters and they were light skinned. This white man was a rolling stone. He moved around and had all these kids, all light skinned by different black women. There was Anna, who married Mason Holly (Holland).

John: All of this is coming into place. I can remember we were kin to the Holly's. They lived in Monroe, Louisiana; I've heard the name called so many times. In fact, they have offspring that lived in Marion. Do you remember Jerry Fields and the Fields over in Marion?

Charles: Yeah, Bill Fields, Ernest Fields.

John: Their mother was kin to us through the Holly's and Ellis's and that line that you just brought up.

Charles: It was because of Anna; Anna was a Bilberry.

John: That's right. I never could connect it up.

Charles: That was Papa Frank's sister.

John: I knew we were related.

Charles: I got a picture of her. I got a lot of it from the internet, but when I get the book done you will get a copy. I got a picture of her and her husband and I'm trying to get another picture. Anna Bilberry-Holland has one daughter still living. Anna had a lot of kids; the youngest one is 82 yrs. old right now and she's still living. She lives in Toledo, Ohio; I talked her on the phone twice. That's how we are related to the Holly's (Holland). It is through Mason Holly. Anna's husband's surname changed over the years. According to the U.S. Census for Union Parish, Mason surname went from Hollis, Hollings to Holly and the last name was Holland. He was born in 1878; she was born around 1888. She was a light-skinned lady sired by the former white slave master name Bilberry. I don't know if it was by the same black lady or not, but it was the same white father.

John: You probably didn't know that you were related to, Britt Bilberry, did you.

Charles: No, I didn't know, not until later on. I used to hear them say cousin this and cousin that, but I didn't know. How could they all be our cousin? I think they called everybody cousin.

John: We were taught that them your kin folk!

Charles: Yeah, and so there was an Anna in Monroe and then there was an Annie; I understand she lived in Crossett, Arkansas. Annie's niece, Clara Waters said that her mother used to take them up there to see her. She said she was a mean old lady! They said that she looked just like a white woman. To confirm it, Paul Bilberry used to go see her too because she was Uncle Lawrence's and Papa Frank's sister too. They knew each other; they all went to see her. Jessie Mae Bilberry just told me the other day, "yeah, we used to go up there to see her." I have some research on her; and I think the Annie, that they're talking

77

about is probably the one General Wallace married. General Wallace was Letha Archie's brother.

John: Letha Archie, that's Benny's grandmother.

Charles: Yes, James Archie was Letha's husband.

John: James Archie and I were first cousins?

Charles: Is that right?

John: Let me get it right now. Uncle Brock Archie married Aunt Chanie Ellis. That's how we are related to Benny Archie; through the Ellis side.

Charles: So, what I also found out was that, Jessie Mae Bilberry from Truxno knew him. She said, "oh yes, I knew General Wallace." She said he was a clean dressing man and that he could walk down a muddy road and got nothing on him, but the sole of his shoes dirty. He and Annie married, but I don't think they were married very long; I think they divorced. Both of them are showed later on in the U.S Census as being widows. I think he ended up working as a servant, for Otis Tugwell according to the 1910 U.S. Census for Union Parish, Ward Six. Annie was living by herself and she had a kid and her kid's name was Bessie Wallace. She had a kid by General Wallace and I think she had another kid named L. C. Wallace. She later married a guy, who was a boarder with her according to the 1920 U.S. Census for Union Parish, Ward Six; his name was Bunk. Bunk Jones, was living up near Junction City; they moved back to Arkansas where he was born and they got married. She married twice; she married General Wallace and then she turned around and married Bunk Jones. I don't know if they got a divorce or not. Maybe they just crossed the state line and said hey, "I'm not married anymore." Maybe they never got a divorce and just remarried; I don't know.

But anyway, I've been doing this research for about 14 years now; and I am learning a little more here and there! I sort of know a little by heart now. I want to just tell the Bilberry story and write about the Ellis', Burchs', Montgomerys', Bridges', and especially close ones that were right around where my great-grandfather lived. I can't write about all of them, but you know it would be nice to throw a white person's story in there too. It would be nice to include some of the Ballard's, the Tugwells' or Honeycutts' that lived in this area and to find some of their descendants that are willing to talk about it.

John: There is a man that lives in Mississippi that comes in and out of here.

Charles: He's a Ballard right?

John: Yes, he's a Ballard.

Charles: John Ballard; he lives in Vicksburg. I have e-mailed him and talked to him too. He did that whole transcription of Meridian Cemetery. I said, "This guy must be from this community." He took all those headstones and put them in alphabetical order; I use it all the time. A lot of Bilberrys, Bridges, Bensons and Roberts from Union Parish moved into Arkansas. In my opinion, Union Parish has done the best job of the Louisiana parishes compared to some of the other states when it comes to having a thorough genealogical website. They are a step ahead of the rest of them. They have taken the U.S. Census of Union Parish and transcribed and indexed it. All you have to do was look for the name alphabetically. I don't look before slavery ended too much because the slaves didn't have surnames then. They only started putting blacks in the census after we were freed. The first census we showed up in as black people was the 1870 Census. Before that we were just listed as male or female owned my Mary Honeycutt, E. B. Bilberry or Otis Tugwell, etc.; two slaves, female age 10 and whether we could read or write that kind of stuff. That's what they wrote then; no first name. They would put whether you were sane, or idiotic, that kind of thing; you were property. You may have had a name, but they did not list your name. Probably 80 percent of them took the name of their white slave master. There were white and black Bilberrys and white and black Ellis's; that's just the way it was! You might have had a first name that they started calling each other. Burch was spelled Birch back then; that's how I found out how my great-great grandmother Liza, Aunt Emma's mother was Liza Roberts. I think she married a Roberts? I was trying to find out who her mother and father were. Later I learned, her mother and father were Thomas Birch and Anna Cook-Birch. I looked and I found Liza and Rodell Burch were her brother and sister. We're related to the Burchs' through Liza Roberts.

John: I knew they were related, but I didn't know how.

Charles: Yes, that was how! I finally found that out and I put that on my *ancestry. com page*. There was another fellow name Ed Thompson. He is listed in the 1900 U.S. Census for Union Parish, Ward Six as living with Robert and Matilda Bridges, the parents of Delia Bridges. Delia Bridges is Ed Thompson's mother.

John: I remember him.

Charles: He lived in Farmerville.

John: He was Angeline's brother.

Charles: Did you know that was her brother?

John: Yes.

Charles: It indicates in the U.S Census that Ed and Dollie living with their grandparents. I can't seem to find Delia Bridges after her application to marry Anderson Thompson in the document I have from the Union Parish's Clerk of Court. I don't know what happened to her, but she probably was Papa Frank's, Ed Thompson' and Dolly Mayfield's mother. I know it wasn't Uncle Lawrence's because his mother was Narsis according to a testimony from his son Paul Bilberry and the death certificate of Lawrence Bilberry. Anyway, this white guy, E. B. Bilberry had kids; he had a kid name after him. E. B. Bilberry, Sr., used to be the postmaster down here in Conway, Louisiana according to the website www.usgwarchives.org/la/union.htm. E. B. Bilberry, he was a top leader in Union Parish; he was a magistrate, justice of the peace and an upstanding man. I looked up the old minutes of Meridian Cemetery. It is a big thick book and I went through every bit of it looking at the slaves that they had in there. Some of them belonged to the Meridian Baptist Church. I highlighted the parts where the slaves accepted the call to be baptized. Most of them said such things as servant of Jacob Garrett Bilberry; servant of John B. Robinson; servant of William Cooper or something in that order. They just gave their first name. This was before 1865; Meridian has been around for a long time. It started as a church around 1850's and lasted to the 1970's; and then it just finally closed as a church.

John: They revamped it.

Charles:	Oh did they?
John:	Oh yeah, you need to drive through there. It looks so different.
Charles:	So they opened up the church and they got a pastor?
John:	Oh yeah, it's a big church.
Charles:	Oh! We were driving through there and I saw where they had cleared the timber on both sides of the road.
John:	They built a big church back there. The little church is still there; they didn't tear it down. They preserved it!
Charles:	That's good because that's a historical church.
John:	Once you get past the clearing it's about a mile down the road. I might go by there.
Charles:	One of things that I did noticed when I was there before was the separation of the races even in death. It was that way when I lived here in the 1950's and 1960's. The cemeteries in Union Parish were separated. They may be in the same cemetery, but whites would be buried on one side and blacks were on the other side. Spring Hill Cemetery is the same way. I went to it too and the races were separated. But I noticed E. B. Bilberry, Sr., who was a white guy and an upstanding citizen children were buried on the same side as the black people. I have a photo of the headstone of E. B. Bilberry's children buried there.
John:	Where?
Charles:	At Meridian Baptist Church Cemetery
John:	There used to be a fence, but it is no longer there. It is all one cemetery now.
Charles:	A road separates them now.
John:	No, I mean within the cemetery, there was a wire fence that separated the whites and blacks within the same cemetery.
Charles:	I was wondering why it was that way. E. B. Bilberry's wife was buried there; he married three times. He was born in 1827 and he married Mary Jane Honeycutt. She died; she had some kids by him. E. B. had a son named George Bilberry and George married Louiser. I'm not sure of her maiden name. Anyway, there is a lady was from Arkansas and her husband was a Marshall; that was his great-great grandfather. I am just trying to get more information on him. I even looked through the Union Parish Gazette, all the way back when they first started printing it. Everything was sort of leading to him. He had a lot of power. He had a son named E. B. Bilberry, Jr. Now he was old enough to impregnate these ladies too. I'm going to try to get to the bottom of things the best I can. I'll see what I come up with at the Union Parish Courthouse tomorrow.
John:	Now back to the Holly guy.
Charles:	Mason (Holland) Holly?
John:	Yeah, now Bill Fields had a brother that got killed. What was his name? He was the oldest boy.
Charles:	Ernest was the youngest. You're talking about Curtis Fields.
John:	I was always told that they were related to us, but I never knew how!
Charles:	Their grandmother was Ella Lowe.
John:	That's right. She died not long ago.
Charles:	She used to say to me, "come here, you're my cousin." She used to live right across the street from us. She had a brother named Willis and one named Columbus and a sister name Ollie Bell. She has a sister still living name Clara

Holland. She married and her name is Clara Waters now; she is 82 years old. I got to talk to her; she did tell me that she remembers going to see Annie Bilberry, her mother's sister in Crossett. I showed her some pictures to hopefully stimulate her mind a little bit.

John: So you're related to the Morgans too!

Charles: The Morgans through Aunt Puss.

John: Through Aunt Lucinda.

Charles: Aunt Lucinda had the other kids with York Morgan; that was her husband and I guess that was our relationship to the Morgans. I'm related to Aunt Puss' mother Lucinda. Like Mama Emma used to tell everybody coming up that they were our cousins; it was just about that way. If you keep going back far enough, then you would circle back around. You could have married your fifth cousin and didn't know it!

Interview ended.

Interview with Leola Wayne-Taylor – August 2, 2010 – Marion, Louisiana

L eola Wayne, a retired school teacher with the City of Chicago School District; she is the granddaughter of Georgia Ann Bilberry-Ellis and Lorenzo Ellis.

Courtesy of Leola Wayne-Taylor

Charles: Leola what is your birth date?

Leola: November 9, 1936.

Charles: Tell me your mother and your father's name.

Leola: My mother's name is Etta Ellis. She was born in 1897 and she died in 1990. She was 93 years old when she passed away. She always told me she had 15 brothers and sisters, but I could account for just 13 so I don't know what happened to the other two. Unfortunately, I was not thinking about asking questions at the time because she could have told me all the names. I know I remember seeing other names in the census. I saw it one time and then I never saw them again. That must have been the two, but we don't have any record of them anywhere. So, I can only account for thirteen. On my dad's side, his parents were Mary Andrews (mother) and Willie Wayne (father); there were six siblings. Daddy, Ollie Wayne had four brothers and one sister. He is the only one still living and he is 104.

Charles: I think, you had a grandmother on your mother's side and she had several names. Could you tell me who she was and what were the names?

Leola: Well, the experience I had with that, was trying to start looking up some of the history for the Ellis family and I kept looking for Georgia Ellis. I couldn't find Georgia Ellis, but in the courthouse, I would see my grandfather's name and then it had another name that I hadn't heard before. John Earl had told me her name was Georgia. The name was Bellzora and I figured it had to be the right one. I called John Earl and he said: "Oh yeah, that's the name!" He said that she didn't like that name so nobody ever used it; that was when I found out. The only thing I knew was Bellzora Georgia. I'm not sure if it was Bellzora Georgia or Georgia Bellzora.

Charles: Do you know how she got the name Aunt Puss?

Leola: That I don't know.

Charles: I will tell you what John Earl told me. He said that was what the white people called her.

Leola:	Well, I knew they called her that, but I don't know how they decided to call her that name. We were little children you know and we used to go visit her and that was what they called her. I don't think we said it too much. We just said grandma.
Charles:	What kind of personality did she have? What was she like; as you remember her as a kid!
Leola:	Well, the only thing I can remember, they said, "you better not get her upset!" She would definitely tell you off. We would go see her and she was in bed and she would say, "you all come in here!" I remember as a little kid they would say, "well, she was sick and not going to make it." Everybody believed it was going to be the end for grandma. The next thing you knew she was up in the kitchen baking some cakes; she just kept coming back. My grandfather lived to be 93 years old. Now that was living back then, when during that time, people just didn't live that long.
Charles:	That was Lorenzo.
Leola:	That was Lorenzo. I'll tell you another story! When we had my mother's funeral, we were doing the obituary. I called John Earl and I said: "Now my grandfather's name was Rance, right!" He said yes, so that was what I wrote on the program because I didn't know it was Lorenzo.
Charles:	Rance was his nickname!
Leola:	Yes, that was his nickname and you will see that on a lot of records, back then, it didn't have to be true what you said; nobody was questioning anything. Whatever you said, they just took your word, but now you have to prove things. I didn't know his name was Lorenzo until after my mom died. Everybody called him Rance and that was all I knew; I never knew him. He died before my mom and dad got married.
Charles:	How did your grandmother look?
Leola:	I don't know if she had Indian in her or something. She kind of had high cheekbones and she was fair skinned, had nice hair and looked like she might have had some Indian in her. I never heard anybody say that, but she looked Indian. She was a nice looking lady.
Charles:	Were there any favorite things that she liked to do or favorite things she liked to cook.
Leola:	I don't know about her favorites, but I would say she loved to cook. I was a little girl and they used to have a house and the kitchen was in the back of the house. I remember in the old house; they had the separated kitchen back there and I don't even know if they were using it, but that was what they used to do; the kitchen part was not attached to the house. My dad said my grandma's house on my dad's side used to be that way, but I don't remember that because when I was small, it wasn't like that to me!
Charles:	Did Aunt Puss belong to any particular church in that area? Did she go to any of those churches?
Leola:	When I remember her, she was old. I don't know what church she attended. John Earl could have told you!
Charles:	I don't think I asked him about it. It was on my mind though.
Leola:	I know my mom's church was Zion Watts Baptist Church, but I'm not sure if all of them didn't used to go Center Branch Baptist Church. I'm not sure, but I

don't remember her at church. I was born in 1936 and my mother was born in 1897, so you know she was real old when I was born so I don't remember her going to church.

Charles: I think Georgia Ann died in 1954 or something like that?

Leola: Yes, was it 1954?

Charles: I think that's what John Earl told me.

Leola: Well, John Earl was right.

Charles: You would have been about 16?

Leola: I would have been around16 or 17. I graduated from high school in 1955. If John Earl said it, then it's true because he was right there. You know she lived with them so he would know. He would know more than I know about what she liked and what she didn't like. We just went over there on Sundays. A lot of Sundays we would go visit grandma. I don't know if I ever spent a night with grandma. I think maybe one or two nights we used to stay.

Charles: I remember my mother said that when she lived down in that community after she married my father they used to walk down the dirt road and they would turn the corner where Aunt Puss lived. She would be sitting on the porch and she would say, "hey, where are you all going!" She was one of the older matriarchs of the community there.

Leola: Oh yes! Another thing about my grandfather, down in the area I think where Lorenzo Burch, where Aunt Hannah Burch stayed, somewhere on the place there, somewhere down in that area there was a white guy that stayed down there. I don't remember his name. Daddy tells this story a lot of times. My grandfather had cows and things and all and they would go on this white guys place. They just stayed in trouble about the cows getting out and going on his place and everything. There was this doctor. I don't know his name, but he was in the community and friends with grandma. You know she was friends to a lot of the whites. He told her, "don't worry about it; I'm going to take of this for you." That's what the doctor told her. I wish I could think of his name.

Charles: Was it Tugwell?

Leola: It might have been. Was there a doc Tugwell?

Charles: There was a Tugwell that was a doctor. His name was Egbert Tugwell.

Leola: That's the guy. He told my grandfather, "don't worry about it. I'm going to take care of this for you." So, the old white guy got sick and he went to the doctor and the doctor told him, "ain't anything wrong with you. You done got this 'nigga' disease" and the man left because he thought he got something from the black folks. He moved out of the community! So he got rid of him by telling him that he done got something from the black folks and he left. You know he was a doctor and he believed him. He probably had nothing but a cold. That's how he got rid of the guy that was giving him a lot of trouble about his cows and things. Dad could tell you all kinds of stories when he was himself. He knew all about that. I don't know if my mother was the last one of grandma's girls to leave home. I believe she was. You know back then, during that time, they called themselves stealing them. You know they'd steal the women. They wouldn't go ask for them, they would steal them. So my dad was going to steal my mom. My dad had his brother in the car and he done got him a little drink. So he told him what time to come down through there, you know. So, he came too early and messed the thing up. So he didn't get to steal her so the next day he had to go and ask for her. He said grandma told him, "I want my last daughter to get married at home." So, his brother messed it up. He went and got drunk. He came by through there too early.

Charles: So, they got married at the house.

Leola: They got married at the house because she told him that she wanted her last daughter to get married at home.

Charles: Who married them?

Leola: It might have been, it probably was daddy's pastor, I believe, Reverend Hawthorn and I think I'm right.

Charles: Here at Mount Union Baptist Church?

Leola: Yeah, he was the Pastor at Mount Union. I think I'm right.

Charles: I saw that in the book.

Leola: I'll have to ask my sister. Now that may not be right, I'm not sure. Dad could tell a lot of tales about what happened back there. As far as my grandma, I just don't know much about her.

Charles: Well, that's good enough. Your mother Etta was the youngest of her kids?

Leola: No, she was the youngest daughter. I think uncle Claude must have been the youngest. I don't know, but I had that information in my book too.

Charles: I can look it up; Aunt Hettie was she older than your mother?

Leola: Oh yes, she was older than my mom. I think the oldest were Aunt Hettie and Aunt Hannah. I'm not sure if she was the oldest child, but I know she was the oldest daughter. My mom was the youngest daughter. I know Uncle Claude was and Uncle Earl too; he was younger than my mom too, although, I didn't really know him. I think one of them died real young. I don't know which one it was though. There were thirteen of them, but I could not come up with the other two. I had some names, but I just ran across those names one time. Did John tell you about the young man that came through here about three years ago? He said he was an Ellis. I don't know if grandpa Lorenzo was his grandfather or great-grandfather or something. He sent me some information too. I really didn't know about them, but he could tell you; he could run it down to you though. I don't know if it was one of those that I couldn't account for or not; it could have been. He sent me some information on them too and he got some information from us. There are a lot of Ellis's. They have a reunion every year, but I don't get to go because it's during dad's birthday time. I know more about the Ellis side than the Bilberry side; I don't know much about the Bilberry side because it goes back into the white folks.

Charles: If you get past Sandy Wayne and then you're into white ancestors.

Leola: I'm talking about the Andrew's side. On the Wayne's side, it's not too many white in that family. On the Andrews side, it's a lot.

Charles: Like the Bilberrys. It doesn't take long, and then all of a sudden you're into the white ancestors.

Leola: You can just look at the older people and see. I wish I had talked more to my mother; you know we just weren't into all of this history. Most of this started when the movie, "Roots" came out. Everybody wanted to know about their family history. I didn't get really into it then. I know a lot about the Wayne's because daddy loved to talk about the Wayne family. Mom never talked too much about the Ellis's. If you asked her a question, she would answer it, but she never would just sit down like daddy and just tell you about all of them. He said he used to crawl under the house so he could listen to them talk. He said: "Mama would have killed me if she knew I was under there!"

Charles: Jessie Mae Andrews in Truxno, she said, "Yeah back when grown folks started talking about, who had a kid by so in so, the kids had to get out."

Leola: Yeah, we used to see somebody coming and we were so trained that they didn't even have to tell us to go play; we would just leave. We were so trained that when you see a grown person coming that meant that you would go outside and play because you were not going to listen to that conversation.

Charles: If you stuck around, you were going to get told to get out of there.

Leola: These days the children take the conversation over. The parents can't get a word in.

Charles: Jessie Mae said the same thing. The kids would get in the conversation and comment on things that they didn't know anything about.

Leola: The older people like us; we just look around and say: "Lord, we would have been on that floor." They would have knocked us out of there.

Interview ended.

Interview with Georgia Willie Mae Bilberry – August 3, 2010 – Monroe, Louisiana

Georgia Willie Mae Benson-Bilberry (aka Aunt Sally) was the wife of the deceased Ed Bilberry; also, Aunt Sally was "scared of cows," much like Prissy, the young slave girl portrayed in the movie "Gone with the Wind."

Georgia Willie Mae Bilberry
Georgia Willie Mae Benson-Bilberry (aka Aunt Sally)
Courtesy of Charles Lee Bilberry

Charles: How did you get the nick name Sally?

Willie Mae: I don't know. Ya'll give it to me.

Charles: Was the reason you took Georgia off of your name is because you didn't like it?

Willie Mae: Yeah, it was too long.

Charles: And the reason you have a long name is because different family members wanted their name in your name.

Willie Mae: It was an old lady name Georgia. I don't know who she was, but mama said she wanted some of her name in my name when I was a baby and that was why the Georgia is in there.

Charles: How did the Willie get in there?

Willie Mae: My uncle. His name was Willie and he wanted his name in my name too.

Charles: Willie Benson?

Willie Mae: Uh Huh!

Charles: And the Mae?

Willie Mae: Aunt Mae Morgan wanted some of hers in their too; she put the Mae in there.

Charles: Was there another reason why you shortened it.

Willie Mae: Yeah. A white man came by selling some candy and said that my name was too long. He said that if I was standing by a stream of water I would drown because my name was too long. And I believed him too!

Charles: You knew Ella Holland-Lowe's mother Anna Holland-Bilberry didn't you. Did you ever see her?

Willie Mae: Oh yes!

Charles:	What did she look like?
Willie Mae:	Big old pretty lady. Looked like a white woman. Yeah, she was beautiful! She was a sweet lady.
Charles:	Did Uncle Ed Bilberry ever visit her?
Willie Mae:	Yeah we did. She didn't live too far from here. I can't think of the name of the street. It was right across the highway over there.
Charles:	Did you go to her funeral?
Willie Mae:	Yeah!
Charles:	Where was it at?
Willie Mae:	Now child you know me; I can't think of anything! I'm eighty-three years old. All of my sense is gone; I don't know what I used to know.
Charles:	What was her husband like?
Willie Mae:	Uncle Mason, he was nice.
Charles:	I looked him up in my research. Anna Bilberry was his second wife, according to the 1910 U. S. Census for Union Parish, Ward Two. His first wife was Mandy Andrews. They married on June 30, 1900. Mason and Anna Bilberry married December 16, 1904.
Willie Mae:	He was! I didn't know that.
Charles:	I don't know if Mandy died or they divorced.
Willie Mae:	I know that Anna was Papa Frank's sister. Now your wife, is she from here or California?
Taryn:	I'm from New York.
Willie Mae:	I love that pretty smile she's got.
Charles:	Do you have a picture of your daddy?
Willie Mae:	My daddy! I don't remember anything about my daddy. They said I was about one and a half years old when he died.
Charles:	Oh, so you never did know him?
Willie Mae:	No, I didn't.
Charles:	You have a sister too.
Willie Mae:	Yeah, her name is Mady. She is six years older that I am. She had a birthday the thirty first of July. She's ninety years old now. She called me the other day. She's doing pretty well. Her daughter came and got her and took her to California? She's been out there a little bit over a year.
Charles:	What part of California?
Willie Mae:	Los Angeles.
Charles:	Did you know a lady name Aunt Puss?
Willie Mae:	Yeah, she kind of reminds me of Aunt Emma. She wasn't quite light skin as Aunt Emma but she was light.
Charles:	Did you know Willie Frank Bilberry?
Willie Mae:	Who is that?
Charles:	Willie Frank Bilberry. He was Uncle Ed Bilberry's brother. But he died in 1940; you were still a young teenage girl then. Did you know Lizza Roberts?
Willie Mae:	It seem like I knew her. Is she Mama Emma's mother?
Charles:	Yes she is! Did you know Corene Bilberry?
Willie Mae:	Yes I did; she was a McGough. Her brother was George McGough.
Charles:	Did you go to school at Center Branch Baptist Church?

Willie Mae:	Yes I did, I had to walk to school by myself because I was the youngest and I didn't have anybody to be with. I would cross the pasture where the cows were and I was scared of cows.
Charles:	Were you scared of just the bulls or all cows?
Willie Mae:	All cows! It didn't have to be a bull. If it was a cow, I was just scared, and they weren't going to bother me. The cows were out there eating what they could find. If I looked up and saw one, I would turn around and go the other way; I had a hard time.

The interview ended with us all looking at pictures on her wall. Also, she gave me several old obituaries for use in researching the family's history.

Interview ended.

Phone Interview with: Clara Waters- September 2010

I had several phone conversations with Clara Waters of Toledo, Ohio. She is eighty two years old and is the only living child of Mason Holland and Anna Bilberry-Holland. Anna Bilberry is the sister of Frank Bilberry.

Courtesy of Sheila Eubank

Charles:	Hello cousin Clara. I just called to check and see how you're doing? Are you doing fine?
Clara:	I wouldn't say fine but I'm doing all right. I'm eighty-two years old now.
Charles:	Yeah. You had a birthday this month didn't you? It was September 10, 1928.
Clara:	I can't get around too much anymore. I have a lot of trouble with my legs and knees. But I can still make it.
Charles:	Well, that's all that matters.
Clara:	When are you coming this way?
Charles:	Well I was in Louisiana this past summer and hopefully I can get there the spring of next year. Where were you born?
Clara:	Right up there in Marion, Louisiana; just like you're going to St. Paul Baptist Church, but we were closer to the town where we lived. I think the church was about four or five miles from where we lived to where they use to go shopping in Marion.
Charles:	Where did they move to from there?
Clara:	After they left Marion they moved to Monroe, Louisiana. My brother Willis was down there. He worked at a funeral home there so we all went there.
Charles:	Did they ever go back to Marion?
Clara:	No. They went to Monroe and that was it.
Charles:	Where was your mother Anna Bilberry-Holland buried?
Clara:	In Monroe.
Charles:	Do you know the name of the cemetery?
Clara:	I know the name but I can't think of the name; the cemetery is up in town. John Davis (her brother) is in there too.
Charles:	What about Mason?
Clara:	He's buried there too.

Charles:	How old were you when your mother passed away?
Clara:	Oh man! Wait a minute now; I was around fifty or sixty. Now I ain't for sure about my actual age. Now my sister Ella, she out lived them all. She out lived Flossie, Lue Emma, Ollie Bell, all of them except me. I was the youngest.
Charles:	What was it like when your parents were in Marion living on a farm?
Clara:	They were on disability at that time. But all of them are gone now but me.
Charles:	What do you remember about your mother's brothers?
Clara:	There was one of them that had gray hair. I'm not talking about Uncle Lawrence.
Charles:	Papa Frank?
Clara:	Yeah, Frank. I used to know them all, but I've gotten away from there and I don't know them anymore.
Charles:	What kind of man was he?
Clara:	All I know is he was big bright man with gray hair; he was kind of heavy and Uncle Lawrence too. Uncle Lawrence wasn't as big as he was though. It was somebody else I knew too!
Charles:	Did your mother have a sister that lived in Crossett, Arkansas ?
Clara:	Oh yeah, Aunt Annie.
Charles:	Was she a twin sister or just another sister?
Clara:	Just a sister. But she was real gray-haired. Her mind wasn't working too well.
Charles:	Was she married?
Clara:	To tell you the truth I don't know, if she was I never seen him. She used to come up there where I lived; you know one of those trailers that you live in. She had a little old raggedy house there too.
Charles:	You lived in Crossett too?
Clara:	Yeah, I lived there and I moved there in 1947 or 1948, and I stayed there until 1950. My husband and my girlfriend's husband moved up to Toledo, Ohio and got jobs. She and I caught a train in Crossett and moved to Toledo later.
Charles:	I've been trying to find her in the census. She must have had another last name. I can't seem to locate her.
Clara:	All I know is Bilberry. Mama had another sister and her name was like that; Aunt Angeline was her name!
Charles:	Now she was dark-skinned. She must have had the same as mother but a different father.
Clara:	They did! There was Aunt Angeline, Uncle Lawrence, Uncle Frank, and Aunt Annie. There were some other ones too but those were the ones I did know.
Charles:	Where did you meet your husband?
Clara:	I met him in Huttig, Arkansas.

We ended our conversation discussing her children and grandchildren in Toledo, Ohio.

Phone Interview with: Charles Henry Bilberry, Jr., November 27, 2010

Charles Henry Bilberry is a retired school teacher and principal in the Detroit Public School system. He is the grandson of Frank Bilberry and Emma Roberts-Bilberry.

Charles Henry Bilberry, Jr.
Photo taken November 2010; courtesy of Taryn D. Bilberry

Charles Henry Bilberry, Jr. is the son of Charles Henry Bilberry, Sr. He mentioned to me in our conversation that his father nickname was "Bud." He resides in Westland, Michigan with his wife, Lillie. Charles is a retired educator from the Detroit, Michigan area School District. He was eighty-one years old at the time of this interview.

Charles: Cousin Charlie, Jesse B. Bilberry, Jr. and you are now the new patriarchs of the family. The stories you both have about your life as a child is a treasure that is relished by the family.

Henry: It's funny how you remember things. I remember vividly the times my parents would drive from Pine Bluff, Arkansas to Papa Frank and Mama Emma's house. All of my father's brothers would come. Uncle Jesse would come over from Farmerville, Louisiana and Uncle Ladell lived right nearby. Uncle Willie was still alive and Uncle Son (Ed Bilberry). They would all come to Mama Emma's and Papa Frank's house. All the men would gather to have dinner together and the women would wait to eat. The men and the boys would all eat

92

together. They had a kitchen that was of built apart from the house. You would walk across a big wide board, like a bridge from the kitchen over to the dining room. I don't know why it was separated. It must have been for fire hazard reasons!

I would remember as a kid I would walk back there in the kitchen where Mama Emma was cooking; she was a good cook. You would walk across that big wide board into the dining room and there was a long table that had a bench on both side. There was a chair at the head of the table where Papa Frank sat. Since I was a guest, I could sat in there and eat with them. When we got through eating, we went into this great big room, much like a living room. I think there might have been a bed in there and a big fireplace. All of the men and boys would sit around the fireplace. I remember your dad, Adell Bilberry and your uncles, me and I guess Jesse B. because Uncle Jesse brought his kids. We would sit there with the men around the fireplace. They would have peanuts, chestnuts or whatever; they would sit way up into the night talking to each other.

I remember once when we went to Papa Frank and Mama Emma's house for Christmas; Jesse B. Jr., Johnny B., and I were not sure how many of Uncle Jesse's kids were born at that time. We were all in the bed together late at night and Papa Frank came in as Santa Claus. He visited us while we were asleep. It wasn't until later on did I find out that that was Papa Frank acting as Santa Claus.

Another thing about Papa Frank and Mama Emma is that they grew all of their own stuff. They had sugar cane and there was a smaller cane called sorghum cane. The sorghum cane was a smaller cane. Whenever I would go down there it was two things that I always wanted. I wanted some sugar cane. Uncle Willie would lead me out there in the fields and cut me some cane. And boy did I have a good time chewing on it! Yes, he and Uncle Son would take me out there. You ever heard of clabbered milk; it was like sour milk and Mama Emma would put sugar in it and give it to me. That was a great treat! Mama Emma would go fishing at D'Loutre River and pickle and can those fish. She would always have a lot of good fish; she was a good cook! It was a real treat and a pleasure whenever we went down to their house.

Charles: That was some good information you just gave me and I like that! I like the stories! How many acres of land did Papa Frank have?

Henry: I'm not sure but they had a big smoke house. Mama Emma made soap. They were very independent and very resourceful. Now Jesse B. would know more about that than I do because they were around them more. We would go for a visit and stay three or four days and then go back to Arkansas.

Charles: That was good and I'm glad you shared the stories with me. Now I understand that Papa Frank and Mama Emma's children lived very close to each other.

Henry: Yeah, they did. They could yell across the way to each other. When we came down they would yell out for everyone to come to see Bud (Charles Henry Bilberry, Sr.). They called my mother sister Dellie and everybody called my dad Bud. They called me Little Charlie.

Interview ended.

Phone Interview with: Jesse Bernard Bilberry, Jr. December 30, 2010

Jesse Bernard Bilberry, Jr.

Photo taken July 2004; courtesy of Taryn D. Bilberry

Jesse B. Bilberry, Sr. is the grandson of Frank Bilberry and Emma Roberts-Bilberry. He is a retired principal and educator in the Louisiana secondary and post-secondary education system. He has been Pastor of the Mt. Pilgrim Missionary Baptist Church for the past 31 years.

Charles: What kind of a man was Papa Frank? I was listening to my father, Adell Bilberry and Uncle Johnny Bilberry discussing Papa Frank one day and they mentioned that he had a little limp in his walk. They mentioned that he got the limp from an injury he received from helping someone move a piano. The piano fell on his foot while it was being move and he's limped ever since that happened.

Jesse: Yes, he had a little limp but I didn't know how he got it. But I would describe Papa Frank as a great man, a real man, a family man and he was a hard-working man. I just knew Papa Frank in so many ways. He had that farm over there and I believe that was his heart. He strived every year to gin the first bail of cotton. At that time, whoever ginned the first bail of cotton would get a prize. Papa Frank would always try to gin the first bail of cotton. He always loved his family. I can remember when he would come to town and sometimes he would ride horse-back to Farmerville, Louisiana if he needed to go to the bank or get one or two small items. If he had to pick up a lot of stuff he would drive his wagon to town. He was a hardworking man and he was also a church man. He was faithful to the church and he was a Christian. He was a family man; he love Mama Emma; he loved his children and he certainly loved his grandchildren. You know Charles, God's primary institution is the family; it's not the church but the family. All of the other institutions depend on the family. I thought Papa Frank was a model man when it came to the family and I admired him for this. He was a hustler; he would work from sun-up to sundown. We lived in Farmerville, Louisiana and I know sometimes we would look up and say: "here comes Papa Frank." Everybody would run out of the house and run down the road and meet him. If he was in that wagon he would stop the wagon and all of us would get up in the wagon and he would ride us on back to the house.

Charles: I'm not sure if Barbra, your sister who told me this but didn't, he have a horse or mule name Molly?

Jesse:	I know he had a horse name Ida, I thought. I don't remember the names of all of the animals.
Charles:	Tell me what you know about Papa Frank's brother Lawrence Bilberry.
Jesse:	I didn't know a lot about Uncle Lawrence. I just knew him; I met him and he was a fine man. I knew more about Uncle Ed (Ed Thompson) than I did Uncle Lawrence. Uncle Ed was his half-brother.
Charles:	What do you know about Ed Thompson.
Jesse:	I knew that he was a family man in Farmerville. He had a real close relationship to our family; he visited us a lot.
Charles:	Papa Frank had another sister name Dolly Mayfield. Did you ever meet her?
Jesse:	No I didn't but I heard of her.
Charles:	Also, Papa Frank had a sister name Anna; he was a Bilberry that married a Holley or Holland. She lived in Monroe, Louisiana in the later years of her life.

Interview ended.

Seab Horn, Sr., Narrates About His Parents to His Daughter Deborah Horn-Reliford

Seab Horn, Sr., was born June 15, 1916; he is the oldest living of the Bilberry and Horn Families

In 1906, John Nabors was born. His father, Wiley Nabors went to Mary McGaskey's house to ask for help with his birth. Wiley McGaskey asked Lola McGaskey to come and help too. The Nabors and McGaskey's were sincere family friends; they lived down on the river near Derry and Cloutierville, Louisiana.

My father was Calvin Horn. He worked for fifty cents a day, six days a week. I'm not sure what type of work he did. Calvin said to Lola (McGaskey), "come with me and I'll marry you." He bought his license and went to a white preacher's house and asked to be married. The white preacher, Louis Frishall said, "Come on in and I'll marry you." Calvin and Lola married that night in 1907. The next day Lola made breakfast for her husband and Calvin's parents Lint and Mary Horn.

Calvin went to a man and asked him to help find him a house to live in. The man said, "Give me a few days." The man got someone to help him clear the land around an old log cabin type house with a shovel and axe. They found a spring for water and then went to let Calvin and Lola know he had found them a house. They moved into the house. Friends gave them a cow, chickens and pigs.

In 1912, Calvin hired a man to build him a new log cabin house. Calvin and Lola had four children; Landola was born in 1908, Mary was born in 1910, Jethro was born in 1912, and I, Seab was born in 1916. Papa Calvin always told me, "If you don't raise it, you don't eat it." They had a horse name Fanny that they used for riding from place to place. Papa Calvin would ride forward but would put mama on the horse sideways to ride.

In 1932 their family was growing so fast; they hired someone to build them another house. They made a crib out of the old log house and then built a smokehouse to cure their own meat. My grandmother Mary would often visit Papa Calvin and Lola. She told Papa Calvin "You married a good cook." Lola would often make biscuits, eggs, and bacon for breakfast. Papa Calvin's dad was Lint Horn. He came from South Carolina on a train to Louisiana.

Grandma Mary Horn died in 1917, at the age of fifty. Louis Frishall donated one acre of land to the Antioch Primitive Baptist Church for a graveyard where the old school was located. Luemmer Bilberry and I married in 1937, and we lived with Papa Calvin and Lola until 1958, until I built a new house for Luemmer and me. When we moved into the house my brother, Jethro complained that the house had too many doors. Jethro built a house for his wife Mary Bilberry and himself and it had the same number of doors!

Interview ended

CHAPTER EIGHT

Adell and Johnny Bilberry's Retirement Party

Excerpts from the Retirement Party for Adell Bilberry and Johnny Bilberry:

Ladell Bilberry, Jr. *Loeast Bilberry-Watkins* *Loreace Bilberry-Watley*

T his retirement party took place on June 18-19, 1994, in Farmerville, Louisiana to honor the retirement of Adell Bilberry and Johnny Bilberry. Johnny Bilberry was 61 years old and had just recently retired. Adell was 67 years old and had been retired for three years. Most of the attendees of the party were relatives and a few friends. The excerpts written here are from a video recording of that event. Loeast and Loreace are their sisters and Ladell is their brother.

Loreace: I remember when we were young; they would both go out and work so we could have food on the table.

Adell Bilberry, son of Ladell Bilberry
Photo Taken July 1992

98

Loeast: I remember when Adell was a teenager. He went to St. Louis, Missouri to get a job but he did not know how to take care of himself. So, he decided to come back home. We missed him so much. When he did come home, he was so poor (skinny). He didn't eat right because he was so lonesome for home. My mama started cooking him food and he started putting weight on and then he got fat. He then went to work for Thad Kennedy. He then got married to this beautiful lady name Bobbie Brown. They had three children, Charles, Peggie, and Princess (Fonda Deleon). Adell was a hardworking man. He stood by his family. Sometimes he would go out to work sick but nobody knew it but him. I would watch him sometimes when he would get up to go; he was always smiling. When you were feeling down, he would make you smile because he was always smiling.

One night I had a long talk with my brother Adell. Who else did I have to talk to other than my older brother? He told me that he started working at the age of 11 years old for an old man, Will Kennedy. He worked for him plowing a mule, from sunrise to sunset until he was 14 years old. He said to me, Loeast, I asked mother to ask dad to let me get another job so I can make more money." Now all the time Adell was working, he was living with us, because he didn't have any kids at that time. He wanted to help out the family.

He then went to work for old man Ross Taylor, cutting pulpwood with a bucksaw making $2.50 to $3.00 a day. He worked there until the age of 17. He then went to work for T. L. Kennedy for $6.00 a day, driving a mule to skid logs. He worked for Mr. Kennedy until he retired in 1991. He worked for Mr. Kennedy for a total of 44 years. That's a long time folks. Let's give him a hand (applause).

Ladell, Jr.: Good evening. I'm here to give recognition to Johnny Bilberry for his years of service in the Union Parish community. I've known Johnny as a big brother from a child up, at home, in school and out of school. He played practically every sport there was. I remember seeing Johnny at the old Union Parish High School. He would go behind the shop, put on boxing gloves and they would box. I use to wonder how he could take those hard hits. He was a running back on the football team. I remember when he got spiked in the face, taken out of the game and taken to the hospital. But he kept coming back for more.

Johnny Bilberry, son of Ladell Bilberry

Johnny Bilberry worked three years with Jethro Horn, who had a contracting business in the pulpwood industry. Johnny graduated from Union Parish High School in May of 1957. In 1959, Johnny got a job working for the IMC Chemical Plant in Sterlington, Louisiana. It was a plant that made fertilizer and distributed it all over the world. The company sold portions of its manufacturing process to other companies for the next few years but for some reason, each new owner kept Johnny Bilberry as one of their employees. Somehow, they recognized the talent that he had. Johnny worked for a total of 37 years in that job at the chemical plant.

I also remember Johnny being involved in community service. I've seen him refereeing basketball games at Eastside High School. I remember seeing him coaching basketball and baseball to young children in the Union Parish community. Also, Johnny was a dedicated church worker and a deacon at Sweet Lilly Primitive Baptist Church, located in Marion, Louisiana. At this time I'd like to present you with this plaque on your retirement (applause).

Courtesy of Loeast Watkins

Where is the D'Loutre River? Three Sisters Visit the Old Family Home Site near Marion, Louisiana

Loeast Bilberry-Watkins **Loreace Bilberry-Watley** **Emma Jean Bilberry-Payne**

On June 19, 1994, family members Loeast Bilberry-Watkins, Loreace Bilberry-Watley and Emma Jean Bilberry-Payne made a family trip to the home site where they were born and raised. They are the daughters of Ladell Bilberry, Sr., and Corene Bilberry. Some of their children and grandchildren accompanied them on this visit. All of them are visiting from Kansas City, Kansas. The videotaping was done by Roy D. Richards Jr., son of Loeast Watkins. It begins as they exit their vehicles and look towards the old home site.

Emma: My room was next to my mama's and daddy's. Richard (son) slept in the room with mama and daddy.

Loreace: If we can just see the old house, we'll be satisfied.

Loeast: I wonder how come nobody has cut all of this down. Why did they let the yard grow up like this? If I had my big long boots on I'd walk up through there; but see I don't have my boots on.

Emma:	Your grandpa killed polecats (skunks) up and down this road Junior (junior is Roy Richards. He is the son of Loeast Watkins and the cameraman in the video of this trip to the old family home site).
Loeast:	He sure did; he would come home stinking a whole lot of nights. We would smell him before he set foot in the house.
Loreace:	Look at those trees.
Loeast:	Boy, I used to climb up trees like that so fast!
Emma:	The D'Loutre bottom is down there (pointing her fingers toward the D'Loutre River bottom). We would go fishing and we would have our smoke in a smoke bucket to keep the mosquitoes off of us.

Loreace and Loeast started running down the small road toward the D'Loutre River.

Cameraman:	Look at them; they're trying to run.
Emma:	They're trying to run; just like little kids! Junior, we had pretty white sand in front of our house; it was beautiful. There wasn't any grass Junior, just sand.
Cameraman:	White sand just like this (pointing camera toward the white sand in the road).
Emma:	Just pure white sand.

Emma started running down the road towards her two older sisters, Loeast and Loreace. The cameraman, Junior, catches up with Emma and they resumed their walking and talking.

Emma:	We had to have our smoke because those mosquitoes would be coming and the smoke kept the mosquitoes off of us too!

The cameraman, zoom the camera in on a sign posted on a tree that read "Sweet Lilly Hunting Club." There were several hunting clubs throughout Union Parish, Louisiana. The hunting clubs would often pay landowners a certain fee for the privilege to hunt on their land. My father, Adell Bilberry was an avid hunter and a member and officer in the Marion Hunting Club. The Bilberry family allowed the Sweet Lilly Hunting Club to hunt on their property without charging them a fee.

Emma:	I need to get my exercise (she started running down the road where she catches up with Loeast and Loreace).
Loeast:	How far is D'Loutre?
Emma:	It's a long way down!
Loreace:	Oh, we can go down there. It's not far! (she starts back running toward the D'Loutre bottom).
Loeast;	Ooh! That's a long stretch!
Emma:	But it's pretty down there.
Loeast:	When was the last time you've been down to the D'Loutre River?
Emma:	Never!

Loeast:	Ooh! Ooh! (getting the attention of the rest of the group). She's never been down here!
Emma:	No, not in 25 years! Not since I was a child growing up. That's what I meant.
Loeast:	But you said never!

A few minutes passed by and it seemed that the D'Loutre River was too far away to continue. The family decided to turn around and go back to their vehicles.

Cameraman: Hey mama! Trina said she want to move down here. She says there is no crime here.

Loeast:	Yes there is. But down here you won't hear any sirens all night. I get tired of hearing all of that mess. Sunflowers! (Loreast picked up a few wild sunflowers, made them into a bouquet and begun running back to her vehicle).
Emma:	Whew, look how far we are from the car!
Loeast:	I told you it was a long way.
Cameraman:	Uh! Huh!

The outing ended with everyone getting back into their vehicles (van and a car) and returning back to their motel in Farmerville, Louisiana.

Courtesy of Loeast Watkins

CHAPTER NINE

Remembering Our Heritage

Mary Lee Roberts-Wayne

Born: August 5, 1920
Parents: Charley H. and Havanah Roberts
Where: Strong, Arkansas
Heritage: Her parents were born in Farmerville, Louisiana
Lineage: Charley's parents were: John Lee and Rachel.
            John Lee was white—and the High Sheriff of Farmerville.
Rachel was a slave married to a Roberts (first name is unknown). Charley was the youngest
            of 16 children. Havanah's parents were: Elisha Smith and Valonia Benson. Both
            Elisha and Valonia were part Cherokee. Elisha and Valonia had 14 children:
            seven boys and seven girls.
Growing Up: Charley and Havanah had six children: four girls and two boys. The children
            called their parents, papa and mama.
Deanna—the oldest, married Roy Williams, and had three girls; Zetilla, Reva, and
            Marie.

Ollie Bell—married Vernie, and had five children; Martha, Vernon, Ruby,
Ollie (Woodrow), John Henry. In later years, he married Laura (last name is
unknown)

Orine—married John L. Henson, and had nine children; Willa Bell, Maxine, John
Phillip, Ralph, Lorraine, Walter, Roger, Bruce.

Robertine—married Mack Henson (brother of John L.), and had three children; Huey, John, and DeLora.

Mary—married Grady Wayne (of Marion, Louisiana), and they had four children; Grady, Marie, Willie, and Sandra.

Charley—married Madessa Gatson, and they had two children; Paul and Charles. Later he married Edith Davis, and they had one daughter, Carla, and her son, Tony.

In all, there were 26 grandchildren.

Mary and her family had a huge farm, and they always had good things to eat from their garden; such as wild berries they picked in the woods, and the animals they raised, slaughtered, and cured. Mary said, because of the beautiful vegetables she was raised on, she has never eaten a vegetable or a fruit she didn't like. They grew sweet potatoes, "Irish" potatoes, okra, sweet peas, black-eyed peas, pole beans, butter beans, squash, cabbage, collards, turnips, mustards, lettuce, cucumbers, onions, and garlic beets and radishes. Also, they had a huge orchard with apples, peaches, plums, pears and strawberries. Mama would cut the apples really fine and put them on top of the tin roof during the day. At night, she would cover them so that the dew wouldn't soften them. Mary said, those dried apples were used to make the most delicious pies she had ever tasted. They picked wild berries, and nuts in the woods, such as huckleberries and chinkeypins (sic) [chinquapins]. They had a melon patch where they grew watermelon and cantaloupe.

In the fields they grew corn, cotton, peanuts, ribbon and sorghum sugar cane. Papa had his own mill in the pasture that he used to grind the sugar cane to make syrup. He traded with everyone in town; and as payment for making syrup to sell; every fourth gallon that he made was for his family and that was all he charged in trade. In the winter, he would take the syrup to the store in Strong, Arkansas and trade it for sugar and flour. He knew exactly how many gallons of syrup would carry the family through the winter. Whatever they didn't eat during the spring and summer, they canned in the fall so that they would have plenty to get them through the winter.

Old King and Old Jim were Papa's mules. King was black and Jim was gray. Also, they raised cows, pigs, chickens, ducks and geese. Mama must have had 100 cats. The family ate well off the hogs, cows, and chickens including chittlins, hog malls, pig feet, pig knuckles, pig tails, pig ears, mountain oysters, ham, bacon, cow tongue, steak, tripe, chicken backs, chicken wings, chicken breasts, chicken legs, chicken thighs and chicken feet. They had squirrel, rabbit, deer, and coon—you name it, they ate it; from the rooter to the tooter.

They never bought eggs, milk or butter. They were totally self-sufficient and never wanted for anything in the way of food. Mama made most of the clothes from Kroger sacks and they were passed down from the girls—Mary being last had lots of hand-me-downs; papa and mama didn't waste anything. Mama stitched quilts and braided rugs from old clothes and handed down that remarkable skill to her girls. They took ashes from the fireplace to make their own soap using hog fat and water in a big barrel. When the water was added to the ashes it turned into lye and mama would pour this caustic mixture into a big wash tub to make the best soap that would clean clothes better than any product on the market today.

Have you ever heard of chinkeypins (sic)? Mary has a unique way of pronouncing things, so for years we thought it was a mispronunciation and then we found it in the dictionary. Chinkeypins (sic) grew on trees in Arkansas. When they ripen, they turn from green to brown in the fall. Mary and her brothers and sisters would shake the trees and come home with a mother lode of these tasty treats. They looked like acorns and had the flavor of pecans. They would boil them in the shell and let them dry; then break them open and enjoy!

One of her favorite beverages was sassafras tea. Papa would dig up the sassafras tree, cut the roots, wash it, and let it dry. Once dried, Mama Havanah would cut them into small pieces, tie them in cheese cloth, and boil them in an old coffee pot. Every spring, papa made everyone drink a concoction sweetened with the honey he gathered from his bees; it was delicious. I used to look forward to the packages from grandpa with these roots; they turned all the pots and cups red. The roots tasted so good and I thought it was more of a type of Kool-Aid. Actually, grandpa distributed it for medicinal purposes; he said it would get the winter 'Yuma' out of your blood.

Papa Charley raised his own bees and that was where the honey came from. There is no sweeter honey than what papa's bees made; he had four hives. He had a homemade mask with screening to protect his face and a tarp to wrap around him to keep from getting stung by the bees. He would pour the honey into pots or pans, leaving enough for the bees to live on. Mama Havanah would squeeze the honey from the comb and the children would get their enjoyment from chewing on the combs like they were gum. Mama put the honey into jars and it would last them through the cold winter months. Mary said, while reminiscing, she could still taste the honey sopped up with mama's good old biscuits; they used more honey than sugar.

Papa was always full of mischief and fun. He kept them entertained and sometimes in terror. He and mama were always concerned about the children getting home from school while it was still daylight. On those long walks down winding country roads and across creeks, Mary and her siblings often had so much fun that they lost track of time. Mary recalls the walk was about three miles each way. School started at 8:00 a.m. and ended at 4:00 p.m. The teacher taught all grades from first to eighth in one room; her name was Miss Emma Jean Burton.

For the most part, Mary and her brothers and sisters weren't afraid of anything—except for Charley; he was the youngest—four years younger than Mary—and he got the rest of them in a lot of trouble being the baby. Even if he wasn't really scared, he would use the experience to torment them because after all "he was mama's baby" and she would get upset if they let anything happen to her baby. One school day, papa conjured up a trick to teach us a lesson about getting home when we were supposed to. He killed an old fox that had been getting into the chicken coup and stretched the fox across the gate with its beady eyes wide open. The sun was setting by the time Deanna, Ollie Bell, Orine, Robertine, Mary, and Charlie made it to the house. There facing them in full stride as if it were about to pounce on them was the old fox. Papa rounded the corner laughing his heart out. Hearing their screams gave him a great deal of satisfaction. Un-huh, he would say: 'dad gum your hide', you won't be late any more. Papa was as sly as that old fox when it came to playing tricks on children.

During the Great Depression times were hard! Mary was unable to complete her education beyond 8th grade. She helped her mama with the household work—cooking, cleaning, washing, ironing, sewing, and tending the garden and the animals, while the others were in school. She was an exceptional learner and to this day reads the newspaper every day and does her "word games." After a brief courtship, at age 18, Mary eloped with Grady Wayne, and moved with him to his home in Marion, Louisiana. Grandpa was really unhappy that Mary had married without his permission, but since Strong and Marion are only 45 minutes apart, there were frequent visits.

Also, the Wayne's had a self-sufficient farm or ranch by today's standards. They made money to purchase acreages of land by hauling paper wood from their land. Papa Willie Wayne and Mary Lee Andrews-Wayne were sweet to Mary, as were Grady's five siblings and their spouses: Ollie (still living at 104 years old) & Etta, Otis & Georgia, Willie (never married), Arniece and Boykin (Persley), and Jay Artis and Maddie (mama's cousin). Two years after they were married, they had their first child, Grady, Jr., on March 10, 1940; and 16 months later, they had their second child, Marie on August 14, 1941.

When Grady Sr., was drafted into the Army during World War II, the Wayne's took good care of Mary, Grady and Marie. The same month that Grady went off to serve this country, their third child, Willie, was born January 4, 1944; he became ill and died at six weeks old. Grady was a member of the now-famous "Red Ball Express," made up primarily of colored soldiers who drove ammunition trucks behind enemy lines during World War II.

In 1950, Grady Sr., followed Mary to Kansas City, Kansas, where she had moved with her brother, Charley and his wife Madessa to start over. On April 30, 1951, their fourth child, Sandra, was born; this is where the rest of the story—the story of the BEGATS continues.

Courtesy of Sandra Campbell

CHAPTER TEN

Short Biographies

Short Biography of Fred Billberry

Born: 1883
Parents: Jack and Francis Billberry
Where: Marion, Union Parish, Louisiana
Died: Unknown

The family bible says that Fred was born in 1883. His parents were Jack and Francis Billberry. He married my Grandmother Rosa and moved to Oklahoma around 1914 or 1915. Rosa's entire family moved to Boley, Oklahoma. Her mother, brothers and sisters all came to Oklahoma. Rosa and Fred settled on some land outside Boley. Boley still exist and is a historical black town founded in 1903. Oklahoma had many black towns but few remain as active towns. My mother, Minerva did not see a white person until she was five years old; there were no white people in Boley. The white people in Okemah, Oklahoma, which is about 20 miles away, decided they were going to come to Boley and kill the black people. The people in Boley found out about it. Every man and boy, old enough to shoot, climbed and lined the building roof tops on Boley's Main Street. My mother said she remembers her dad and brothers getting on top of the buildings. She said that her mother and the girls got in the cellar. The county police stop the whites on the road to Boley. They told them that they were going to get massacred by the blacks; and they turned around and went back.

My mother said, that she remembered her dad being gentle and loving and she really missed him when he was gone. While in Union Parish, Louisiana they had five sons; Columbus, Morris Lee, Henry, Pratis, and Sidney. The 1910 U. S. Census list Fred's trade as laborer on a logging gang. They had six more children after arriving in Oklahoma. Minnie, Minerva, Bessie, Marie, Pearlena, and Willie Lee. Pearlena and Willie Lee both died before age five. Bessie died of throat cancer at age 16. Morris Lee died in 1950; he was murdered. Sidney died December 25, 1972. Minnie died August 1994. Columbus died in his 20's. Henry died in 1998 in Detroit, Michigan; he had moved to Detroit to be with my mom. My mother, Minerva left after high school to attend Wayne State

University. She came back to Oklahoma in 1960, but had lived in Detroit for over 20 years. She married Bervin Winans. So the singing Winans (Be Be, Ce Ce, Marvin, etc.) are my cousins on my dad's side. Pratis left with Fred in the fall of 1928; they went down south to earn some extra money. Neither Fred nor Pratis came back home. Some men in Boley came back and said there was some trouble with the white men. They last saw Fred being held by some white men. They believed he was lynched; no one ever saw him again. The men told my grandmother that they thought Pratis got away. My grandmother moved the family to Seminole, Oklahoma in 1929; Seminole had plenty of jobs because of the oil boom. She could not handle the farm with the girls and boys so she moved to go to work. In 1950, someone in Seminole sent a letter from Pratis to my grandmother who then lived in Oklahoma City. She did not get the envelope with the address so they never knew what happen to him. Also, Fred's sister Mattie and her family move to Oklahoma. Mattie's daughter was Mary Arbertha Thurmond. The only child of Fred's that is still alive is Marie; we call her "Tootsi," and she is 87 years old. My aunt had seven children and she has outlived all but three; Urban, Sidney, Fred, and William are all deceased. She has twin girls who are named Mae and Marie. She has one son who goes by the surname Bilbury. His name is James Bilbury and he lives in California and is a lawyer. He presently runs a cleaning business and has several contracts with the state, counties, and restaurants in Chinatown.

Courtesy of Nancy Winans-Garrison;
Granddaughter of Fred and Rosa Billberry

Short Biography of Rosa Lee Staples-Billberry

Born: May 5, 1874
Parents: Columbus Staples and Lizzie Davis
Where: Marion, Union Parish, Louisiana
Died: October 9, 1977

Rosa Staples married Fredrick Billberry on September 3, 1906. Fredrick is the son of Jack and Francis Billberry of Conway, Louisiana. They had eleven children. In 1915, the family moved from Louisiana to Oklahoma. In 1922, Rosa became a member of the Church of God In Christ. During the 1940's, Rosa moved to Oklahoma City, Oklahoma; and united with the Page Sanctuary Church of God in Christ. She was a missionary and founded a mission on Second Street and Central Street in Oklahoma City, Oklahoma. She labored at this mission for years. Rosa was involved with civic work in the Oklahoma City community. She worked with the Boy Scouts, Girl Scouts and a Community Action Program where she served as a senior citizen recruiter. Sunday, October 9, 1977, Rosa died while singing a gospel song in church.

Short Biography of Minerva Billberry-Winans

Born: April 10, 1919
Parents: Fred and Rosa Staples-Billberry
Where: Boley, Oklahoma
Died: December 22, 1994
Heritage: Her parents were born in Conway, Louisiana; Union Parish.
Lineage: Fred's parents were: Jack Billberry and Francis Jones-Billberry.

Minerva Billberry was born April 10, 1919, in Boley, Oklahoma to Fred and Rosa Billberry. Her parents moved to Seminole, Oklahoma when she was eight years old. Minerva graduated from Booker T. Washington High School where she was an honor student; and she won several debate awards and graduated early.

She moved to Detroit, Michigan to attend Wayne State University to study Psychology and Sociology. She was united in holy matrimony to Bervin Winans, and has two daughters, Rosa Marie Wiggins and Nancy Ann Winans-Garrison.

Minerva was awarded the highest civilian medal from the United States government during World War II. The Medal was awarded by Admiral Nimitz of the Navy for her inspection of thousands of rounds of navy shells with none being defective. She attended the University of Oklahoma and Oklahoma City University where she completed a nursing program. She worked for the Community Action Program in 1965, Oklahoma City Housing Authority in 1967, and Greater Urban League in 1971; and as a social worker for the Department of Human Services in 1972, and she retired in 1984. Minerva loved people and was active in the community. She was president of the PTA and scout leader of the Girl Scouts and Camp Fire Girls. She was a member of the Bethlehem-Wesley Center Board, Neighborhood Service Organization Board, Legal Aid of Western Oklahoma Board and the Oklahoma City Police Citizen Advisory Board. She organized the Mothers' Club to aid young mothers in employment and education. She was a member of the Black Social Workers Association.

Minerva received Christ under the direction of Bishop E. M. Page and Elder Joe Statum in Seminole, Oklahoma. She began singing at revival at an early age. She was a world known singer, and she sang with great professionals, such as Mahalia Jackson and others. Minerva was famous for her rendition of the song "This Train." Also, she held many offices in the church. Minerva died at home with her three grandchildren on December 22, 1994. Ta'ron was playing the piano and they were singing, "I'll fly away." Three minutes later she was gone.

Courtesy of Nancy Winans-Garrison

Short Biography of Elsey (E. B.) Bilberry, Sr.

Born: 1827 circa
Parents: McDuel Bilberry and Mary Simmons
Where: Alabama
Lineage: Father was McDuel Bilberry

Elsey B. Bilberry (aka Britt or Britton) was a farmer and held positions of prominence (magistrate, justice of the peace, and postmaster) in Union Parish. There are variations in the spelling of his name throughout. He was born in Alabama; and his father was William McDuel Bilberry and mother was Mary Simmons. Elsey B. Bilberrys' (aka E. B.) first marriage was to Mary Jane Honeycutt in 1851. She was the daughter of John Honeycutt, Sr., an early settler of Union Parish and Mary Feazel. Mary Jane died in 1865. She and some of her children are buried at the Meridian Baptist Church cemetery near Marion, Louisiana. Elsey B. married Cynthia Smith in 1868. When Cynthia passed away he then married Leona Kerr in 1907 in Arkansas. Elsey B. and Cynthia had a son by the name of John Henry who was buried in the West Cemetery at Meridian Baptist Church. According to the State of Arkansas' death certificates, Elzie [sic] Bilberry was the father of a slave name Jordan Bilberry. Jordan's mother name is Martha Gilbert.

The Conway, Louisiana post office was established on April 19, 1881. Elsey B. Bilberry was the village first postmaster. He held that position from April 19, 1881, until June 18, 1908. He was listed as a magistrate in the Gazette Newspaper in 1888. E. B. Bilberry died around 1920. The State of Louisiana, Parish of Union, and Third District Court office indicates E. B. Bilberry as the Justice of the Peace that performed the marriage between Robert Bridges, Jr. and Josie Smith on December 10, 1892. Lincoln Burch was listed as security on the marriage application and the witnesses for the marriage ceremony were J. H. Bilberry, J. D. Conley, and Robert Bridges, Sr.

(Source: http://usgwarchives.net/la/lafiles.htm)
Courtesy of Larry Edwards

Short Biography of Jordan Billberry

Born: 1857
Died: February 14, 1915
Parents: Elzie Billberry and Martha Gilbert (servant)

Jordan Billberry was born in Conway, Louisiana in Union Parish. His death certificate lists his father as Elzie Bilberry. Elzie Bilberry was a white slave owner, farmer and served as a magistrate in Union Parish for many years. As an adult, Jordan became a farmer. According to the United States Census records of 1880, he was married to Amanda Dertin (Durden). Amanda was originally from Arkansas. Jordan and Amanda had three children residing in their household; John, Abe and Domien. The 1900 United States Census list Jordan as married to Mattie Carson.; and it shows that he and his family had moved to the Liberty Township area of Ouachita County, Arkansas. J. C. Menser, W. L. Menser and R.J. Rodgers were witnesses at their marriage ceremony in Union Parish Louisiana. Four more children were born to this union; Frank, Mary, Margurther and Fanny. Jordan died on February 14, 1915, in Chidester, Arkansas from cirrhosis of the liver and mitral insufficiency.

Short Biography of Adell Billberry

Born: December 15, 1877
Died: January 8, 1953, Stockton, San Joaquin County, California
Parents: Jordan Ellis Billberry and Amanda Dertin

Adell Billberry (aka A. D. or Abe) was born in Conway, Louisiana in Union Parish. He came to Arkansas in 1896, where he settled in Chidester, Arkansas in Ouachita County. He married Annie Ross on January 18, 1900. According to the 1930 U. S. Census records, Abe and Annie had eight children; Henry, Mimie, Mandolph, Linsee, James E., Amanda, Edward and Hayaree; and one niece, Madailee Woods who resided in their household. Abe's father name was Jordan Billberry and his mother was named Amanda (Mandy Dertin). Abe had one aunt by the name of Cindy Billberry. She was the sister of Jordan Billberry. His grandfather's name was Elzie Bilberry; a slaveholder in Marion, Louisiana of Union Parish.

Courtesy of Joyce Billberry-Cofer

Short Biography of Sarah Alabama Montgomery-Ellis

Born: March 15, 1911
Died: July 21, 1986
Parents: George Montgomery and Minnie Ann Roberts-Montgomery
Town: Marion, Louisiana

Sarah Alabama Montgomery "Bama" was born on March 15, 1911, in Louisiana. She died on July 21, 1986, in Marion, Louisiana. She was buried in Meridian Cemetery, Conway, Louisiana. Sarah, as she was often called, was only six months old when her mother died. Her grandmother Eliza Jane and grandfather Will Roberts reared her along with the help of her uncles' Lee, Genie, C. C., Charlie Roberts, and Aunt Emma Bilberry. Many loved Aunt Bama. She married John Ellis in 1942; there were no children born to this union.

She and Uncle Johnnie did not have a formal education, but they wanted to see our people succeed and enjoy the finer things in life. I can remember her bragging on John's new car that had revealing/concealing lights. It was such a nice car; it even had "blinking eyes." She had him go out and start the car and turn the lights off and on to demonstrate its ability.

Aunt Bama was a big talker and as you can tell, she was a hoot. She had many funny stories, which carried a lot of our history – she was a historian in her own right. Some of the stories we can fondly recount, but others we regrettably let slide by the wayside. Sarah married Johnnie H. Ellis son of Lorenzo Ellis, Sr., and Georgia Bellzora Bilberry. Johnnie was born on March 14, 1903, in Louisiana. He died on November 28, 1990, in Louisiana; he was buried in Meridian Cemetery, Conway, Louisiana.

Courtesy of Linda Lou Evans

Short Biography of Gordie Etta Bilberry-Burch

Born: October 12, 1893
Died: July 30, 1983
Parents: John (Jack) Bilberry and Francis Jones
Town: Marion, Louisiana

Gordie Burch was fondly known as "Aunt Gordie." She was married to John Burch of Marion, Louisiana. She moved to Farmerville, Louisiana in later years. She became a member of Blooming Grove Baptist Church in 1921; where she served as an usher, treasurer of the Southside Home Mission, chairperson of the cooking department and a mother of the church.

Short Biography of John Hiram Montgomery

Born: April 15, 1835
Died: April 25, 1916
Parents: Slaves from Africa
Town: Perry County, Alabama

John Hiram Montgomery was a slave of slaveholder Samuel Montgomery. His father was a slave from Africa that kept and tended the heating pots on the ship to keep the crew feet warm on the ship according to an oral testimony of his great granddaughter Ruby Montgomery-Wayne. John Hiram's African father lived among the Indians and was one of the first black people to settle in Union Parish, Louisiana. Samuel died circa June 28, 1855. Catharine, Samuel's wife, died circa October 4, 1855. William C. Smith was appointed administrator of the estate and Samuel oldest son James P. Montgomery became the tutor of the minor children. By an order of the 12th Judicial Court, William C. Smith sold the slave Hiram, age 20, to the highest bidder who was George R. Murphy for $1305. After emancipation John Hiram Montgomery acquired land near Big Cane Creek in Marion, Louisiana. He married Caroline Nelson and they had the following children: James, Benjamin, Susan, Jane, Eliza, Sarah, Martha, Earlia, Harriet, John, and George. James was sired by a white man name "Old Man Atkins" that lived near Litroe, Louisiana. He was born prior to the marriage of Hiram and Caroline. John Hiram Montgomery died April 25, 1916 from organic heart failure. Porter T. Holley was the informant on his death certificate.

Their youngest child George Montgomery was born May 15, 1875. He married Minnie Roberts, the daughter of Will and Liza Roberts. They had the following children: Victoria, George, Jr., Calline, John, Jessie, Mary L., Liza, Adelle, Rodelle, J. C. and Sarah. Minnie Roberts-Montgomery died six months after the birth of her daughter Sarah. George later married Lettie and fathered more children, Ollie, Joseph, and Birdie. Ruby Montgomery-Wayne whose father is Rodelle Montgomery stated to me that her grandfather George was sent to prison for allegedly fathering a child by his oldest daughter Victoria. The statement supposedly was made by Will Roberts whom with his wife Liza was raising George's daughter Sarah. George spent 18 months in prison and Victoria had the baby. According to Ruby, Will Roberts wanted Victoria to go and cook for Thurman/Thornton Tugwell. They apparently took Victoria from George Montgomery in order to cook for the Tugwells. As a result of this George Montgomery and his family became estranged to Will Roberts and his family. George never recovered from the sickness he got while in prison. According to Ruby Wayne Victoria had a baby after George got out of prison. He died April 11, 1924 of tuberculosis and arthritis. Also, Ruby mentioned that Caroline Montgomery was the sister of Branch Nelson. Branch Nelsons' first wife was Hannah Bilberry the sister of Georgia Bellzora Bilberry-Ellis. Hannah died and Branch Nelson petitioned the courts to allow Sandy Goldsby to be appointed the Under Tutor for Branch and Hannah's children. The appointment was granted. A family meeting composing of Hannah Bilberry's nearest relatives was held on January 20, 1906, between Branch Nelson, Rance Ellis, Hiram Montgomery, Jack Bilberry, Sam Morgan and Henry Bilberry. The meeting was held to settle the children's interest in Hannah's estate.

Source: Union Parish Succession Book E, pages 96 -101 and 753 – 755; Union Parish Succession Hannah Bilberry.

Short Biography of York Honeycutt

Courtesy of Grace Nezworski

Born: March 12, 1855
Died: February 16, 1940
Parents: Honeycutt and Mariah

York Honeycutt was a mulatto. His mother's name was Mariah, a slave woman given by Joseph M. Warren to his daughter, Sarah Ann Warren, in 1851. Sarah married John Honeycutt in 1852, and they moved to Hunt and Henderson Counties in Texas.

Sarah Ann Warren 1836-1884
daughter of Joseph M. Warren
probably about the time she   married
her first husband John Honeycutt

Courtesy of Grace Nezworski

York was born March 12, 1855, on Elm Creek, thirteen miles west of Greenville. He died February 16, 1940, and he was buried in Center Point Cemetery in Greenville, Hunt County, Texas. The cause of death was acute paralysis of the throat. He would tell stories to all the children; and he was fondly remembered as "Uncle York".

Courtesy of Grace Nezworski

York Honeycutt and family; wife Hattie sitting to York's right side; youngest son Buddy sitting to York's far left York married Hettie Winn.

York Honeycutt and Hettie Winn had the following children:

Alfred Honeycutt was born October 10, 1881 in Texas. He died March 26, 1938, in San Angelo, Texas—Tom Green County. He was buried in Center Point Cemetery in Greenville, Texas—Hunt County. Alfred was a janitor and he was working in an elevator shaft and the elevator malfunctioned crushing and severing his head.

Maggie Honeycutt was born September 21, 1883 in Texas. She died March 30, 1938, in Greenville, Texas—Hunt County from liver cancer. She was buried in Center Point Cemetery in Greenville, Texas—Hunt County. Maggie was a housekeeper. She married **Jim Polk**.

Myrtle Honeycutt was born January 20, 1884, in Texas. She died January 22, 1920, in Texas—Hunt County from dropsy (Bright's disease). She was buried in Center Point Cemetery in Greenville, Texas—Hunt County. Myrtle was a domestic. Myrtle married **Henry Scott**.

Jannie Honeycutt was born December 25, 1888, in Texas. She died March 25, 1942, in Texas—Hunt County from complications of mitral regurgitation and general edema. She was buried in Center Point Cemetery, Greenville, Texas—Hunt County. Jannie married **Charlie Henry Scott**.

Georgie Honeycutt was born April 8, 1891, in Texas. She died March 29, 1934, in Greenville, Texas—Hunt County from complications of Bright's disease. Georgie was a cook. She was buried in Center Point Cemetery in Greenville, Texas—Hunt County.

Melvin Honeycutt "Buddy" was born March 19, 1895, in Texas. He died January 17, 1977. He was buried in Center Point Cemetery in Greenville, Texas—Hunt County. Melvin was a PVT in World War I. Buddy was remembered for his delicious lemon pies.

Upon the death of Hettie, York married Lorena E. Johnson. Lorena was born November 7, 1892, in Texas. She died January 3, 1960, in San Angelo, Texas—Tom Green County from acute pneumonia combined with cerebral accident. She was buried in Center Point Cemetery in Greenville, Texas—Hunt County.

When John Honeycutt entered the Army he and some of the others in his group believed the war would last only a few months and the Confederates would soon win. It did not turn out that way. The war had gone on four years and they could see that the War was lost. They were tired of army life and their Confederate money was almost valueless. John Honeycutt was a leader in the group. He made up a company of eighty men and started for Mexico. He told his wife to follow.

York Honeycutt, a former slave of John Honeycutt recalls their journey: "We started with an ox wagon, a hack and a pair of mules. Parson Atterberry, his wife and two children went with us and a colored boy named Levi Warren. Captain Honeycutt told us he would leave a sign at each fork of the road. We left Hunt County in February 1865, and got as far as Williamson County. Men followed us on the hunt for the company. They surrounded us two or three times trying to find the location of the company. We made a crop in Williamson County and there heard that the Company had all been killed. It was presumed the entire band was 'butchered' by Indians. We came back in the fall to Mrs. Honeycutt's people, her father, Mr. Warren. We left Parson Atterberry in Williamson County." York was well liked among both white and black people. He wore long pig tails. One of York's sons was in a rest home in Greenville. He said that York's father was a white man. A picture of York and his family is at the Greenville Library.

War materials, food, and clothing were in short supply during the war. Families were being neglected and their spirits were low; not only in Hunt County but elsewhere men were disserting the Army. It was believed that some of the soldiers had fulfilled their time but others disserted. The desertions were so great that the General sent a group of soldiers to look for deserters. Some of the relatives believed John Honeycutt and his followers were killed by their own men (Confederate Soldiers). The story is told of a little pony from the lost group making his way back to Hunt County but could not tell the story.

Courtesy of Grace Nezworski

Short Biography of John Honeycutt, Sr.
Union Parish Pioneer Picked Bride in Bold Manner

Wooing was different in the frontier pioneer days when what is now known as the Honeycutt and Feazel families of Union Parish were united. No soda pops, no automobiles, no crooning radios nor tin-pan jazz bands for the first adventurer. John Honeycutt won the hand at first sight of one of the original Union Parish Feazel girls. This was a romance that has been woven into the folk lore of Union Parish as the beginning of what have today become two families prominent in that section. It was with his new leather suit trimmed with fine fringe, his silver belt buckle and coon skin cap that John Honeycutt caught the eye on first sight of Miss Feazel.

John was a fisherman and trapper. His livelihood necessitated his seasonal travel between New Orleans and Camden, Arkansas. This pioneer was fortunate in having obtained a grant of land from the Spanish government before the Louisiana Purchase from France was made by the United States. The records of this grant are available today on Union Parish land files. Over this large domain, John roamed at large, but roamed alone leading the customary hard life of the trapper and fisherman. On his way out of his wilderness en route on one of his periodic trips to New Orleans, this Beau Brummell of the backwoods learned from the Indians that a settler with some daughters had moved onto property adjacent to his land. John was glad to have neighbors and decided to pay the newcomers a visit on his return. In those days travel was slow and a trip to New Orleans and return by boat gave ample time for thought. During this lengthy trip, John's reflections turned to introspection and as he began wondering if it was not the time in his life for him to wed. He thought too, it was probably spring, following as it does with its inducements to thoughts of love in the wake of the hard winter.

Returning from the Crescent City, John continued upstream to Camden becoming more obsessed with the idea of seeking a wife. Another trapper confirmed the report that the newcomer Feazel had several daughters. Returning to his cabin on his claim, John pondered over thoughts of a bride. In those times distances meant days; John reasoned the thing out. At the bottom of the strong box reposing in the cabin of this backwoodsman there lay a new buckskin suit trimmed with fine trappings; a prize dress possession in those days which divulged one's calling as plainly as the badge and bluecoat today designates the minion of the law. This fine new pioneer suit was augmented by an equally fine specimen of a coon's skin cap; a necessary accessory to the leather suit of the backwoods trapper dressed his best. Further augmenting this array in finery was the ornament of a silver buckled belt, which the trapper had bought in New Orleans. Thus attired, John Honeycutt fared forth across the forest to seek his bride, if his new neighbor's daughter would look with favor upon him; and that was the day when father had the say. Today he hears about it later, probably from friends of his daughter.

"My name is John Honeycutt" the trapper introduced himself to George Feazel upon arriving in his neighbor's home. "I live in this country" continued John, "and have a grant of land from the Spanish government. I hear you have some daughters and as I think I am getting old enough to get married, I will take one of yours." Thus, Honeycutt made the frank proposal to the father rather than to the girl as yet unseen by the prospective bridegroom. George Feazel evidently liked the looks of this young trapper for he called his three daughters into the room and had them stand in a row along the wall to view the trio; like '*the young Lochinvar, the hero of a ballad in Scotland, who boldly rides off with his sweetheart'.* "Which one would you like?" Father George Feazel inquired of his visitor in reference to the three daughters. "That One" said John as he quickly made his choice from among the three. His choice being that of Mary Mae. "Will you go with him?' George Feazel asked of his daughter, in those days when father's wish was a command. She was willing to cast her lot with this "handsome trapper" arrayed so attractively in his fancy trimmings. The couple was thus summarily wedded; and to John's cabin on his Spanish grant of land they went. Thus the Honeycutt family, who make Farmerville their home today, was founded in Union Parish.

Article copied out of an old newspaper—no date, author unknown.
Courtesy of Eleanor Singleton

York was sold to John Honeycutt, Jr., by A. J. Morgan
Courtesy of Grace Nezworski

copied 1956
G. Nezworski

OUACHITA PARISH LOUISIANA

<u>DEEDS</u>

John Honeycutts only

BOOK/ PAGE
No.   No.

Z / 45 - Jean Hunicut to Zador Harmon, 400 arpents of land
This deed written in French - dated 21 G^{bre} 1797 - not recorded until
22 Jan. 1833

AB / 97   John Honeycutt, Sen'r to Thomas B. Franklin for $500 land on
Bayou D'Arbone, west side of Ouachita River, about 1 league from
and above mouth of Bayou on southside called Walnut Ridge where
Honeycutt formerly lived - 26 Aug. 1809

D / 140   John Honeycutt, Jr. - deed of slaves from Thomas B. Franklin- 1816

F / 137   A. J. Morgan - deed of negroes to John Honeycutt, Jr. - negro
named York age 3 and negro girl, Fortune, age 5 - 6 Nov. 1816

F / 276   John Honeycutt to Margaret A. Bougeat, wife of James Fort Muse, $2,000
land in Ouachita Parish - 15 Nov. 1823
Plat proceeds this deed dated 1 Nov. 1802 and perhaps is plat of
land grant confirmed to John Honeycutt by U. S.

F / 277   John Hunnicutt, Junr. - deed of stock to James Fort Muse and wife
in return for so much prepared meat - 15 Nov. 1823

Z / 188   John Honeycutt, Junr. to Enoch Drake of Miss. Territory, 800 acres
on NW side of Ouachita River and south of Bayou D'Arbonne adjoining
his tract of 400 acres on said Bayou whereon he now lives about
1 leages from its mouth. - 1804
Wit: J. McLauchlin, Charles Betin

G/ 192   John Stow to John Honnicut - half of SE/4 of Section 22 and east half
of SW/4 of Section 22, Township 19, Range 1 E - containing 160 5/10 acres
27 Oct. 1828

G / 131   John Honeycutt to Margaret A. Muse - deed of negro - 14 March 1828

G / 132   Margaret A. Muse to John Honeycutt - deed of negro - 14 March 1828

G / 195   Joseph Friend to John Honnicutt, Senr. - 20 Nov. 1828   "Pine Hills"

G / 489   George Girado of Madison County, Miss. to John Honeycutt, Senr.
Deed of negroes - 22 Oct. 1832

H / 205   William May to John Honeycutt, Sr. 9 March 1835

H / 466   John Honeycutt to Philip Feazel - deed of negro - 12 Nov. 1836

H / 548   Thomas N. Warren of Williamson County Tenn. to John Honeycutt, Senr.
Deed of slaves - 11 May 1837

H / 548   John H. Grice - deed of land to John Honeycutt Senr. - 5th _____ 1837

F / 269   Phillip Feazel - sale of negroes to Hiram Aswell - 23 April 1821
Wit: Solomon Aswell. John (his mark) Honeycutt

Short Biography of Mary Feazel-Honeycutt

Born: circa 1793
Died: March 31, 1863
Parents: John George Feazle and Magret Pear
Town: Hawkins County, Tennessee

Mary Feazel was born to John George Feazel and Margret Pear about 1793, in Hawkins County, Tennessee. She died March 31, 1863, in Union Parish, Louisiana; and she was buried in Feazel Cemetery in Union Parish, Louisiana. Mary married John Honeycutt Jr., son of John Honeycutt, Sr., March 31, 1814, in Ouachita Territory, Louisiana. John was born about 1779 in Holstein Settlements, Sullivan County, Tennessee. He died March 24, 1857, in Hunt County, Texas; and he was buried in Hunt County, Texas. John Honeycutt, Jr., later known as Sr. He was the only child of John Honeycutt, Sr., and he was a young boy of about the age of 10 when his family moved into North Louisiana. They pushed their way through the untamed wilderness of Alabama and Mississippi to get to Union Parish then known as Ouachita Territory.

John's father had been granted a land Grant from the Spanish government. They were among the first white settlers in Union Parish. The Honeycutt's were trappers and hunters and they found plenty in the wilds of Union Parish sharing the land with the Indians. They settled not far from D'Arbonne Bayou and Cornie Bayou. It was the Indians who told John of another white family down on the Cornie with young girls that were his neighbors. He decided to visit them in search of a wife. Upon reaching the wilderness home of the people an introduction was made. He boldly asked his neighbor for the hand of one of his daughters in marriage. The daughters were lined up and John Honeycutt made his pick. Her name was Mary Feazel. They were married March 31, 1814. They had seven children, which were all born in Louisiana. In November 1856, they moved to Hunt County, Texas, along with one of their sons, Alfred, and purchased land near another son, John. John Honeycutt, by now called Sr., died there March 24, 1857. He was probably buried on the land he had bought, which was located about eight miles southwest of Greenville, Texas on Elm Creek formerly known as Bears Creek. Mary returned to Union Parish and died there in March 1863. John Honeycutt and Mary Feazel had the following children:

Austin Honeycutt was born about 1815. He died May 7, 1911.

Elizabeth Honeycutt was born about 1817. She died August 8, 1862.

John Honeycutt, Jr., was born about 1825.

George W. Honeycutt was born in 1827, in Ouachita Territory, Louisiana; he died in 1850, in Union Parish, Louisiana apparently unmarried. The administration of his estate was filed December 1850, in Union Parish, Louisiana.

Alfred Honeycutt was born about 1829.

Britton Dalton Honeycutt was born January 7, 1832; he died February 13, 1908.

Mary Jane Honeycutt was born July 24, 1835; she died March 2, 1865.

The application for the administration of Mary Feazle Honeycutt's estate was filed October 24, 1864, by Alfred Honeycutt (recorded in Union Parish Succession Record A-2, P. 122) and states: "*the petitioner represents that Mrs. Mary Honeycutt, late of said parish of Union, departed this life in said Parish intestate March 1863. She left small property consisting of land, negroes and some personal property and her children; Elizabeth Wilhite (represented by her minor heirs), Austin Honeycutt, John Honeycutt, Britton Honeycutt, Mary Jane wife of E. B. Bilberry and your petitioner. The property cannot be divided and a sale is not advisable at the present time.*" Alfred Honeycutt was made administrator of her estate and no further records were found.

Courtesy of Eleanor Singleton

More on the Honeycutts and their Extended Families

Levi Warren circa 1838-1905?

Notes by Grace Lamm Nezworski

In Ouachita Parish, Louisiana, deed records in 1848, Joseph M. Warren was described as a resident of Newton County, Mississippi, and he appears in the 1850 Census of Newton County. His previous residences had included Rankin and Lauderdale Counties, Mississippi. In October 1851, Joseph M. Warren, a former resident of Newton County, Mississippi; made deeds of slaves to some of his children. Records of these transactions can be found in Union Parish, Louisiana Courthouse, deed books:

"*To daughter Jane Warren, a negro girl, Susan, age 22 - witnessed by Abner Green, Jasper Warren*"

"*To son, Jasper Warren, a negro boy, Isaah, age eight - Witness Abner Green, Sarah Warren*"

"*To daughter, Sarah Warren, a negro woman, Marier (Mariah), age 22 - Witness Abner Green, Jasper Warren*"

The following year on July 24, 1852, he makes a deed to another son.

"*To son, Joseph L. Warren, a negro boy, Levi, age 14 - witnesses, Jasper Warren and John Honeycutt.*" John Honeycutt had married Sarah Ann Warren the previous January 1852.

It was possible that all of these slaves were related as Mariah's son, York, and Levi would stay together or close to each other following emancipation in 1865. Exactly why Joseph M. Warren was in Union Parish is unclear. The only deeds for him are in March

1852, when he is conveyed 40 acres for $700. He deeds this land on the same date to William R. Mayo for $800. These transactions are apparently pursuant to some previous oral agreement. One family story said: Joseph M. Warren went to Louisiana to visit and later came to Texas with the Honeycutts. If this was true, who he was visiting is unknown. Who came with whom and when is an unanswered question. In November 1852, Joseph M. Warren acquired rights to over 900 acres of land in Henderson County, Texas. He gives 160 acres to Jasper Warren and John Honeycutt, but title to this land was not patented until after Joseph M. Warren's death. The Honeycutts, John and his brother, Alfred, and his father, John Honeycutt, Sr., acquired land in Hunt County in October 1854. Joseph M. Warren died in May 1855, in Henderson County, leaving his entire estate to his youngest daughter, Louisa. This land consisted of 916 acres in Henderson County; and included a negro woman named Charity, age 28, a child named Mandy, age one, another negro woman named Emeline, age 29, and her child, James, age one. His son, Jasper Warren is appointed administrator and guardian to Louisa.

Peyton S. Bethel is appointed administrator of the Joseph M. Warren Estate and guardian of Louisa in January 1856, because the estate was without a lawful administrator. In December 1855, the second death had occurred in the family with Jasper Warren's death in Hunt County. Louisa apparently returned to Mississippi to her older brother, John Warren. The last mention of Charity and Emeline and their children was in January 1856, when they were to be hired out to the highest bidder.

In Hunt County, Issac Penrod was appointed administrator of Jasper Warren's estate, and was replaced by Hardin Hart in March 1857. The final account of Jasper's Estate could not be located in Hunt County records. In January 1857, the administrator was to sell the Negro, boy Isaah on 12 months credit at the courthouse door in the City of Greenville. In January 1863, Joseph L. Warren died in Hunt County, and his brother-in-law, John Honeycutt, became administrator of his estate. Two months later, the administration of Joseph L. Warren's Estate is given to his sister, Sarah Ann Honeycutt. As administrator of her brother's estate, she kept the original deed for Levi Warren in her possession, which explains why it was found with Lennie Garrison's papers (daughter of Sarah Ann) many years later.

In 1864, the Hunt County Tax list of 'Slave Owners' listed John Honeycutt as agent for J. L. Warren with one male slave valued at $1,800, the second most valuable slave in the county. One wonders what skills or strengths Levi Warren possessed. The inventory of his owner, J. L. Warren Estate does not indicate he was a farmer.

Following the Civil War, Mariah, York Honeycutt, and Levi Warren, although emancipated, remained with Sarah Ann and her seven children for some time. The black and white families seem to have clung together during the radical rule in Texas when so much lawlessness occurred. Her husband, John Honeycutt, had disappeared with other Hunt County men on their way to Mexico between 1864 and 1865. She was a widow for some five years before she married a second time to George W. Garrison. When the former slaves left Sarah Ann was uncertain. Levi Warren was separately listed in the 1880 Census for Hunt County as well as York Hunnicutt (spelled that way in Census).

When Mariah died is not known. York was born March 12, 1855, on Elm Creek, 13 miles west of Greenville, and married March 6, 1879, Hattie Winn. He died February16, 1940. These dates were given to me by 'Buddy', Melvin's youngest son of York, who also gave me a family picture of York's Family. Buddy said that York's birth date and place were given to him by Sarah Ann Warren at the time he left Sarah Ann. He had a picture of Sarah Ann, which York had kept in remembrance of his white family. Also, Buddy had the death date of Levi Warren as March 4, 1903, and Joe Aner Warren, Levi's wife, death as July 19, 1912. Their marriage records – Hunt County, Texas for Levi Warren and J. E. Wynn – January 19, 1882 – Book D/110.

Courtesy of Grace Nezworski
Sarah Ann Warren photo in later years
Courtesy of Grace Nezworski

Sarah Ann Warren (1836 – 1884) dau of
Joseph M & Lavinia Warren md (1)John
Honeycutt
(2)George Garrison
This picture in her later years)

Conclusion

Most Americans are able to trace their family's history back to where their ancestors sought hope for a better life. America was the democracy – the promise land where all people are created equal, endowed by their Creator with certain inalienable rights, among which are life, liberty, and the pursuit of happiness. It was a dream that was realized by many.

But not all Americans shared this dream. There were Native Americans that were already here when the Europeans crossed the Atlantic Ocean to seek their place in the New World. Also, there were those who were brought to this land against their will, chained in the holds of slave vessels so that they could be used as laborers to help develop the rich land in America. The starting point for the black man in this nation did not begin on equal grounds. Likewise, they were the only American immigrant that did not choose to come here.

Tom Skinner, evangelist and former Chaplin of the Washington Redskins used the illustration of a baseball game to demonstrate what has happened to black people in America. He said that the game began with Team-A quickly taking the lead over Team-B. It wasn't too long before Team-A was leading Team-B by the score of 10-0. Team-B had been complaining throughout about the rules of the game. It was not until the sixth inning that Team-A realized that the baseball players on Team-B were playing the game with one of their hands tied behind their backs. Team-A decided that it was now okay to change the rule and let Team-B untie their hands. With two innings left to go in the game, Team-A was now leading by a score of 20-0. Throughout the game, Team-A had been free to use all of their mental and physical abilities to master the game. Team-B, though now with the ability to use both hands because of the change in the rule had not acquired the same level of skills as Team-A; and the outcome of the game was very predictable.

The black Bilberrys and extended families in Union Parish, Louisiana overcame the struggle of a system that kept their hands tied for many years. Yet, they remained steadfast in their desire to be somebody. During the nineteenth and twentieth centuries the bond between families and extended families was crucial for the survival of the black man and black woman. The family consisted of more than just a husband, wife, and children. A family became the union of two or more families forming a "network of extended kin," which accepted the responsibility of protecting and nurturing the family.[57]

The Bible said there are times for everything: a season for every activity under heaven: a time to be born and a time to die (Ecclesiastes 3:1-2 NIV). Frank Bilberry's name will eventually fade away in time like the setting sun. This research may hinder that process but there is nothing I can do to stop it. We must die one day and our names will be mentioned less and less as our families multiply in the future. The new families will create new stories. Let us never forget that our family story just get us ready to talk about the real story of how God brought us this far by faith. When we think of it that way then we can all tell the story. We can endure the seasons, rejoice at the births, build memories of good times and rise into the sunsets!

Appendix A

Family Death Certificate Collection

This family and extended family collection is used to help validate the deaths dates of family members. Each death certificate contains vital genealogical information, which includes mother, father, age, medical data, and death records that are used for researching. Note: The letter "W" stands for those that are of Caucasian descent.

NAMES OF THE DECEASED	
Adell (Abe) Billberry	John Mack Bilberry (**W**)
Adell Bilberry	Jordan B. Nelson
Alcandor Ewing	Jordan Ellis Billberry, Sr.
Anderson Thompson	Jordan Ellis Billberry
Andie Julks	Lawrence Bilberry
Annie Bilberry	Levonia Nelson-Wyatt
Barbara Neal Bilberry	Liza Roberts
Bill (William) Bridges	Maggie Bilberry
Brock Archie	Mammie (Mary) Bohanna (Bohannon)
Dolly (Dollie) Mayfield	Mary Horn
Elza Billberry Robinson (**W**)	Monroe Finley
Emma Bilberry	Ollie Bell Holland
Frances Bilberry	Ollie Henderson-Roberts
Frank Bilberry	Rachel Thompson
George McGough	Rodelle Burch, Sr.
George Montgomery	Sally Washington
George Willie Bilberry	Sandy Wayne, Jr.
Georgia Bilberry	Stella Billberry

Georgia (aunt Pus) Ellis	Will Roberts
James Alfred Honeycutt (**W**)	Will Roberts
John Burch	Willie Frank Bilberry
John Hiram Montgomery	

Adell (Abe) Billberry's Death Certificate
Son of Jordan E. Bilberry

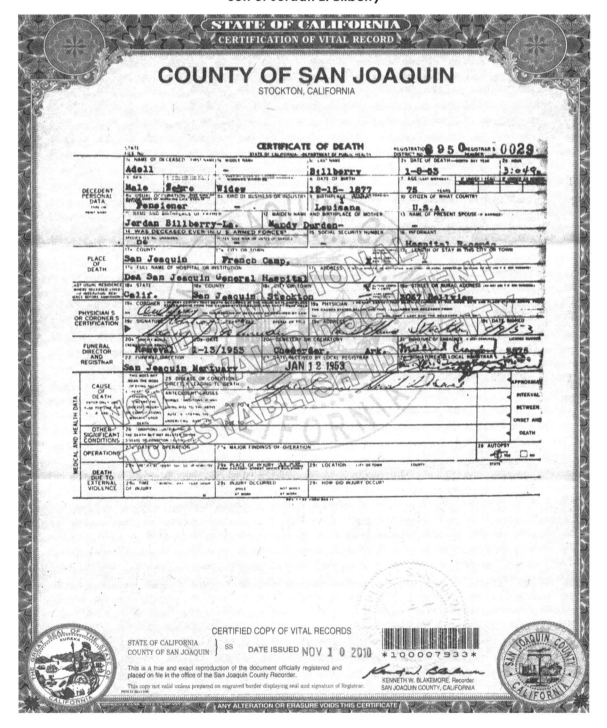

Adell Bilberry's Death Certificate
Son of Ladell Bilberry

Adell Bilberry's Death Certificate — State of Louisiana, Certificate of Death No. 586041. Decedent: Adell Bilberry, Male, Black, Married to Barbara Brown. Date of death April 28, 1997. Born March 14, 1927 in Marion, LA, age 70. Occupation: Log Cutter (Logging). Died at HCA North Monroe Hospital, Monroe, Ouachita Parish. Residence: Thomas St (P.O. Box 103), Marion, Union Parish, LA 71260. Father: Ladell Bilberry (Marion, LA); Mother: Maggie Washington (Marion, LA). Informant: Barbara Bilberry. Burial May 3, 1997, Sweet Lily Cemetery, Marion, LA. Union Funeral Home, Farmerville, LA 71241. Cause of death: Lung Cancer.

Alcandor Ewing's Death Certificate

IMPORTANT! This is a Permanent Record. Use Typewriter or Ink. For Typewriter Set Tabs	LOUISIANA STATE DEPARTMENT OF HEALTH DIVISION OF PUBLIC HEALTH STATISTICS	**CERTIFICATE OF DEATH**	STATE FILE NO.	512 1433

PERSONAL DATA OF DECEASED *Byen.*

1a. Last Name of Deceased	1b. First Name	1c. Second Name	DATE OF DEATH: 2a. Month Day Year 2b. Hour
Ewing	Alcandor	D.	1-1-44 7 A.M.

3. Sex — Male or Female?	4. Color or Race	5. Single, Married, Widowed or Divorced	6a. Name of Husband or Wife 6b. Age
Male	negro	Married	Ada 76

7. Date of Birth of Deceased	8. Age of Deceased	If under 1 day	9a. Birthplace (City or town)	9b. (State or Foreign Country)
Aug 4-1864	79 4		Union Pr	La

10. Usual Occupation	11. Industry or Business	12. Social Security Number	13. If veteran name war
Farmer			

PLACE OF DEATH 56 X

14. City or Town — (If outside city or town limits write RURAL)	15. Parish and Ward No.	16. Length of Stay in this Community (Yrs. months or days)
Farmerville	Union 1	Life

17. Name of Hospital or Institution (If not in hospital or institution give street no. or location)	18. Length of Stay in Hospital or Institution (Yrs. months or days)

USUAL RESIDENCE OF DECEASED 56 X

19. City or Town — (If outside city or town limits write RURAL)	20. Parish and Ward No.	21. State
Farmerville La R)	Union 1	La

22. Street Address — (If rural give location)	23. Is deceased a citizen of a foreign country? If yes, name country

PARENTS

24. Name of Father	25. Birthplace of Father	26. Name of Mother	27. Birthplace of Mother
Hiram Ewing	Not Known	Louise Wagner	Kentucky

INFORMANT'S CERTIFICATION

I certify that the above stated information is true and correct to the best of my knowledge.	28. Signature of Informant	29. Date of Signature
	Ada Ewing — by (her)	1-1-44

CAUSE OF DEATH 033 a

30. Immediate Cause of Death	Pneumonia	Duration
31. Due to	Influenza	Duration
32. Other Conditions (Include pregnancy within three months of death)		Duration

33. Major Findings of Operations	34. Major Findings of Autopsy

DEATHS DUE TO EXTERNAL VIOLENCE

35. Accident, Suicide, or Homicide (Specify)	36. Date of Occurrence	37. Where did injury occur? (City or town, parish and state)

38. Did injury occur in or about home, on farm, in industrial or public place? (Specify type of place)	39. Did injury occur at work? (Yes or No)	40. Means of Injury

PHYSICIAN'S CERTIFICATION

41. I certify that I attended the deceased, and that death occurred on the date and hour stated above.	42. Signature of Physician	43. Date of Signature
	Dr J Taylor Corona	1-1-44

FUNERAL DIRECTORS CERTIFICATION

44. Burial ... on Date Thereof From Cremation ... Removal .. 1-3-44	45. Place of Burial or Cremation	46. Signature of Funeral Director	47. Signature of Local Registrar
	Farmerville Cem	Kilpatrick	

080441—70M—PHS 16   In cooperation with the U. S. Department of Commerce—Bureau of the Census. FEB -3 1944 Dr. N. A. Giles, M.D.

Anderson Thompson, Jr.'s Death Certificate
His father was the husband of Delia Bridges
See Marriage document in Appendix B

Andie Julks' Death Certificate
Husband of Dollie (Letha) Burch-Julks
See Photo in Appendix G

OCT -9 1936

LOUISIANA STATE BOARD OF HEALTH
Bureau of Vital Statistics
CERTIFICATE OF DEATH

1—PLACE OF DEATH

Parish *Union*

Ward *1*

District No. *56-5544*

File No. ....
(1, 2, 3, etc., in the order Certificates are filed.)

City or Town *Farmerville*

Registered No. **11114**
(To be given in Central Bureau.)

No. .... St. .... Ward
(If death occurred in a Hospital or Institution, give its Name instead of Street and Number.)

2—FULL NAME *Andie Julks*

(a) Residence. No. *Farmerville* St., Ward. *1*
(Usual place of abode)   (If non-resident give city or town and State)

Length of residence in city or town where death occurred.   yrs.   mos.   ds.   How long in U. S.; of foreign birth?   yrs.   mos.   ds.

PERSONAL AND STATISTICAL PARTICULARS	MEDICAL CERTIFICATE OF DEATH

3. SEX *Male*   4. COLOR OR RACE *Colored*   5. SINGLE, MARRIED, WIDOWED, OR DIVORCED (WRITE the word) *M*

21. DATE OF DEATH (month, day, and year) *8/12*, 19*36*

5a. If married, widowed, or divorced
HUSBAND of (or) WIFE of *Letha Julks*

22. I HEREBY CERTIFY, That I attended deceased from
19....
I last saw h...... on...................., 19...., death is said
to have occurred on the date stated above, at...............m.
Died without medical attention

6. DATE OF BIRTH (month, day, and year) *1850*

7. AGE   Years *86*   Months *✓*   Days *✓*   If LESS than 1 day, ...hrs. or....min.

The principal cause of death and related causes of importance in order of onset were as follows: Date of onset

8. Trade, profession, or particular kind of work done, as SAWYER, BOOKKEEPER, etc. *Farmer*

9. Industry or business in which work was done, as cotton mill, saw mill, bank, etc.

Cardio Renal disease   *95?*

10. Date deceased last worked at this occupation (month and year)   11. Total time (years spent in this occupation *Life Time*

Contributory causes of importance not related to principal cause:

11a. Veteran past wars *no* (yes or no)   (name war)

12. BIRTHPLACE (city or town) *Louisiana*
(State or Parish)

Name of operation............... Date of...............
What test confirmed diagnosis?............... Was there an autopsy?...............

FATHER   13. NAME *Mose Julke*

14. BIRTHPLACE (city or town) *unknown*
(State or Parish)

23. If death was due to external causes (violence) fill in also the following:

Accident, suicide, or homicide?............... Date of injury............... 19....

MOTHER   15. MAIDEN NAME *Ann Julks*

16. BIRTHPLACE (city or town) *unknown*
(State or Parish)

Where did injury occur? ....
(Specify city or town, parish, and State)
Specify whether injury occurred in industry, in home, or in public place

17. INFORMANT *O. B. Julks*
(Address)

Manner of injury ....
Nature of injury ....

18. BURIAL, CREMATION, OR REMOVAL
Place *Zion Hill*   Date *C.* ...., 19....

24. Was disease or injury in any way related to occupation of deceased?...............
If so, specify ....

19. UNDERTAKER ....
(Address)

(Signed) *George A. Ramsey*

20. FILED *8/12/36* 19.... *Mr. Geo. A. Ramsey*
Registrar.

Oct-5-1936

(Address) *Farmerville La*

Ramsey, Coroner

Annie Bilberry's Death Certificate
Daughter of Jack and Francis Bilberry

134

Barbara Neal Bilberry's Death Certificate
Wife of Adell Bilberry

STATE OF NEVADA — DEPARTMENT OF HUMAN RESOURCES
DIVISION OF HEALTH — VITAL STATISTICS

CERTIFICATE OF DEATH

STATE FILE NUMBER: 2009010520

DECEDENT
- 1a. DECEASED-NAME: Barbara N BILBERRY
- 2. DATE OF DEATH: July 19, 2009
- 3a. COUNTY OF DEATH: Clark
- 3b. CITY, TOWN, OR LOCATION OF DEATH: Las Vegas
- 3c. HOSPITAL OR OTHER INSTITUTION: Heights of Summerlin
- 3e. Inpatient
- 4. SEX: Female
- 5. RACE: Black
- 6. Hispanic Origin: No - Non-Hispanic
- 7a. AGE: 74
- 8. DATE OF BIRTH: October 23, 1934
- 9a. STATE OF BIRTH: Louisiana
- 9b. CITIZEN OF WHAT COUNTRY: United States
- 10. EDUCATION: 8
- 11. MARRIED...: Widowed
- 12. SURVIVING SPOUSE:
- 13. SOCIAL SECURITY NUMBER: 439-90-0723
- 14a. USUAL OCCUPATION: Nurses Aide
- 14b. KIND OF BUSINESS OR INDUSTRY: Medical
- Ever in US Armed Forces? No
- 15a. RESIDENCE - STATE: Nevada
- 15b. COUNTY: Clark
- 15c. CITY: Las Vegas
- 15d. STREET AND NUMBER: 300 Promenade Blvd.
- 15e. INSIDE CITY LIMITS: Yes

PARENTS
- 16. FATHER - NAME: Charlie BROWN
- 17. MOTHER - NAME: Willie MOORE
- 18a. INFORMANT - NAME: Charles BILBERRY
- 18b. MAILING ADDRESS: 6215 Cape Canaveral Court Las Vegas, Nevada 89149

DISPOSITION
- 19a. BURIAL, CREMATION...: Cremation
- 19b. CEMETERY OR CREMATORY - NAME: Palm Crematory
- 19c. LOCATION: Las Vegas Nevada 89101
- 20a. FUNERAL DIRECTOR - SIGNATURE: BART BURTON (SIGNATURE AUTHENTICATED)
- 20b. FUNERAL DIRECTOR LICENSE: 50
- 20c. NAME AND ADDRESS OF FACILITY: Palm Mortuary-Northwest, 6701 N. Jones Blvd. Las Vegas NV 89131

TRADE CALL

CERTIFIER
- 21a. ... SIGNATURE AUTHENTICATED DEAN TSAI MD
- 21b. DATE SIGNED: July 22, 2009
- 21c. HOUR OF DEATH: 06:00
- 23a. NAME AND ADDRESS OF CERTIFIER: DEAN TSAI MD 1701 W. Charleston Blvd. Las Vegas, NV 89102
- 23b. LICENSE NUMBER: 9130

REGISTRAR
- 24a. REGISTRAR: CHRISTINE JOHNSON (SIGNATURE AUTHENTICATED)
- 24b. DATE RECEIVED BY REGISTRAR: July 22, 2009
- 24c. DEATH DUE TO COMMUNICABLE DISEASE: NO [X]

CAUSE OF DEATH
- 25. IMMEDIATE CAUSE: (a) Metastatic kidney cancer
- 26. AUTOPSY: No
- 27. WAS CASE REFERRED TO CORONER: Yes

STATE REGISTRAR

"CERTIFIED TO BE A TRUE AND CORRECT COPY OF THE DOCUMENT ON FILE WITH THE REGISTRAR OF VITAL STATISTICS STATE OF NEVADA." This copy was issued by the Southern Nevada Health District from State certified documents as authorized by the State Board of Health pursuant to NRS 440.175.

NOT VALID WITHOUT THE RAISED SEAL OF THE SOUTHERN NEVADA HEALTH DISTRICT

Lawrence K. Sands, D.O., M.P.H.
Registrar of Vital Statistics
By:
Date Issued: JUL 24 2009

SOUTHERN NEVADA HEALTH DISTRICT ♦ 625 Shadow Lane P.O. Box 3902 ♦ Las Vegas, Nevada 89127 ♦ 702-759-1010 ♦ Tax ID# 88-0151573

Bill (William) Bridges' Death Certificate
Son of Robert and Matilda Bridges

Death Certificate — State of Louisiana, Certificate of Death, State File No. 13,621

- 1a. Last Name of Deceased: Bridges
- 1b. First Name: Bill
- 1c. Second Name:
- 2a. Date of Death: Month 10 Day 29 Year 51; 2b. Hour 10:30 P.M.
- 3. Sex: Male
- 4. Color or Race: Col - Negro
- 5. Single, Married, Widowed, or Divorced: Married
- 6a. Name of Husband or Wife: Bill Bridges
- 6b. Age: 50
- 7. Date of Birth of Deceased: Unknown
- 8. Age of Deceased: 92
- 9a. Birthplace: Union Parish La.
- 9b. State or Foreign Country:
- 10a. Usual Occupation: Farming
- 10b. Kind of Industry or Business: Tenant Farm
- 11. Was deceased ever in U.S. Armed Forces?: No

PLACE OF DEATH — 56X
- 12a. City or Town: Lillie Rt. 3 - Rural
- 12b. Parish and Ward No.: Union 3
- 12c. Length of Stay in this Place: 80 yrs
- 12d. Name of Hospital or Institution: 14 Mi. South East

USUAL RESIDENCE OF DECEASED — 56X
- 13a. City or Town: Lillie Rt. 3 - Rural
- 13b. Parish and Ward No.: Union 3
- 13c. State: La
- 13d. Street Address: 14 Miles South East
- 14. Citizen of what Country: U.S.A.

PARENTS
- 15a. Name of Father: Bob Bridges
- 15b. Birthplace of Father: Virginia
- 16a. Maiden Name of Mother: Unknown
- 16b. Birthplace of Mother: Don't Know

INFORMANT'S CERTIFICATION
- I certify that the above stated information is true and correct to the best of my knowledge.
- 17a. Signature of Informant: Sarah Ann Benton
- 17b. Date of Signature: 10-29-51

CAUSE OF DEATH
- 18. I. Disease or Condition Directly Leading to Death (a): Myocarditis & Nephritis
- Antecedent Causes, Due to (b): Pneumonia & Complications — Interval: 60 days
- Due to (c):
- II. Other Significant Conditions: Arterio Sclerosis and Senility
- 19a. Date of Operation: None
- 19b. Major Findings of Operation: None
- 20. Autopsy: No

DEATHS DUE TO EXTERNAL VIOLENCE
- 21a. Accident, Suicide, or Homicide:
- 21b. Place of Injury:
- 21c. City, Town, or Ward No.: Lillie 3
- Parish: Union
- State: La.
- 21d. Time of Injury:
- 21e. Injury Occurred: Not While at Work
- 21f. How did injury occur?: Natural Causes

PHYSICIAN'S CERTIFICATION
- 22. I certify that I attended the deceased and that death occurred on the date and hour stated above: After Death
- 23a. Signature of Physician: C. H. Gunner M.D. Union Parish La.
- 23b. Date of Signature: 10-29-51

FUNERAL DIRECTOR'S CERTIFICATION
- 24a. Burial — Date Thereof: Nov 1st
- 24b. Name and Location of Cemetery or Crematory: Fellowship Un. Pa.
- 25. Signature and Address of Funeral Director: E. H. Kilpatrick

BURIAL TRANSIT PERMIT
- 26. Burial Transit Permit Number: 962
- 27. Parish of Issue: Union
- 28. Date of Issue: 10-30-51
- 29. Signature of Local Registrar: Wm. M. Funderburk

3M Bks. 2-51 PHS 16 (Rev.) — LOUISIANA STATE DEPARTMENT OF HEALTH, DIVISION OF PUBLIC HEALTH STATISTICS

NOV 6 - 1951

Brock Archie's Death Certificate
Son of Jacob Archie

Dollie Mayfield Death Certificate
Daughter of Delia Bridges-Thompson and Anderson Thompson

Public Health - Seattle & King County Vital Statistics

CERTIFIED COPY OF DEATH CERTIFICATE

STATE OF WASHINGTON DEPARTMENT OF HEALTH
VITAL RECORDS

CERTIFICATE OF DEATH

64:37 LOCAL FILE NUMBER

NAME FIRST MIDDLE LAST	SEX	DEATH DATE	STATE FILE NUMBER
DOLLIE MAYFIELD	FEMALE	7-12-1991	146

AGE LAST BIRTH	UNDER 1 YEAR MOS DAYS	UNDER 1 DAY HOURS MINS	BIRTHDATE	BIRTH STATE	CITIZEN OF WHAT COUNTRY	COUNTY OF DEATH
95			12-25-1895	LOUISIANA	USA	KING

CITY TOWN OR LOCATION OF DEATH	PLACE OF DEATH	SMOKING IN LAST YEARS
SEATTLE	RESTORATIVE CARE CENTER	NO

MARITAL STATUS	SURVIVING SPOUSE	WAS DECEDENT EVER IN U.S. ARMED FORCES?	SOCIAL SECURITY NO	HIGH SCHOOL GRADUATE?
WIDOWED		NO	532-26-4970	NO

USUAL OCCUPATION	KIND OF BUSINESS OR INDUSTRY	WAS DECEDENT OF HISPANIC ORIGIN	RACE
DOMESTIC			BLACK

RESIDENCE NUMBER AND STREET	CITY TOWN OR LOCATION	INSIDE CITY LIMITS	COUNTY	STATE	ZIP CODE
4628 SOUTH HOLLY #224	SEATTLE	YES	KING	WA	98118

FATHER'S NAME FIRST MIDDLE LAST	MOTHER'S NAME FIRST MIDDLE MAIDEN SURNAME
JOHN THOMAS	DEALIE BRIDGES

INFORMANT NAME	MAILING ADDRESS STREET OR RFD NO	CITY OR TOWN	STATE	ZIP
RUTH DAVIS	9745-44th AVENUE S.W.	SEATTLE	WASHINGTON	98136

BURIAL CREMATION OTHER	DATE	CEMETERY/CREMATORY NAME	LOCATION CITY TOWN STATE
BURIAL	7-20-1991	ABBEYVIEW CEMETERY	BRIER, WASHINGTON

FUNERAL DIRECTOR SIGNATURE	NAME OF FACILITY	ADDRESS OF FACILITY
X *Philip Morris*	SOUTHWEST MORTUARY	9021 RAINIER AVE. S., SEATTLE,

TO BE COMPLETED ONLY BY CERTIFYING PHYSICIAN | TO BE COMPLETED ONLY BY MEDICAL EXAMINER OR CORONER

TO THE BEST OF MY KNOWLEDGE DEATH OCCURRED AT THE TIME, DATE, AND PLACE AND DUE TO THE CAUSE(S) STATED

SIGNATURE AND TITLE X

DATE SIGNED	HOUR OF DEATH
7/19/91	7:30 AM

NAME AND ADDRESS OF CERTIFIER - PHYSICIAN MEDICAL EXAMINER OR CORONER

1001 BROADWAY #746 - SEATTLE WA 98122

PART I ENTER THE DISEASES INJURIES OR COMPLICATIONS WHICH CAUSED THE DEATH

IMMEDIATE CAUSE		INTERVAL BETWEEN ONSET AND DEATH
(A)	CARDIAC ARREST	
DUE TO OR AS A CONSEQUENCE OF		
(B)	HYPERTENSIVE ARTERIO SCLEROTIC HEART DISEASE	
DUE TO OR AS A CONSEQUENCE OF		
(C)	SENESCENCE	

OTHER SIGNIFICANT CONDITIONS	AUTOPSY
CHRONIC RENAL INSUFFICIENCY	NO

REGISTRAR SIGNATURE X *Susan Stanley*

DATE RECEIVED JUL 18 1991

Elza Billberry Robinson's Death Certificate
Son of John Bishop Robinson

Emma Bilberry's Death Certificate
Daughter of Lawrence Bilberry and Lula Kilgore-Bilberry

LOUISIANA STATE BOARD OF HEALTH
BUREAU OF VITAL STATISTICS
CERTIFICATE OF DEATH

1—PLACE OF DEATH

Parish *Union*   FEB 14 1918   Registration District No. *56164*   File No. *82*
(1, 2, 3, etc., in the order Certificates are filed.)

Police Jury Ward *6*

Village *Truxno*   Primary Registration District No. ....   Registered No. *1444*
(Applies only to an incorporated town.)   (To be given in Central Bureau.)

or

City ....   (No. ....   St. ....Ward   (If death occurred in a hospital or institution, give its name instead of street and number.)

2—FULL NAME *Emma Bilberry*

PERSONAL AND STATISTICAL PARTICULARS			MEDICIAL CERTIFICATE OF DEATH

3—SEX   4—COLOR or RACE   5—Single Married Widowed or Divorced *Single*

Female   *Colored*
(Write White or Col.)   (Write the word)

16—DATE OF DEATH *Nov 12*, 191*7*
(Must always be given.)   (Month)   (Day)   (Year)

6—DATE OF BIRTH

June 5, 19*13*
(Month)   (Day)   (Year)

17—I HEREBY CERTIFY, that I attended deceased from ...., 191..., to ...., 191...
that I last saw h.... alive on *Nov 12*, 191*7*
and that death occurred, on the date stated above, at *9.00* m. The CAUSE OF DEATH* was as follows:

Burned to death

7—AGE (If in doubt, write "about.....years")   IF LESS than 1 day..........hrs. or..........min.

4 yrs. *5* mos. *7* ds.

hit

(Duration)..........yrs..........mos..........ds.

Contributory (Secondary)..........

8—OCCUPATION
(a) Trade, profession, or particular kind of work   *none*
(b) General nature of industry, business or establishment in which employed (or employer)

(Duration)..........yrs..........mos..........ds.

(Signed)..........

9—BIRTHPLACE (City or Town, State or foreign country)   *Truxno*

10—NAME OF FATHER   *Alonzo Bilberry*

11—BIRTHPLACE OF FATHER (City or Town, State or foreign country)   *Conway La*

.............., 191...   (Address)..........

(If no Physician, Registrar must write "No Physician.")
*State the Disease causing Death, or, in deaths from Violent Causes, state (1) Means of injury; (2) whether Accidental, Suicidal or Homicidal.

12—MAIDEN NAME OF MOTHER   *Lula Kilgore*

13—BIRTHPLACE OF MOTHER (City or Town, State or foreign country)   *Truxno*

18—LENGTH OF RESIDENCE (for Hospitals, Institutions, Transients or Recent Residents.)

14—The above is true to the best of my knowledge.

(Informant) *J. Bilberry*

(Address)..........

At place of death.....yrs.....mos.....ds.   In the State.....yrs.....mos.....ds.
Where was disease contracted if not at place of death?
Former or usual residence..........

15—Filed *Jan 12*, 191*8*   *J. Z. Holler*
(Date certificate is received.)   Registrar.
(This MUST be signed.)

19—PLACE OF BURIAL or REMOVAL   DATE OF BURIAL
Central Cemetery   *Nov 13*, 191*7*

20—UNDERTAKER   ADDRESS
J. Bilberry

Form V. S. No. 2.

Frances Bilberry's Death Certificate
Wife of Jack Bilberry

141

Frank Bilberry's Death Certificate
Husband of Emma Roberts-Bilberry
Son of Delia (Eliza) Bridges and Britt

George McGough's Death Certificate
Father of Corene McGough-Bilberry

LOUISIANA STATE BOARD OF HEALTH
BUREAU OF VITAL STATISTICS
CERTIFICATE OF DEATH

1 PLACE OF DEATH

Parish _Union_

Police Jury Ward _6_

Village _Truxno_
or
City _____

Registration District No. _565548_
(For deaths outside an incorporated town, write X after its District No.)

Primary Registration District No. _____
(Applies only to an incorporated town)

File No. _2_
(1, 2, 3, etc., in the order Certificates are filed.)

Registered No. _13311_
(be given in Central Bureau.)

DEC 15 1923

2 FULL NAME _George McGough_ _McGough_ (No. _____ St. _____ Ward) (If death occurred in a hospital or institution, give its name instead of street and number.)

PERSONAL AND STATISTICAL PARTICULARS	MEDICAL CERTIFICATE OF DEATH

3 SEX _Male_

4 COLOR OR RACE _Black_ (Write White or Col.)

5 Single / Married _Married_ / Widowed or Divorced (Write the word)

6 DATE OF BIRTH _Sept_ _9_ _1854_
(Month) (Day) (Year)

7 AGE (If in doubt, write "about ...... years") _69_ yrs. _9_ mos. _0_ ds. IF LESS than 1 day ...... hrs. or ...... min.

8 OCCUPATION
(a) Trade, profession, or particular kind of work _Farming_
(b) General nature of industry, business or establishment in which employed (or employer) _____

9 BIRTHPLACE (City or Town, State or foreign country) _Union Parish La_

PARENTS

10 NAME OF FATHER _Unknown_

11 BIRTHPLACE OF FATHER (City or Town, State or foreign country) _Unknown_

12 MAIDEN NAME OF MOTHER _Betsie Stoples_

13 BIRTHPLACE OF MOTHER (City or Town, State or foreign country) _Unknown_

14 The above is true to the best of my knowledge.
(Informant) _Francis Ollison_
(Address) _Truxno La_

15 Filed _Nov 8_, 1923 _Jon Ardum_
(Date certificate is received.)
(This MUST be signed.) _Registrar._

Form V. S. No. 2 _W. & R. 1-9-24_

16 DATE OF DEATH _Nov_ _9_, 19_23_
(Must always be given.) (Month) (Day) (Year)

17 I HEREBY CERTIFY, that I attended deceased from _____, 191..., to _____, 191...
that I last saw h...... alive on _____, 191...
and death occurred, on the date stated above, at _____ m. The CAUSE OF DEATH was as follows:
Cancer of the Bladder
Dr Dudley come to see him one time
Dr Ramsey one time but was not there when he Died (Duration) _____ yrs. _7_ mos. _____ ds.

Contributory (Secondary) _____ (Duration) _____ yrs. _____ mos. _49_ ds.

(Signed) _Dr Dudley by Jon Ardum_
Nov 9, 1923 (Address) _Spearsville La_ _Downsville La_

(If no Physician, Registrar must write "No Physician.")
*State the Disease Causing Death, or, in deaths from Violent Causes, state (1) Means of injury, (2) whether Accidental, Suicidal or Homicidal.

18 LENGTH OF RESIDENCE (or Hospitals, Institutions, Transient or Recent Residents)
At place of death _3_ yrs. _9_ mos. _____ ds. In the State _69_ yrs. _2_ mos. _____ ds.
Where was disease contracted if not at place of death?
Former or usual residence _Usual Residence_

19 PLACE OF BURIAL OR REMOVAL _Antioch La_ DATE OF BURIAL _Nov 10_, 1923

20 UNDERTAKER _Prince Dawkins_ ADDRESS _Truxno La_
home made casket

143

George Montgomery's Death Certificate
Husband of Minnie Ann Roberts-Montgomery
Father of Sarah Alabama Montgomery-Ellis
(See note about letter to L. Bilberry at bottom of certificate)

LOUISIANA STATE BOARD OF HEALTH
BUREAU OF VITAL STATISTICS
CERTIFICATE OF DEATH

1 PLACE OF DEATH	
Parish *Union*	Registration District No. *SL-554*
Police Jury Ward *6*	(For deaths outside an incorporated town, write X after the District No.)
Village *Marion*	Primary Registration District No.
or *Conway*	(Applies only to an incorporated town.)
City (No. St. Ward)	
2 FULL NAME *George Montgomery*	

File No. *279*
(1, 2, 3, etc., in the order Certificates are filed.)

Registered No. *5375*
(To be given in Central Bureau.)

5395

(If death occurred in a hospital or institution, give its name instead of street and number.)

PERSONAL AND STATISTICAL PARTICULARS

MEDICAL CERTIFICATE OF DEATH

3 SEX *Male*
4 COLOR OR RACE *Colored* (Write White or Col.)
5 Single Married *Married* Widowed or Divorced (Write the word)

16 DATE OF DEATH *April 11*, 19*24* (Month) (Day) (Year)

6 DATE OF BIRTH
May 15 1875 19
(Month) (Day) (Year)

17 I HEREBY CERTIFY, that I attended deceased from *Jan. 5*, 19*24* to *10-*, 19*24*
that I last saw her alive on, 191
and death occurred, on the date stated above, at m. The CAUSE OF DEATH* was as follows:
Chthiri- Pulmonar
(T. B.)

7 AGE (If in doubt, write "about......years")
48 yrs. *10* mos. *26* ds.
IF LESS than 1 day......hrs. or......min.

(Duration) *3.5* yrs. mos. ds

8 OCCUPATION
(a) Trade, profession or particular kind of work *Farmer*
(b) General nature of industry, business or establishment in which employed (or employer)

Contributory (Secondary)
(Duration) yrs. mos. ds

9 BIRTHPLACE (City or Town, State or foreign country) *Union Parish La*

(Signed) *Milo Matkin M.D.*
4/96 191 (Address) *Marion La*

PARENTS
10 NAME OF FATHER *Green Montgomery*
11 BIRTHPLACE OF FATHER (City or Town, State or foreign country) *Ala*
12 MAIDEN NAME OF MOTHER *Caroline Nelson*
13 BIRTHPLACE OF MOTHER (City or Town, State or foreign country) *Ala*

(If no Physician, Registrar must write "No Physician.")
*State the Disease Causing Death, or, in deaths from Violent Causes, state (1) Means of injury, (2) whether Accidental, Suicidal or Homicidal.

14 The above is true to the best of my knowledge.

(Informant) *J. H. Montgomery*
(Address) *Marion La*

18 LENGTH OF RESIDENCE (or Hospitals, Institutions, Transient or Recent Residents)
At place of death yrs. mos. ds. In the State yrs. mos. ds.
Where was disease contracted if not at place of death?
Former or usual residence

19 PLACE OF BURIAL OR REMOVAL *Antioch Cemetery* DATE OF BURIAL *April 12, 1924*

15 Filed *Apr. 11*, 19*24* *J. L. ...* Registrar

20 UNDERTAKER *J. H. Montgomery* ADDRESS *Marion L*

Form V. S. No. 8 *Letter to L. Bilberry ... death as ...*

George Willie Bilberry's Death Certificate (One month and three days old)
Son of Ladell and Maggie Washington-Bilberry

Georgia Bilberry's Death Certificate
Wife of Henry Bilberry

IMPORTANT! This is a Permanent Record. Use Black Typewriter Ribbon or Black Ink.	BIRTH No. _____	STATE OF LOUISIANA CERTIFICATE OF DEATH	STATE FILE No. 3 958

PERSONAL DATA OF DECEASED
(Type or print names. Do not use numerals for date of death.)

1a. Last Named of Deceased	1b. First Name	1c. Second Name	2a. Month Day Year	2b. Hour
Bilberry	Georgia		Date Of Death: 3 - 7 - 57	2 P.M.

3. Sex — Male or Female	4. Color or Race	5. Married ☐ Never Married ☐ Widowed ☒ Divorced ☐	6a. Name of Husband or Wife	6b. Age
Female	Colored			

7. Date of Birth of Deceased	8. Age of Deceased	If under 24 Hrs.	9a. Birthplace (City and State)	9b. Citizen of what Country
2/2/79	Years 98 Months Days	Hours Min.	Louisiana	U.S.A.

10a. Usual Occupation	10b. Kind of Industry or Business	11. Was Deceased ever in U. S. Armed Forces?	11a. Social Security No.
none		m.	

PLACE OF DEATH

12a. City, Town, or Location	12b. Parish	12c. Length of Stay in this Place
Monroe	Ouachita	50 hours

12d. Name of Hospital or Institution	12e. Is Place of Death inside City Limits?
E. A. Conway Memorial Hospital	Yes ☐ No ☒

USUAL RESIDENCE OF DECEASED

13a. City of Town	13b. Parish	13c. State
Farmerville	Union	Louisiana

13d. Street Address	13e. Is Residence inside City Limits?	13f. Is Residence on a Farm?
Box 222	Yes ☐ No ☐	Yes ☐ No ☐

PARENTS

14a. Name of Father	14b. Birthplace of Father	15a. Maiden Name of Mother	15b. Birthplace of Mother
Branson Holly	unknown	unknown	unknown

INFORMANT'S CERTIFICATION

16a. Signature of Informant	16b. Date of Signature
I certify that the above stated information is true and correct to the best of my knowledge. ► Morean Benson	3/2/57

CAUSE OF DEATH
Enter only one cause per line for (a), (b) and (c)

17. Part I. Death was caused by:		Interval Between Onset and Death
Immediate cause (a)	Cardiac Insufficiency	
Conditions, if any, which gave rise to above cause (a), stating the underlying cause last. Due to (b)	Renal Failure	
Due to (c)	cerebro Vascular accident	

Part II. Other significant conditions contributing to death but not related to the Terminal Disease condition given in Part I (a)

18. Autopsy
Yes ☐ No ☐

DEATHS DUE TO EXTERNAL VIOLENCE

19a. Accident ☐ Suicide ☐ Homicide ☐	19b. Describe how Injury Occurred.

19c. Time Of Injury Hour a.m. p.m.	Month, Day, Year

19d. Injury Occurred While at Work ☐ Not While At Work ☐	19e. Place of Injury	19f. City, Town, or Location	Parish	State

PHYSICIAN'S CERTIFICATION

20. I certify that I attended the deceased From To	and that death occurred on the date and hour stated above.	21a. Signature of Physician	21b. Date of Signature
		R. Holly	3/7/57

FUNERAL DIRECTOR'S CERTIFICATION

22a. Burial .... ☐ Date Thereof Cremation . ☐ Removal .. ☐ 3-10-57	22b. Name and Location of Cemetery	23. Signature and Address of Funeral Director
	Concord Cemetery Union Parish	

BURIAL TRANSIT PERMIT

24. Burial Transit Permit Number	25. Parish of Issue	26. Date of Issue	27. Signature of Local Registrar
56-27	Union	March 8, 1957	W. Carroll Plummer M.D.

LOUISIANA STATE DEPARTMENT OF HEALTH, DIVISION OF PUBLIC HEALTH STATISTICS MAR 15 1957 Per J. Cabus

Georgia Ann Bilberry-Ellis's (aka Aunt Puss) Death Certificate
Daughter of Lucinda (Cinda) Morgan and Elsa Bilberry
Husband of Lorenzo (Rance) Ellis

James Alfred Honeycutt's Death Certificate
Son of Alfred Honeycutt

DEC 22 1917

LOUISIANA STATE BOARD OF HEALTH
BUREAU OF VITAL STATISTICS
CERTIFICATE OF DEATH

N. B. Every item of information should be carefully supplied—AGE should be stated EXACTLY. PHYSICIANS should state CAUSE OF DEATH in plain terms, so that it may be properly classified. Exact statement of OCCUPATION is very important.

WRITE PLAINLY WITH UNFADING INK—THIS IS A PERMANENT RECORD

MARGIN RESERVED FOR BINDING

1—PLACE OF DEATH

Parish *Union*

Police Jury Ward *1*

Village *Farmerville*
or
City

Registration District No. *5-6 0 8*

Primary Registration District No.
(Applies only to an incorporated town.)

File No. *5-*
(1, 2, 3, etc., in the order Certificates are filed.)

Registered No. *13048*
(To be given in Central Bureau.)

(If death occurred in a hospital or institution, give its name instead of street and number.)

2—FULL NAME *James Alfred Honeycutt*

(No.   St.   Ward

PERSONAL AND STATISTICAL PARTICULARS	MEDICIAL CERTIFICATE OF DEATH

3—SEX *Male*

4—COLOR or RACE *white*
(Write White or Col.)

5—Single *Widowed* **Married Widowed or Divorced**
(Write the word)

16—DATE OF DEATH *Sept 22*, 1917
(Must always be given.) (Month) (Day) (Year)

6—DATE OF BIRTH *Sept 6*, 1852
(Month) (Day) (Year)

17—I HEREBY CERTIFY, that I attended deceased from *January 1*, 1917, to *Sept 22*, 1917,
that I last saw h... alive on *Sept 22*, 1917,
and that death occurred, on the date stated above, at....m. The CAUSE OF DEATH* was as follows:
Rheumatism, old age, and general nervous breakdown

7—AGE (If in doubt, write "about...years)
65 yrs. ...mos. *16* ds.
IF LESS than 1 day...hrs. or ...min.

(Duration) yrs. *8* mos. *21* ds.
Contributory (Secondary)

8—OCCUPATION
(a) Trade, profession, or particular kind of work *Farmer*
(b) General nature of industry, business or establishment in which employed (or employer)

(Duration) yrs. ...mos. ...ds.
(Signed) *J. G. Taylor M. D.*
, 191... (Address) *Farmerville, La.*

9—BIRTHPLACE
(City or Town, State or foreign country) *Union Pa.*

10—NAME OF FATHER *Alfred Honeycutt*

11—BIRTHPLACE OF FATHER *Louisiana*
(City or Town, State or foreign country)

12—MAIDEN NAME OF MOTHER *Miss Ratief*

13—BIRTHPLACE OF MOTHER *Louisiana*
(City or Town, State or foreign country)

PARENTS

(If no Physician, Registrar must write "No Physician.")
*State the Disease causing Death, or, in deaths from Violent Causes, state (1) Means of injury; (2) whether Accidental, Suicidal or Homicidal.

18—LENGTH OF RESIDENCE (for Hospitals, Institutions, Transients or Recent Residents.)
At place of death...yrs....mos....ds.
In the State...yrs....mos....ds.
Where was disease contracted if not at place of death?
Former or usual residence

14—The above is true to the best of my knowledge.

(Informant) *J. G. Taylor M. D.*

(Address) *Farmerville, La.*

15—Filed *Nov 25*, 1917 *J. C. Toler*
(Date certificate is received.) (This MUST be signed.) Registrar

19—PLACE OF BURIAL or REMOVAL *near Farmerville*

DATE OF BURIAL *Sept 23*, 1917

20—UNDERTAKER *Farmerville Merc. Co.*
ADDRESS *Farmerville La*

Form V. S. No. 2.

148

John Burch's Death Certificate
Son of Tom Burch

**John Hiram Montgomery's Death Certificate
Father of George Montgomery**

MAY 15 1916

LOUISIANA STATE BOARD OF HEALTH
BUREAU OF VITAL STATISTICS
CERTIFICATE OF DEATH 4520

PLACE OF DEATH
Parish *Union*
Township or Village *Marion*
or City

Registration District No. *56/6X*
Primary Registration District No.
File No. *40*
Registered No.

[If death occurred in a hospital or institution, give its NAME instead of street and number.]

FULL NAME *John Hiram Montgomery*

PERSONAL AND STATISTICAL PARTICULARS

MEDICAL CERTIFICATE OF DEATH

SEX *Male* | COLOR or RACE *Black* | Single Married Widowed or Divorced (*Write* the word) *Married*

DATE OF DEATH *April 25, 1916*

DATE OF BIRTH *April 15, 1835*

AGE *81* yrs. mos. *10* ds.

I HEREBY CERTIFY, that I attended deceased from *April 20*, 1916, to , 191
that I last saw him alive on *April 20*, 1916
and that death occurred, on the date stated above, at *12* m. The CAUSE OF DEATH was as follows: *Organic Heart Disease*

OCCUPATION
(a) Trade, profession, or particular kind of work *Farmer*
(b) General nature of industry, business, or establishment in which employed (or employer)

(Duration) yrs. *4* mos. ds.
Contributory (Secondary)
(Duration) yrs. mos. ds.

BIRTHPLACE (City or Town State or foreign country) *Perry County Ala.*

(Signed) *O H Thompson* M. D.
May 3, 1916. (Address) *Marion La*

NAME OF FATHER *Don't know*
BIRTHPLACE OF FATHER *Don't know*
MAIDEN NAME OF MOTHER *Don't know*
BIRTHPLACE OF MOTHER *Don't know*

LENGTH OF RESIDENCE
At place of death *38* yrs. mos. ds. In the State yrs. mos. ds.
Where was disease contracted if not at place of death?
Former or usual residence *Near Marion*

THE ABOVE IS TRUE TO THE BEST OF MY KNOWLEDGE
(Informant) *P T Hally*
(Address) *MARION, LA.*

PLACE OF BURIAL OR REMOVAL *Antioch Cemetery*
DATE OF BURIAL *April 26, 1916*

Filed *May 4, 1916* *J L Hopkins* Registrar

UNDERTAKER *P T Hally*
ADDRESS *Marion La*

150

John Mack Bilberry's Death Certificate
Son of Elzy Bilberry

1—PLACE OF DEATH	LOUISIANA STATE BOARD OF HEALTH
Parish....*[illegible]*	Bureau of Vital Statistics
Police Jury Ward....*6*	*56-5549* CERTIFICATE OF DEATH
	Registration District No.......... File No.
Village..........	(1, 2, 3, etc., in the order Certificates are filed.)
or	Primary Registration District No.......... Registered No. *23328*
City..........	(Applies only to an incorporated town.) (To be given in Central Bureau.)

No.......... St.......... Ward..........
(If death occurred in a Hospital or Institution, give its Name instead of Street and Number.)

2—FULL NAME.... *John Mc morn Bilberry*

(a) Residence. No.... *Conway* St.... Ward.... *6*
(Usual place of abode) (If non-resident give city or town and State)
Length of residence in city or town where death occurred.... yrs. mos. ds. How long in U. S., if of foreign birth? yrs. mos. ds.

PERSONAL AND STATISTICAL PARTICULARS	MEDICAL CERTIFICATE OF DEATH
3 SEX 4 COLOR OR RACE 5 Single, Married, Widowed, or Divorced (write the word)	16 DATE OF DEATH *July 15 1918*
Male white single	(Month) (Day) (Year)
5a If married, widowed, or divorced HUSBAND of (or) WIFE of *Single*	17 I HEREBY CERTIFY, That I attended deceased from.......... 19...... to.......... 19......
	that I last saw h....alive on.......... 19......
6 DATE OF BIRTH (month, day, and year)	and that death occurred, on the date stated above, at.......... m.
	The CAUSE OF DEATH* was as follows:
7 AGE Years Months Days If LESS than 1 day....hrs. or....min.	
June 24 1884	*Measles*
8 OCCUPATION OF DECEASED	(duration)....yrs....mos....ds.
(a) Trade, profession, or particular kind of work *farmer*	CONTRIBUTORY (Secondary)..........
(b) General nature of industry, business, or establishment in which employed (or employer)..........	(duration)....yrs....mos....ds.
(c) Name of employer	18 Where was disease contracted if not at place of death?..........
9 BIRTHPLACE (city or town) *county* (State or country)	Did an operation precede death?.......... Date of..........
10 NAME OF FATHER *Elzy B Bilberry*	Was there an autopsy?..........
11 BIRTHPLACE OF FATHER (city or town).......... (State or country)	What test confirmed diagnosis?..........
12 MAIDEN NAME OF MOTHER *dont no*	(Signed).......... M. D.
13 BIRTHPLACE OF MOTHER (city or town).... *dont no* (State or country)	, 19 (Address) *Dr W T Patterson*
	*State the Disease Causing Death, or in deaths from Violent Causes, state (1) Means and Nature of Injury, and (2) whether Accidental, Suicidal, or Homicidal. (See reverse side for additional space.)
14 Informant.......... (Address)	19 PLACE OF BURIAL, CREMATION, OR REMOVAL DATE OF BURIAL 19
15 Filed *Aug 8* 19*18* *A C Atkins Out* Registrar	20 UNDERTAKER ADDRESS

151

Jordan B. Nelson's Death Certificate
Son of Jordan (Branch) Nelson and Hannah Bilberry-Nelson

Jordan E. Billberry, Sr.'s, Death Certificate
Husband of Amanda Durden (First) and Mattie Carson (Second wife)
Son of Martha Gilbert (black) and Elzie Billberry (white); see death certificate below

Jordan Ellis Billberry's Death Certificate
Son of Adell (Abe) and Annie Ross-Billberry

Lawrence Bilberry's Death Certificate
Husband of Lou Kilgore-Bilberry
Son of Norsis Armstrong and Britt/Bridges (white)

Certificate of Death — State of Louisiana, State File No. 18 443. Deceased: Bilberry, Lawrence. Male, Colored. Date of Death: Oct. 8, 1965. Born 1883. Birthplace Truxno, LA. Cause of death: Cerebrovascular Accident due to Arteriosclerosis & Senility. Father: Bridge Bilberry; Mother's maiden name: Norsis. Informant: Paul Bilberry.

155

Levonia Nelson-Wyatt's Death Certificate
Daughter of Branch Nelson and Hannah Bilberry-Nelson

Death certificate for Levonia Wyatt, State file no. 2848, Louisiana State Department of Health, Division of Public Health Statistics, Baton Rouge Louisiana

Liza Roberts's Death Certificate
Wife of Will Roberts
Daughter of Thomas and Ann Burch

Maggie Bilberry's Death Certificate
Wife of Ladell Bilberry
Daughter of James and Sara Ann Washington

Mammie (Mary) Bohanna's (Bohannon's) Death Certificate
Daughter of Narsis Armstrong
Wife of Will Bohannon; half-sister of Lawrence Bilberry

Mary Horn's Death Certificate
Wife of Jethro Horn
Daughter of Frank and Emma Bilberry

IMPORTANT! This is a Permanent Record. Use Black Typewriter Ribbon or Black Ink.	STATE OF LOUISIANA	STATE FILE No. 11 433

CERTIFICATE OF DEATH

BIRTH No. _____

PERSONAL DATA OF DECEASED
(Type or print names. Do not use numerals for month of death.)

1a. Last Named of Deceased	1b. First Name	1c. Second Name	2a. Month Day Year	2b. Hour
Horn	Mary		Date Of Death: 8-21-56	M.

3. Sex — Male or Female	4. Color or Race	5. Married ☑ Never Married ☐ Widowed ☐ Divorced ☐	6a. Name of Husband or Wife	6b. Age
Female	Col		Jethro Horn	44

7. Date of Birth of Deceased	8. Age of Deceased Years Months Days / If under 24 Hrs. Hours Min.	9a. Birthplace (City and State)	9b. Citizen of what Country
11-1st-1910	46	La	U.S.A.

10a. Usual Occupation (Give kind of work done during most of working life, even if retired)	10b. Kind of Industry or Business	11. Was Deceased ever in U. S. Armed Forces? (Yes, no, or unknown) (If yes, give war or dates of service)	11a. Social Security No.
House Maid	Home	no	

PLACE OF DEATH 56X

12a. City, Town, or Location	12b. Parish	12c. Length of Stay in this Place
Larmerville La.	Union	11 years

12d. Name of Hospital or Institution (If not in hospital or institution give street address or location)	12e. Is Place Of Death inside City Limits? Yes ☑ No ☐

USUAL RESIDENCE OF DECEASED
(Where deceased lived. If institution: Residence before admission)

13a. City or Town	13b. Parish	13c. State
Larmerville, La	Union	La

13d. Street Address—(If rural give location)	13e. Is Residence inside City Limits? Yes ☐ No ☑	13f. Is Residence on a Farm? Yes ☐ No ☑
Gen-Del		

PARENTS 56X

14a. Name of Father	14b. Birthplace of Father (City or town)	15a. Maiden Name of Mother	15b. Birthplace of Mother (City or town)
Frank Billbury	La	Emma Robert	La

INFORMANT'S CERTIFICATION
I certify that the above stated information is true and correct to the best of my knowledge.

16a. Signature of Informant	16b. Date of Signature
Jetho Horn	8-21-56

CAUSE OF DEATH
Enter only one cause per line for (a), (b) and (c)

443X

17. Part I. Death was caused by:		Interval Between Onset and Death
Immediate cause (a)	Pulmonary Edema	
Conditions, if any, which gave rise to above cause (a), stating the underlying cause last. Due to (b)	Hypertensive Cardiovascular Disease	
Due to (c)		

Part II. Other Significant conditions contributing to death but not related to the Terminal Disease condition given in Part I (a)

18. Autopsy Yes ☐ No ☐

DEATHS DUE TO EXTERNAL VIOLENCE

19a. Accident ☐ Suicide ☐ Homicide ☐	19b. Describe how Injury Occurred. (Enter nature of injury in Part I or Part II of item 17.)

19c. Time Of Injury Hour Month, Day, Year a. m. p. m.			

19d. Injury Occurred While at ☐ Work Not While At ☐ Work	19e. Place of Injury (e. g., in or about home, farm, factory, street, office bldg., etc.)	19f. City, Town, or Location	Parish	State

PHYSICIAN'S CERTIFICATION

20. I certify that I attended the deceased From To and that death occurred on the date and hour stated above.	21a. Signature of Physician	21b. Date of Signature
	G. C. Wadlington	8-23-56

FUNERAL DIRECTOR'S CERTIFICATION

22a. Burial ☑ Cremation ☐ Removal ☐ Date Thereof 8-23-56	22b. Name and Location of Cemetery or Crematory	23. Signature and Address of Funeral Director
	Sweet Lilly Cemetery	Charlie Darby

BURIAL TRANSIT PERMIT

24. Burial Transit Permit Number	25. Parish of Issue	26. Date of Issue	27. Signature of Local Registrar
56-93	Union	8-23-56	A. Ciaccio, R.G.M.

25M 10-55 PHS 16 (Rev.) LOUISIANA STATE DEPARTMENT OF HEALTH, DIVISION OF PUBLIC HEALTH STATISTICS SEP 4- 1956 ☆ 440

Monroe Finley's Death Certificate
Son of Osborn and Narcissa Finley

1—PLACE OF DEATH		NOV 10 1937	LOUISIANA STATE BOARD OF HEALTH

Parish *Union*

NOV 10 1937

LOUISIANA STATE BOARD OF HEALTH
Bureau of Vital Statistics
CERTIFICATE OF DEATH

Ward *1*

District No. *56-5544*

File No. *49*
(1, 2, 3, etc., in the order Certificates are filed.)

City *Farmerville*
or
Town *La. R#2*

Registered No. **12452**
(To be given in Central Bureau.)

No. .... St., ... Ward.
(If death occurred in a Hospital or Institution, give its Name instead of Street and Number.)

2—FULL NAME *Monroe Finley*

(a) Residence. No. *Farmerville La* St., ... Ward.
Length of residence in city or town where death occurred *65* yrs. ✓ mos. ✓ ds. How long in U. S.; of foreign birth? .... yrs. .... mos. .... ds.
(Usual place of abode.) (If non-resident give city or town and State)

PERSONAL AND STATISTICAL PARTICULARS	MEDICAL CERTIFICATE OF DEATH

3. SEX *male* 4. COLOR OR RACE *colored* 5. SINGLE, MARRIED, WIDOWED, OR DIVORCED (WRITE the word) *widowed*

21. DATE OF DEATH (month, day, and year) *July 11*, 19 *37*

5a. If married, widowed, or divorced
HUSBAND of
(or) WIFE of *Martha James Finley*

22. I HEREBY CERTIFY That I attended deceased from *July 9* 19 *37*, to *July 11*, 19 *37*
I last saw h..... on *July 10* 19 *37* death is said
to have occurred on the date stated above, at *7 P* .... m.

6. DATE OF BIRTH (month, day, and year) *1872*

7. AGE Years *65* Months ✓ Days ✓ If LESS than 1 day, ...hrs. or ....min.

The principal cause of death and related causes of importance in order of onset were as follows: Date of onset

8. Trade, profession, or particular kind of work done, as SAWYER, BOOKKEEPER, etc. *Farmer*

Diabetes

9. Industry or business in which work was done, as cotton mill, saw mill, bank, etc.

10. Date deceased last worked at this occupation (month and year) *1935* 11. Total time (years spent in this occupation)

Contributory causes of importance not related to principal cause:

11a. Veteran past wars *No* (yes or no) .... (name war)

12. BIRTHPLACE (city or town) *Farmerville La*
(State or Parish) *Union*

Name of operation .... Date of ....
What test confirmed diagnosis? .... Was there an autopsy? ....

13. NAME *Osborn Finley*

14. BIRTHPLACE (city or town) *Greenville County Ala.*
(State or Parish)

23. If death was due to external causes (violence) fill in also the following:
Accident, suicide, or homicide? .... Date of injury .... 19...

15. MAIDEN NAME *Narcis Watson*

16. BIRTHPLACE (city or town) *Not Known*
(State or Parish)

Where did injury occur? ....
(Specify city or town, parish, and State)
Specify whether injury occurred in industry, in home, or in public place

17. INFORMANT *Asby Finley*
(Address) *Farmerville La*

Manner of injury ....

18. BURIAL, CREMATION, OR REMOVAL
Place *Liberty Hill* Date *July 12, 19*

Nature of injury ....

19. UNDERTAKER *Kilpatrick & Kilpatrick*
(Address) *Farmerville, La.*

24. Was disease or injury in any way related to occupation of deceased? ....
If so, specify ....

20. FILED *Oct. 5, 1937, Mrs. Lee Ramsey*
Registrar

(Signed) .... M.D.
(Address) ....

Ollie Bell Holland's Death Certificate
Daughter of Mason and Anna Bilberry-Holland

Ollie Henderson-Roberts's Death Certificate
Wife of Lee Roberts

APR 13 1931

1—PLACE OF DEATH

LOUISIANA STATE BOARD OF HEALTH
Bureau of Vital Statistics
CERTIFICATE OF DEATH

Parish _Union_

Police Jury Ward _1_

Ward District No. _56-5542_

File No. _____
(1, 2, 3, etc . in the order Certificates are filed.)

3974

City
or _Farmerville_
Town

Incorporated Town District No. _56-5544_ Registered No. _____
(Applies only to an incorporated town.)

(To be given in Central Bureau.)

No. _____ St. _____ Ward
(If death occurred in a Hospital or Institution, give its Name instead of Street and Number.)

2—FULL NAME _Ollie Henderson Roberts_

(a) Residence. No. _____ St., _____ Ward. _____
(Usual place of abode)
(If non-resident give city or town and State)
Length of residence in city or town where death occurred. yrs. mos. ds. How long in U.S.; of foreign birth? yrs. mos. ds.

PERSONAL AND STATISTICAL PARTICULARS	MEDICAL CERTIFICATE OF DEATH

3 SEX _female_

4 COLOR OR RACE _negro_

5 Single, Married, Widowed or Divorced (write the word) _married_

16 DATE OF DEATH _Mch 15_ _1931_
(Month) (Day) (Year)

6a If married, widowed, or divorced HUSBAND of (or) WIFE of _Lee Roberts_

17 I HEREBY CERTIFY, That I attended deceased from _Mch 1_, 19_31_ to _Mch 15_, 19_31_
that I last saw h__ alive on _Mch 15_, 19_31_
and that death occurred, on the date stated above, at. _6 8_ m.

6 DATE OF BIRTH (month, day, and year) _May 16 1884_

7 AGE Years _46_ Months _9_ Days _29_ If LESS than 1 day, ___hrs. or ___min.

(54)

The CAUSE OF DEATH* was as follows:

Pellagra + ulcer stomach

(duration) _2_ yrs. ___mos. ___ds.

8 OCCUPATION OF DECEASED
(a) Trade, profession, or particular kind of work _house keeper_
(b) General nature of industry, business, or establishment in which employed (or employer) _own home_
(c) Name of Employer

CONTRIBUTORY (Secondary) _____
(duration) ___yrs. ___mos. ___ds.

9 BIRTHPLACE (city or town) _Louisiana_
(State or country)

18 Where was disease contracted if not at place of death? _____

Did an operation preceed death? _____ Date of _____

10 NAME OF FATHER _Willis Henderson_

Was there an autopsy? _____

11 BIRTHPLACE OF FATHER (city or town) _Louisiana_
(State or country)

What test confirmed diagnosis? _____

(Signed) _J H Taylor_ M.D.

12 MAIDEN NAME OF MOTHER _Matilda_

19 (Address) _Farmerville La_

13 BIRTHPLACE OF MOTHER (city or town) _Louisiana_
(State or country)

*State the Disease Causing Death, or in deaths from Violent Causes, state (1) Means and Nature of Injury, and (2) whether Accidental, Suicidal or Homicidal. (See reverse side for additional space.)

14 Informant _Lee Roberts_
(Address) _Farmerville, La_

19 PLACE OF BURIAL, CREMATION, OR REMOVAL. _Zion Hill_

DATE OF BURIAL _March 19_

15 Filed _Mar 15_ 31 _J H Taylor_
Registrar

20 UNDERTAKER _home made coffin_

ADDRESS

Rachel Thompson's Death Certificate
Daughter of Darky Thompson

Rodelle Burch's Death Certificate
Husband of Hanna Burch
Son of Thomas and Ann Burch

LOUISIANA STATE BOARD OF HEALTH
Bureau of Vital Statistics
CERTIFICATE OF DEATH

1—PLACE OF DEATH
Parish *Union*
Ward 6
City or Town *Marion La*
District No. *56-5550*
File No. *115*
Registered No. *9679*
Ward *131*

2—FULL NAME *Rodelle Burch*
(a) Residence. No. *Marion La Rt-1* St. Ward 6

PERSONAL AND STATISTICAL PARTICULARS

3. SEX *Male*
4. COLOR OR RACE *Colored*
5. SINGLE, MARRIED, WIDOWED, OR DIVORCED *married*
5a. HUSBAND of (or) WIFE of *Hanna Burch*
6. DATE OF BIRTH *1874*
7. AGE Years *65*
8. Trade *Farmer*
11a. Veteran past wars *no*
12. BIRTHPLACE *Louisiana*
13. NAME *Tom Burch*
14. BIRTHPLACE *Louisiana*
15. MAIDEN NAME *Unknown*
16. BIRTHPLACE *Unknown*
17. INFORMANT *Edward Burch Marion La*
18. BURIAL *Marion* Date *4-8-39*
19. UNDERTAKER *Kilpatrick & Kilpatrick Farmerville La*
20. FILED *April 10 1939* *Geo. A. Ramsey* Register

MEDICAL CERTIFICATE OF DEATH

21. DATE OF DEATH *April 6 1939*
22. I HEREBY CERTIFY, That I attended deceased from *April 3 1939* to *April 6 1939*. I last saw him alive on *April 6 1939*, death is said to have occurred on the date stated above, at *2:30 P* m.

24. Was disease or injury in any way related to occupation of deceased? *No*
(Signed) *Charles C. Francis* M.D.
(Address) *Farmerville La*

Sally Bridges-Washington's Death Certificate
Sister of Delia Bridges

		STATE OF LOUISIANA		
IMPORTANT! This is a Permanent Record. Use Typewriter or Ink.	**BIRTH No.**	**CERTIFICATE OF DEATH**	**STATE FILE No.**	**9 168**

PERSONAL DATA OF DECEASED

1a. Last Name of Deceased	1b. First Name	1c. Second Name	2a. Month Day Year 2b. Hour
Washington	*Salley*		DATE OF DEATH: *7-3-52* *6* M.

3. Sex—Male or Female	4. Color or Race	5. Single, Married, Widowed, or Divorced	6a. Name of Husband or Wife	6b. Age
Female	*Colored*	*Widowed*		

7. Date of Birth of Deceased	8. Age of Deceased — If under 1 day	9a. Birthplace (City or town)	9b. (State or Foreign Country)
unknown	*76*	*Union Parish*	*La*

10a. Usual Occupation	10b. Kind of Industry or Business	11. Was deceased ever in U.S. Armed Forces? (Yes, no, or unknown) (If yes, give war or dates of service)
Domestic		

PLACE OF DEATH

12a. City or Town	12b. Parish and Ward No.	12c. Length of Stay in this Place
930 Ridge Drive W. Monroe *Ouchita*		

12d. Name of Hospital or Institution	12e. Length of Stay in Hospital or Institution

USUAL RESIDENCE OF DECEASED

13a. City or Town	13b. Parish and Ward No.	13c. State
930 Ridge Drive W. Monroe *Ouchita*		*La*

13d. Street Address	14. Citizen of what Country

PARENTS

15a. Name of Father	15b. Birthplace of Father	16a. Maiden Name of Mother	16b. Birthplace of Mother
Bob Bridges	*unknown*	*Matilda Bridges*	*unknown*

INFORMANT'S CERTIFICATION

I certify that the above stated information is true and correct to the best of my knowledge.

17a. Signature of Informant	17b. Date of Signature
Rabell Hampton	*7/4/52*

CAUSE OF DEATH

Enter only one cause per line for (a), (b), and (c)

*This does not mean the mode of dying, such as heart failure, asthenia, etc. It means the disease, injury, or complication which caused death.

18. I. Disease or Condition Directly Leading to Death* (a)		Interval Between Onset and Death
Antecedent Causes	*Cerebral Hemorrhage*	
Diseases or conditions, if any, giving rise to the above cause (a) stating the underlying cause last. Due to (b)	*Hypertension*	
Due to (c)	*Hypertensive Cardiovascular Disease*	

II. Other Significant Conditions: Conditions contributing to the death but not related to the disease or condition causing death.

19a. Date of Operation	19b. Major Findings of Operation	20. Autopsy Yes ☐ No ☐

DEATHS DUE TO EXTERNAL VIOLENCE

21a. Accident, Suicide, or Homicide (Specify)	21b. Place of Injury	21c. City, Town, or Ward No.	Parish	State

21d. Time of Injury (Month)(Day)(Year)(Hour)	21e. Injury Occurred While at Work ☐ Not While at Work ☐	21f. How did injury occur?

PHYSICIAN'S CERTIFICATION

22. I certify that I attended the deceased, From To and that death occurred on the date and hour stated above.	23a. Signature of Physician	23b. Date of Signature
	J Truck - Coroner	*7/6/52*

FUNERAL DIRECTOR'S CERTIFICATION

24a. Burial ☐ Date Thereof Cremation ☐ Removal ☐	24b. Name of Cemetery or Crematory	24c. Location (City, town, or parish)	25. Signature of Funeral Director
7/6/52	*Pine Cemetery*	*Farmerville, La.*	*S Douglas*

BURIAL TRANSIT PERMIT

26. Burial Transit Permit Number	27. Parish of Issue	28. Date of Issue	29. Signature of Local Registrar
1611A	*Ouachita*	*7-6-52*	

2M Bks. 12-48 PHS 16 (Rev.)   LOUISIANA STATE DEPARTMENT OF HEALTH, DIVISION OF PUBLIC HEALTH STATISTICS

JUL 21 1952

Sandy Wayne, Jr. – Death Certificate

PERSONAL DATA OF DECEASED	1a. Last Name of Deceased *Wayne*	1b. First Name *Sandy*	1c. Second Name *Jr.*	Second Name	2a. Month Day Year *1-28-53* 2b. Hour *9:15* M.	DATE OF DEATH:		

3. Sex — Male or Female *Male*	4. Color or Race *Colored*	5. Single, Married, Widowed, or Divorced *Married*	6a. Name of Husband or Wife *Beulah*	6b. Age *70*	

7. Date of Birth of Deceased *Oct. 3, 1878*	8. Age of Deceased Years *74* Months *4* Days *25*	If under 1 day Hours Min.	9a. Birthplace (City or town) *Marion*	9b. (State or Foreign Country) *La.*	

10a. Usual Occupation (Give kind of work done during most of working life, even if retired) *Farming*	10b. Kind of Industry or Business *Own Farm*	11. Was deceased ever in U.S. Armed Forces? (Yes, no, or unknown) (If yes, give war or dates of service) *no*

PLACE OF DEATH 56X	12a. City or Town—(If outside corporate limits write RURAL) *5 miles north of Marion*	12b. Parish and Ward No. *Union #2*	12c. Length of Stay in this Place *50 yr.*
	12d. Name of Hospital or Institution (If not in hospital or institution give street address or location) *5 miles north of Marion*		12e. Length of Stay in Hospital or Institution *" "*

USUAL RESIDENCE OF DECEASED 56X	13a. City or Town—(If outside corporate limits write RURAL) *Marion (Rural)*	13b. Parish and Ward No. *Union #2*	13c. State *La.*
	13d. Street Address—(If rural give location) *5 miles north*		14. Citizen of what Country *U.S.A.*

PARENTS	15a. Name of Father *Sandy Wayne Sr.*	15b. Birthplace of Father *Unknown*	16a. Maiden Name of Mother *Mary Douglas* 16b. Birthplace of Mother *Marion, La.*

INFORMANT'S CERTIFICATION	I certify that the above stated information is true and correct to the best of my knowledge. ▶ 17a. Signature of Informant *King Wayne*	17b. Date of Signature *1-29-53*

CAUSE OF DEATH Enter only one cause per line for (a), (b), and (c) *This does not mean the mode of dying, such as heart failure, asthenia, etc. It means the disease, injury, or complication which caused death.*	18. I. Disease or Condition Directly Leading to Death* (a) *Cerebral Hemorrhage* Antecedent Causes Diseases or conditions, if any, giving rise to the above cause (a) stating the underlying cause last. Due to (b) *Hypertension* Due to (c)	Interval Between Onset and Death *3*
	II. Other Significant Conditions Conditions contributing to the death but not related to the disease or condition causing death.	
	19a. Date of Operation	19b. Major Findings of Operation	20. Autopsy Yes ☐ No ☐

DEATHS DUE TO EXTERNAL VIOLENCE	21a. Accident, Suicide, or Homicide (Specify)	21b. Place of Injury (e.g., in or about home, farm, factory, street, office bldg., etc.)	21c. City, Town, or Ward No.	Parish State
	21d. Time (Month) (Day) (Year) (Hour) of Injury M.	21e. Injury Occurred While at ☐ Not While ☐ Work at Work	21f. How did injury occur?	

PHYSICIAN'S CERTIFICATION	22. I certify that I attended the deceased, From To and that death occurred on the date and hour stated above. 23a. Signature of Physician *Virgil B. Kelly MD*	23b. Date of Signature

FUNERAL DIRECTOR'S CERTIFICATION	24a. Burial ☒ Cremation ☐ Removal ☐ Date Thereof *2-1-53*	24b. Name and Location of Cemetery or Crematory *Concord Marion La.* 25. Signature and Address of Funeral Director *Hatton Farmerville La.*

BURIAL TRANSIT PERMIT	26. Burial Transit Permit Number *56-13*	27. Parish of Issue *Union*	28. Date of Issue *Jan. 30, 1953* 29. Signature of Local Registrar *Sam M Funderburk MD* E Dean

3M Bks. 2-51 PHS 16 (Rev.)   LOUISIANA STATE DEPARTMENT OF HEALTH, DIVISION OF PUBLIC HEALTH STATISTICS   FEB 4- 1953

Stella Billberry's Death Certificate

Wife of Jesse Billberry; daughter of Scott and Helia-Roberts Jackson. Stella was the niece of Will Roberts. At 18 years old, she was counted in the 1910 U. S. Census as living with lived with Liza and Will Roberts.

Source: 1910 U.S. Census

Will Roberts' Death Certificate – Number 1
Husband of Eliza (Liza) Roberts
Son of Will and Angeline Roberts

Will Roberts' Death Certificate Number 2
Husband of Eliza (Liza) Roberts
Son of Will and Angeline Johnson-Roberts

Willie Frank Bilberry's Death Certificate
Husband of Lettie Warren-Archie
Son of Frank Bilberry and Emma Roberts-Bilberry

Appendix B

Family Marriage License Collection

Prior to the emancipation proclamation of 1865, many southern states prohibited slaves from legally marrying. Most before-the-war, slave marriages were informal ceremonies; they consisted of an agreement witnessed by the slave owner. It was a common occurrence for female slaves to birth one or more children with one father, but then find themselves forced to establish a different relationship with a man whom she may or may not want to marry. Likewise, some slave women were sexually exploited against their will by white men. The victimized women were left with no option and, often, with one or more children as a result.

This family and extended family collection is used below to help validate the marriage of family members. A person can use the witnesses listed in these marriages to further research family and extended family relationships. <u>Note</u>: The letter "W" stands for those who are of Caucasian descent.

NAMES – MARRIAGE LICENSES COLLECTED	
Anderson Thompson and Delia Bridges	Jesse Fuller and Lula Bridges
Bunk Jones and Annie May Bilberry	Joe Frank Bilberry and Emma Roberts
Dennis Canaly (Conley) and Anna Bridges	John Bishop (Robertson) Robinson and Frances Bilberry (**W**)
Eddie Bilberry and Georgia Willie Mae Benson	John Bishop (Robertson) Robinson and Frances Bilberry (**W**)
Ed Thompson and Fronia Kemp	John Clark and Cinda Bilberry
Elsey B. Bilberry and Mary Jane Honeycutt (**W**)	J. Henry Bilberry and Bessie Rowler (**W**)
Elsey B. Bilberry and Mary Jane Honeycutt (**W**)	Jordan B. Bilberry and Mattie Carson
Elzy B. (E. B.) Bilberry and Cintha Smith (**W**)	Ladell Bilberry and Maggie Washington
E. B. Bilberry and Leona Kerr (**W**)	Ladell Bilberry and Corinne (Corene) McGough
Erass Bridges and Hattie Creath	Lawrence Bilberry and Lou Killgore
Fred Bilberry and Rosa Lee Staples	L. A. (Lee) Burgay and E. Bernice Bilberry (**W**)
General Wallace and Annie Bilberry	Lorenzo Ellis and Bellzora (Georgia Ann/Aunt Pus) Bilberry

George N. Cobb and Lou Bilberry (**W**)	Mason (Holland) Hollings and Anna Bilberry
George Gaines and Fannie Bridges	Mason (Hollis) Holland and Mandy Andrews
Guy Bilberry and Mollie Steel	Prartus Billberry and Dora Gibson
Henry Bilberry and Georgia B. Ellis	Robert Bridges, Jr., and Josie Smith
Isaac (Ike) Douglas and Angeline Bilberry	Sam Tucker and Amy Bilberry
Jackson Bilberry and Lucy Fuller (**W**)	Thomas Birch (Burch) and Ann Cook
James Bilberry and Lou Emma Daniels	Will Bohannon and Mary (Mamie) Armstrong
Jesse Bilberry and Stella Jackson	William (Bill) Bridges and Sarah Montgomery
Jesse Bridges and Pink Young	Willie Bilberry and Lettie Warren Archie

Anderson Thompson and Delia Bridges – Marriage Application
Delia is the mother of Frank Bilberry, Dollie Mayfield and Ed Thompson

4 ??

Know all Men by these Presents.

That we *Anderson Thompson* as principal

and *Fin Ewing* as security, we are held and firmly bound

unto THE STATE OF LOUISIANA, in the sum of *One Hundred*

DOLLARS; and for the true and final payment thereof, we bind ourselves, our heirs, administrators and assigns.

Signed and dated on this *6th* day of *Jany* A. D., 189*7*

THE CONDITION OF THE ABOVE OBLIGATION IS SUCH,

That Whereas, A MARRIAGE is about to take place between the above bound

Anderson Thompson and Miss *Delia Bridges*

and if there shall not exist any legal impediments why the marriage should not take place, then the above obligation to be void; else to remain in full force and virtue, according to law.

Signed and acknowledged before me, this *6th* day of *Jany* A. D. 189*7*

IN THE PRESENCE OF

Edw Everett

Dy Clerk District Court, &c.

Anderson X Thompson
his mark

F. Ewing

174

Bunk Jones and Annie May Bilberry – Marriage License
Annie May Bilberry was formerly married to General Wallace of
Union Parish, Louisiana

Dennis Canaly (Conley) and Anna Bridges – Marriage License
Dennis Conley was a Minister of the Gospel (see other marriage documents in this book)
Anna Bridges is the daughter of Robert and Matilda Bridges

STATE OF LOUISIANA,
PARISH OF UNION,

Clerk's Office Third District Court.

To any ordained Minister of the Gospel, or to any Justice of the Peace, legally authorized according to law, to celebrate **MARRIAGES** within the same place,—GREETING:—

You are hereby authorized and fully empowered to unite in the Bonds of Matrimony, and Holy Wedlock, Mr. *Dennis Canaly* and Miss *Anna Bridges* agreeable to Law and the usual forms and ceremonies of the State of Louisiana, in the presence of at least three male witnesses, residing within the said Parish; and that you certify the same, signed by the parties and the witnesses, with your official signature, and the due return thereof make to this office within thirty days from this date.

Given under my Hand and Seal of Office, on this the *16th* day of *December* A. D., 1880

Jas M Smith
CLERK DISTRICT COURT, &c.

STATE OF LOUISIANA,
PARISH OF UNION.

I do hereby certify, That I have, on this day, in pursuance of the foregoing License, celebrated and solemnized a **MARRIAGE** between Mr. *Dennis Canaly* and Miss *Anna Bridges* agreeable to the Laws and Customs of the State of Louisiana. In faith whereof, I have, together with the parties, and in the presence of the undersigned witnesses, signed the present, on this the *17th* day of *December* A. D., 1885

WITNESSES:
R. J. Gardner
J. W. Goldsby
Alphonso Nelson

Dennis Canaly
Anna x Bridges
her mark

A true record. This *16th* day of *Dec* 1885

Jas M Smith
CLERK DISTRICT COURT, &c.

Eddie Bilberry and Georgia Willie Mae Benson – Marriage License
Eddie Bilberry is the son of Frank Bilberry

STATE OF LOUISIANA,
Parish of Union.

KNOW ALL MEN BY THESE PRESENTS:

THAT WE, _Eddie Bilberry_ ..... as Principal, and
Frank Bilberry ..... as Security, acknowledge to owe to the Governor of the State of Louisiana, or his successor or successors in office, the sum of ONE HUNDRED DOLLARS, the payment of which we hereby bind ourselves, our heirs and administrators, in solido.

Given under our hands at _Farmerville, La_ this _6_ day of _Nov._, A. D. 19 _41_.

The Condition of the above Obligation is such,

That, whereas, the above bounden _Eddie Bilberry_ has this day obtained a license from the Clerk of the District Court of the PARISH OF UNION, STATE OF LOUISIANA, to marry with _Georgia Willie Mae Benson_.

Now, if at the time said license was granted, there existed no legal impediments or obstacles to the celebration of said marriage, then, and in such case, this obligation to be null and void; otherwise to remain in full force and virtue in law.

Eddie Bilberry
Frank his X mark Bilberry

Name of Man _Eddie Bilberry_
Age _28_ Residence _Marion, La._
Occupation _Public Works_
Mother _Emma Bilberry_
Residence _Marion, La_
Father _Frank Bilberry_
Residence _Marion, La._
Former Wife _None_ Dead/Living

Name of Woman _Georgia Willie Mae Benson_
Age _21_ Residence _Marion, La._
Occupation _None_
Mother _Bessie Benson_
Residence _Marion, La._
Father _Robert Benson_
Residence _Dead_
Former Husband _None_ Dead/Living

Relationship of contracting parties .....

MARRIAGE LICENSE

STATE OF LOUISIANA,
Parish of Union.

CLERK'S OFFICE, THIRD DISTRICT COURT

To any Ordained Minister of the Gospel, or any Justice of the Peace, or any Person Legally Authorized According to Law, to Celebrate Marriages Within the Same Place—GREETING

YOU ARE HEREBY AUTHORIZED AND FULLY EMPOWERED TO UNITE IN THE BONDS OF

MATRIMONY AND HOLY WEDLOCK

Mr. _Eddie Bilberry_ and M _Georgia Willie Mae Benson_ agreeable to Law and the usual forms and ceremonies in the State of Louisiana in the presence of at least three male witnesses, residing within the said Parish, and that you certify the same, signed by the parties and witnesses, with your official signature, and due return hereof make to this office within thirty days from this date.

Given under my hand and seal of office on this the _6_ day of _Nov._ A. D. 19_41_.

J M Hawkins Clerk District Court.

STATE OF LOUISIANA, PARISH OF UNION

I DO HEREBY CERTIFY, That I have, on this day, in the pursuance of the foregoing License, celebrated and solemnized

A MARRIAGE BETWEEN

Mr. _Eddie Bilberry_ and Miss _Georgia Willie Mae Benson_ agreeable to the Laws and customs of the State of Louisiana.

IN FAITH WHEREOF, I have, together with the parties, and in the presence of the undersigned witnesses, signed these presents on this the _8_ day of _November_ A. D. 19. _41_

Witnesses:
Charley Bilberry
Joe Benson
Almer Roberts

Eddie Bilberry
Georgia Willie Mae Benson
Eddie X Bilberry

Filed and Recorded in the office of Clerk of Court, Parish of Union, State of Louisiana, this _11_ day of _Dec_, A. D. 19_41_.

Mary Miller, Dy Clerk,

177

Ed Thompson and Fronia Kemp – Marriage License
Ed Thompson is the half-brother of Frank Bilberry

Full name of man _Ed Thompson_ Occupation _Public Work_
Man's age _59_ Residence _Farmerville La_ Color _Col_ Nativity _—_
Previously married or not _yes_ Name of former wife _Maria Thompson_
Former wife, dead or alive _Decd_ Divorced or not _—_ Where _—_ When _—_
Man's father _Emerson Thompson_ Dead or alive _Dead_ Residence _—_
Man's Mother _Dela Thompson_ Dead or alive _—_ Residence _—_
Full name of woman _Fronnie Kemp_ Occupation _None_
Woman's age _61_ Residence _Farmerville La_ Color _Col_ Nativity _—_
Previously married or not _yes_ Name of former husband _Den Kemp_
Former husband, dead or alive _Dead_ Divorced or not _—_ Where _—_ When _—_
Woman's father _—_ Dead or alive _—_ Residence _—_
Woman's mother _—_ Dead or alive _—_ Residence _—_
Relationship of parties _None_ Date of License _Aug 13, 1951_

Before me the undersigned authority, personally came and appeared Mr. _Ed Thompson_, who first being sworn by me, deposes and says that he is about to contract a marriage with M _Fronnie Kemp_, and that he and she are not related within the degree prohibited by the laws of the State of Louisiana, and are not prohibited from intermarrying by the said laws, and that if they, or either of them reside in another State, they are not prohibited from inter-marrying by the laws thereof, and that the answers given to the questions above on this page are true.

Sworn to and subscribed before me, this _13th_ day of _August_, A. D. 19_51_
Ed his + mark Thompson _A. A. Britton_ Dy Clerk, District Court.

STATE OF LOUISIANA, }
PARISH OF UNION. } CLERK'S OFFICE, THIRD DISTRICT COURT

To any Ordained Minister of the Gospel or any Justice of the Peace, or any Person legally authorized according to law, to celebrate marriage within the same place—

GREETING: You are hereby authorized and fully empowered to unite in the bond of

Matrimony and Holy Wedlock

MR. _Ed Thompson_ AND Mrs _Fronnie Kemp_

agreeable to law and the usual forms and ceremonies in the State of Louisiana in the presence of at least three legal and competent witnesses and that you certify the same, signed by the parties and witnesses, with your official signature and due return thereof make to this office within thirty days from date of celebration.

GIVEN UNDER MY HAND and seal of office on this the _13th_ day of _August_ 19_51_.
_at 1:0 PM_ _A. Britton_ Dy Clerk of District Court.

STATE OF LOUISIANA, PARISH OF UNION

I DO HEREBY CERTIFY, That I have on this day, in pursuance of the foregoing License, celebrated and solemnized

A Marriage Between

MR. _Ed Thompson_ AND M _Fronnie Kemp_

agreeable to the laws and customs of the State of Louisiana.

IN FAITH WHEREOF, I have, together with the parties, and in the presence of the undersigned witnesses, signed these presents on this the _16_ day of _August_ 19_51_ at _5:00_ o'clock PM —

WITNESSES:
Ada Holland _Ed Thompson_
Duke E. Fields _Fronnie Thompson_
Vada Fields Kemp _Rev J B Bilberry_

Filed and recorded in the office of Clerk of Court, Parish of Union, State of Louisiana the _5_ day of _November_, A. D., 19_51_.
Bess Paine Dy Clerk.

Elsey B. Bilberry and Mary Jane Honeycutt – Marriage Application

STATE OF LOUISIANA,

Parish of Union.

12th DISTRICT COURT.

KNOW ALL MEN BY THESE PRESENTS, That we, *Elsey B. Bilberry*

as principal and *John Honeycutt* his security are held and firmly bound

Joseph Walker Governor of the State of Louisiana for the time being, and his succe

in office, in the sum of *Two thousand dollar* to the true and faithful payment thereof we

ourselves, our heirs and assigns on this the *2nd* day of *June* A. D. 185*1*

The condition of the above obligation is such, that whereas the said *Elsey B. Bilbe*

has applied to the Clerk of the said 12th District Court in and for said parish, for license to marry *Mar*

J Honeycutt Now, therefore, if it shall appear that no legal cause exist why said license sh

not be granted, and said marriage consumated, the above obligation to be null and void, or else to remain in

force and effect. Signed and acknowledged on the day and date above written *E. B. Bilberr*

C. T. Barton Clerk. *John Honeycutt*

Elsey B. Bilberry and Mary Jane Honeycutt – Marriage License

Elzy B. (E. B.) Bilberry and Cintha Smith – Marriage Application

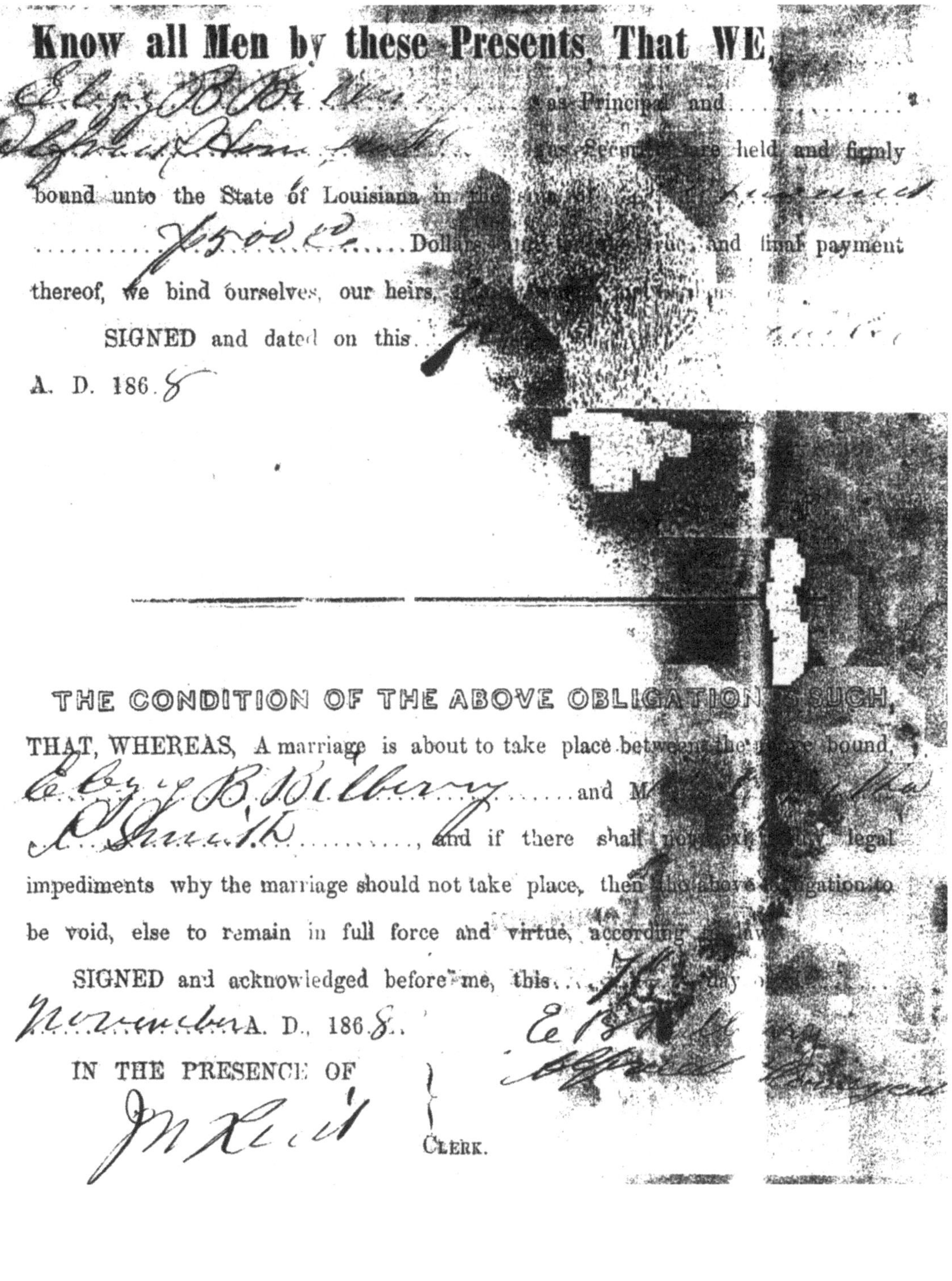

Know all Men by these Presents, That WE,

[handwritten] .... as Principal and ....

[handwritten] .... as Security, are held and firmly

bound unto the State of Louisiana in the sum of ....

.... *[handwritten]* ....Dollars, for the true and final payment

thereof, we bind ourselves, our heirs, ...

SIGNED and dated on this ....

A. D. 186.*8*

THE CONDITION OF THE ABOVE OBLIGATION IS SUCH,

THAT, WHEREAS, A marriage is about to take place between the above bound

[handwritten] E. B. Bilberry .... and M ....

[handwritten] S. Smith ...., and if there shall .... legal

impediments why the marriage should not take place, then the above obligation to

be void, else to remain in full force and virtue, according to law.

SIGNED and acknowledged before me, this ....

[handwritten] November A. D., 186.*8*.

IN THE PRESENCE OF

[handwritten signatures]

}

CLERK.

E. B. Bilberry and Leona Kerr – Marriage License

Erass Bridges and Hattie Creath – Marriage License
Erass is the brother of Delia Bridges

STATE OF LOUISIANA,
PARISH OF UNION

Clerk's Office, Third District Court.

...any ordained Minister of the Gospel, or to any Justice of the Peace, legally, authorized according to law, to celebrate **MARRIAGES** within the same place.—GREETING:—

You are hereby authorized and fully empowered to unite in the Bonds ...mony, and Holy Wedlock, Mr. *Erass Bridges* ...*Hattie Creath* agreeable to Law ...usual forms and ceremonies of the State of Louisiana, in the presence of at least ...witnesses, residing within the said Parish; and that you certify the same, ...by the parties and the witnesses, with your official signature, and the due return ...make to this office within thirty days from this date.

...**under my Hand and Seal of Office,** on this the _1_ ...*Jan* A. D., 1896

B. F. Pleasant
Dy Clerk District Court, &c.

...OF LOUISIANA,
PARISH OF UNION.

I hereby Certify, That I have, on this day, in pursuance of the foregoing License, ...and solemnized a **MARRIAGE** between Mr. *Erass Bridges* ...*Hattie Creath* agreeable to the Laws and Customs of ...Louisiana. In faith whereof, I have, together with the parties, and in the pre- ...undersigned witnesses, signed the present, on this the _2_ *Jan* A. D., 1896

WITNESSES:

Hattie Creath
Eras Bridges
Rev. E. H. Watson Minister

...record. This *13th* day of *Jany* 1896

Jas M Smith
Clerk District Court, &c.

183

Fred Bilberry and Rosa Lee Staples – Marriage Application

Know All Men By These Presents:

That we *Fred Bilberry* as principal

and *Jas Morgan* as security, we are held and firmly bound

unto THE STATE OF LOUISIANA, in the sum of *One Hundred*

DOLLARS; and for the true and final payment thereof, we bind ourselves, our heirs,

administrators and assigns, and I do solemnly swear that I am not related within the degrees

prohibited by law to the party whom I am to marry.

Signed and dated on this *3rd* day of *Sept* A. D. 190 *6*

THE CONDITION OF THE ABOVE OBLIGATION IS SUCH,

That Whereas, A *MARRIAGE* is about to take place between the above bound

Fred Bilberry and Miss *Rosa Lee Staples*

and if there shall not exist any legal impediments why the marriage should not take place,

then the above obligation to be void; else to remain in full force and virtue, according

to law.

Signed and acknowledged before me, this *3* day of *Sept* A. D. 190 *6*

IN THE PRESENCE OF

Edw Everitt

CLERK DISTRICT COURT, ETC.

his
Fred X *Bilberry*
mark

Jas Morgan

General Wallace and Annie Bilberry – Marriage License

STATE OF LOUISIANA, } Clerk's Office, Fourth District Court.
PARISH OF UNION.

To any ordained Minister of the Gospel, or to any Justice of the Peace, legally authorized, according to law, to celebrate MARRIAGES within the same place,--GREETING:

You Are Hereby Authorized and fully empowered to unite in the Bonds of Matrimony, and Holy Wedlock, Mr. *General Wallace* Miss *Annie Bilberry* agreeable to law the usual forms, do solemnly swear that I am not related, within the degrees at least male witnesses, residing within the said parish, and that you certify the same, to the person whom I am to marry. signed by the parties and the witnesses officially and make the due return of make to this office within thirty days from *General X Wallace*

Given under my hand and seal of office, on this the subscribed before me this *14* day of *Dec* 190 *4*
of

Clerk District Court.
CLERK DISTRICT COURT, Etc.

STATE OF LOUISIANA, }
PARISH OF UNION.

I Do Hereby Certify, That I have, on this day, in pursuance of the foregoing License, celebrated and solemnized a MARRIAGE between

Mr. *General Wallace* and Miss *Annie Bilberry*

agreeable to the laws and customs of the State of Louisiana. In faith whereof, I have, together with the parties, and in the presence of the undersigned witnesses, signed the present, on this the *15* day of *Dec* A. D., 190 *4*

General his Wallace
Annie X Bilberry
R. A. Gibson
Justice of the Peace
of Union Parish

WITNESSES:
Job his Warren
marke
Josh. his Bridges
marke

A true record. This *24* day of *June* 190 *5*

CLERK DISTRICT COURT, Etc.

George N. Cobb and Lou Bilberry – Marriage License

STATE OF LOUISIANA, }
PARISH OF UNION,

Clerk's Office Third District Court.

To any ordained Minister of the Gospel, or to any Justice of the Peace, legally authorized according to law, to celebrate MARRIAGES within the same place,—GREETING:—

You are hereby authorized and fully empowered to unite in the Bonds

of Matrimony, and Holy Wedlock, Mr. *George N. Cobb*

and Mrs *Lou Bilberry* agreeable to Law

and the usual forms and ceremonies of the State of Louisiana, in the presence of at least three male witnesses, residing within the said Parish; and that you certify the same, signed by the parties and the witnesses, with your official signature, and the due return hereof make to this office within thirty days from this date.

Given under my Hand and Seal of Office, on this the _____ 24 _____ day of

_____ December _____ A. D., 188 8

W. H. Heard Dy
CLERK DISTRICT COURT, &c.

STATE OF LOUISIANA, }
PARISH OF UNION.

I do hereby certify, That I have, on this day, in pursuance of the foregoing License, celebrated and solemnized a **MARRIAGE** between Mr. *George N. Cobb*

and Mrs *Lou Bilberry* agreeable to the Laws and Customs

of the State of Louisiana. In faith whereof, I have, together with the parties, and in the presence of the undersigned witnesses, signed the present, on this the _____ 26 _____

day of _____ December _____ A. D., 188 8

WITNESSES:

W. H. Brashu

G. F. Cobb

A. A. Cobb

M. G) M. P. Newsom

G. N. Cobb

Lou Bilberry

George Gaines and Fannie Bridges – Marriage Application
Fannie Bridges is the Sister of Delia Bridges

Know all Men by these Presents,

That we *George Gaines* as principal

and *Sam Phillips* as security, we are held and firmly bound

unto THE STATE OF LOUISIANA, in the sum of *One hundred*

DOLLARS; and for the true and final payment thereof, we bind ourselves, our heirs, ad-

ministrators and assigns.

Signed and dated on this *2* day of *May* A. D., 1885

THE CONDITION OF THE ABOVE OBLIGATION IS SUCH,

That Whereas, A **MARRIAGE** is about to take place between the above bound

George Gaines and Miss *Fannie Bridges*

and if there shall not exist any legal impediments why the marriage should not take place,

then the above obligation to be void; else to remain in full force and virtue, according

to law.

Signed and acknowledged before me, this *2* day of *May* D., 188

IN THE PRESENCE OF

W. W. Heard

CLERK DISTRICT COURT, &c.

George W. ^{his} + ^{mark} Gaines

Sam + ^{his} _{mark} Phillips

Guy Bilberry and Mollie Steel – Marriage License

STATE OF LOUISIANA,
PARISH OF UNION. } Clerk's Office, Fourth District Court.

To any ordained Minister of the Gospel, or to any Justice of the Peace, legally authorized, according to law, to celebrate MARRIAGES within the same place,—GREETING:

You Are Hereby Authorized and fully empowered to unite in the Bonds of Matrimony, and Holy Wedlock, Mr. *Guy Bilberry* and Mrs *Mollie Steel* agreeable to law and the usual forms and ceremonies of the State of Louisiana, in the presence of at least three male witnesses, residing within the said parish; and that you certify the same, signed by the parties and the witnesses, with your official signature, and the due return hereof make to this office within thirty days from this date.

Given under my hand and seal of office, on this the *17* day of *Oct* A. D., 190*6*

O Baughman dy
CLERK DISTRICT COURT, ETC.

STATE OF LOUISIANA, }
PARISH OF UNION. }

I Do Hereby Certify, That I have, on this day, in pursuance of the foregoing License, celebrated and solemnized a MARRIAGE between Mr. *Guy Bilberry* and Miss *Mollie Steel* agreeable to the laws and customs of the State of Louisiana. In faith whereof, I have, together with the parties, and in the presence of the undersigned witnesses, signed the present, on this the *18* day of *Oct* A. D., 190*0*

Guy his mark Bilberry
Mattie Steel marle

WITNESSES:
John Honeycutt
Lonnie F Isur
Wise Goldsby
J. D. Cooley M G

A true record. This *12th* day of *June* 190*5*

CLERK DISTRICT COURT, ETC.

Henry Bilberry and Georgia B. Ellis – Marriage License

STATE OF LOUISIANA, }
PARISH OF UNION.

Clerk's Office, Fourth District Court.

To any ordained Minister of the Gospel, or to any Justice of the Peace, legally authorized, according to law, to celebrate MARRIAGES within the same place,--GREETING:

You Are Hereby Authorized and fully empowered to unite in the Bonds of Matrimony, and Holy Wedlock, Mr. *Henry Bilberry*

and Miss *Georgia B Ellis* agreeable to law and the usual forms and ceremonies of the State of Louisiana, in the presence of at least three male witnesses, residing within the said parish; and that you certify the same, signed by the parties and the witnesses, with your official signature, and the due return hereof make to this office within thirty days from this date.

Given under my hand and seal of office, on this the *fifteenth*

day of *January* A. D., 190*4*

JF Breed Dc
CLERK DISTRICT COURT, ETC.

STATE OF LOUISIANA, }
PARISH OF UNION.

I Do Hereby Certify, That I have, on this day, in pursuance of the foregoing License, celebrated and solemnized a **MARRIAGE** between

Mr. *Henry Bilberry* and Miss *Georgia B Ellis* agreeable to the laws and customs of the State of Louisiana. In faith whereof, I have, together with the parties, and in the presence of the undersigned witnesses, signed the present, on this the *16th* day of *January* A. D., 190*4*

WITNESSES:

M J Killy

J C Ellis

J D Couly M G

Gil his mark Bilberry

A true record. This *6th* day of *April* 190*1*

JF Breed Dc
CLERK DISTRICT COURT, ETC.

Isaac (Ike) Douglas and Angeline Billberry – Marriage License
Angeline Bilberry is the half-sister of Frank Bilberry

STATE OF LOUISIANA,

PARISH OF UNION

Know All Men by These Presents:

THAT WE, *Isac Duglas* _____ as Principal, and

Lee Roberts _____ as Security, acknowledge to owe to the Governor of the State of Louisiana, or his successor or successors in office, the sum of ONE HUNDRED DOLLARS, the payment of which we hereby bind ourselves, our heirs and administrators, in solido.

Given under our hands at *Farmerville* this 27 day of *May* A. D., 1916

The Condition of the above Obligation is Such,

That, whereas, the above bounden *Isac Duglas*

has this day obtained a license from the Clerk of the District Court of the PARISH OF UNION, STATE OF LOUISIANA,

to marry with *Angeline Billberry*

Now, if at the time said license was granted, there existed no legal impediments or obstacle to the celebration of said marriage, then, and in such case, this obligation to be null and void; otherwise to remain in full force and virtue in law.

Isac his Duglas
mark
Lee Roberts

Name of Man *Isac Duglas*	Name of Woman *Angeline Billberry*
Age *21* Residence *Conway*	Age *21* Residence *Conway*
Mother *Sefronie Duglas*	Mother *Dont Know*
Residence *Conway*	Residence *Dead*
Father *Anderson Duglas*	Father *Jordon Billberry*
Residence *Strong Arks*	Residence *Dont Know*
Former Wife *none* Dead/Living	Former Husband *none* Dead/Living
Relationship of contracting parties *no Kin*	

MARRIAGE LICENSE

STATE OF LOUISIANA,

PARISH OF UNION

Clerk's Office, Fourth District Court

To any Ordained Minister of the Gospel, or any Justice of the Peace, or any Person Legally Authorized According to Law, to Celebrate Marriages Within the Same Place—GREETING:

YOU ARE HEREBY AUTHORIZED AND FULLY EMPOWERED TO UNITE IN THE BONDS OF

MATRIMONY AND HOLY WEDLOCK

Mr. *Isac Duglas* and Miss *Angeline Billberry*

agreeable to Law and the usual forms and ceremonies in the State of Louisiana in the presence of at least three male witnesses, residing within the said Parish, and that you certify the same, signed by the parties and witnesses, with your official signature, and due return hereof make to this office within thirty days from this date.

Given under my hand and seal of office on this the 27 day of *May* A. D., 1916

J M Dawkins
Clerk District Court.

STATE OF LOUISIANA, PARISH OF UNION

I DO HEREBY CERTIFY, That I have, on this day, in the pursuance of the foregoing License, celebrated and solemnized

A MARRIAGE BETWEEN

Mr. *Isac Duglas* and Miss *Angeline Billberry*

agreeable to the Laws and customs of the State of Louisiana.

IN FAITH WHEREOF, I have, together with the parties, and in the presence of the undersigned witnesses, signed these presents on this the *28th* day of *May* A. D., 1916

Witnesses:
W B Cooper
many not legible
Lee Roberts

Isac Duglas
Angeline Billberry
Rev W M Larkin

Filed and Recorded in the office of Clerk of Court, Parish of Union, State of Louisiana, this 9 day of *June* A. D., 1916

J M Dawkins Dy Clerk.

Jackson Bilberry and Lucy Fuller – Marriage Application

Know all Men by these presents, That we,

Jackson Bilberry as principal and

George Harris as security, are held and firmly bound unto THE STATE OF LOUISIANA, in the sum of *Five hundred*

$500 Dollars; and for the true and final payment thereof, we bind ourselves, our heirs, administrators and assigns.

Signed and dated on this *28th* day of *December* 186

The Condition of the above Obligation is such, That Whereas,

A Marriage is about to take place between the above bound

Jackson Bilberry and M *Lucy Fuller*

and if there shall not exist any legal impediments why the Marriage should not take place, then the above Obligation to be void; else to remain in full force and virtue, according to law. Signed and acknowledged before me, this *28th* day of *December* A. D. 186

IN THE PRESENCE OF

J W Kirkland

Jackson + Bilberry mark

George + Harris mark

Charles Lee Bilberry

James Bilberry and Lou Emma Daniels – Marriage License

STATE OF LOUISIANA,
PARISH OF UNION.   *Clerk's Office, Fourth District Court.*

To any ordained Minister of the Gospel, or to any Justice of the Peace, legally authorized, according to law, to celebrate MARRIAGES within the same place,--GREETING:

𝔜ou 𝔄re 𝔥ereby 𝔄uthorized and fully empowered to unite in the Bonds of Matrimony, and Holy Wedlock, Mr. *James Bilberry* and M*iss* *Lou Emma Daniel* agreeable to law and the usual forms and ceremonies of the State of Louisiana, in the presence of at least three male witnesses, residing within the said parish; and that you certify the same, signed by the parties and the witnesses, with your official signature, and the due return hereof make to this office within thirty days from this date.

Given under my hand and seal of office, on this the _16_

day of _Oct_ A. D. 190_6_

E. L. Ramsey D.
CLERK DISTRICT COURT, ETC.

STATE OF LOUISIANA,
PARISH OF UNION.

¶ 𝔇o 𝔥ereby 𝔠ertify, That I have, on this day, in pursuance of the foregoing License, celebrated and solemnized a *MARRIAGE* between

Mr. *James Bilberry* and M*iss* *Lou Emma Daniel* agreeable to the laws and customs of the State of Louisiana. In faith whereof, I have, together with the parties, and in the presence of the undersigned witnesses, signed the present, on this the _17_ day of *October* A. D. 190_6_

WITNESSES:

J. W. Kendrix
John Bright
Lee McEnery

James X Bilberry
Lou Emma Daniel
J. D. Cauly, M.G.

A true record. This _28_ day of _Oct_ 190_6_

192

Jesse Bilberry and Stella Jackson – Marriage License

Jesse Jackson _____ as principal and *Joe. M. Dawkins*

are held and firmly bound unto THE STATE OF LOUISIANA, in the sum of *100* _____ Dollars; and for the true and fina

d, we bind ourselves, our heirs, administrators and assigns, and I do solemnly swear that I am not related within the degrees prohibited by law t

I am to marry.

I dated on this _____ *1 st* _____ day of *Aug.* _____ A. D. 191*2*

THE CONDITION OF THE ABOVE OBLIGATION IS SUCH,

Whereas, A MARRIAGE is about to take place between the above bound *Jesse Bilberry*

Stella Jackson _____ and if there shall not exist any legal impediments why the marriage

ce place, then the above obligation to be void; else to remain in full force and virtue, according to law.

nd acknowledged before me, this _____ *1 st* _____ day of *Aug.* _____ A. D. 191*2*

IN THE PRESENCE OF

A J Hammons
Clerk District Court, Etc.

Jesse his x mark Bilberry
J. M. Dawkins

---

f Louisiana }
sh of Union }

Clerk's Office, Fourth District Court.

To any ordained Minister of the Gospel, or to any Justice of the Peace, legally authorized, according
to law, to celebrate MARRIAGES within the same place—GREETING:

are hereby authorized and fully empowered to unite in the Bonds of Matrimony, and Holy Wedlock, Mr. *Jesse Bilberry*

Stella Jackson _____ agreeable to law and the usual forms and ceremonies of the State of Louisiana, in the presence of at least three male

residing within the said parish; and that you certify the same, signed by the parties and the witnesses, with your official signature, and the due return

e to this office within thirty days from this date.

under my hand and seal of office, on this the _____ *1 st* _____ day of *Aug.* _____ A.D. 191*2*

A J Hammons
Clerk District Court, Etc.

---

of Louisiana }
sh of Union }

hereby Certify, That I have, on this day, in pursuance of the foregoing License, celebrated and solemnised a MARRIAGE between

Jesse Bilberry _____ and Miss *Stella Jackson* _____ agreeable to the laws,

s of the State of Louisiana. In faith whereof, I have, together with the parties, and in the presence of the undersigned witnesses, signed the present

_____ *4* _____ day of *Aug* _____ A. D. 191*2*

WITNESSES:

llie Boyd
D. Conly, Jr
hn Bright

Jesse his x mark Bilberry
Stella her x mark Jackson
J. D. Conly. M.H

nd correct record. This _____ *7 th* _____ day of *Aug* _____ 191*2*

Jesse Bridges and Pink Young – Marriage Application

Know all Men by these Presents,

That we *Jesse Bridges* as principal

and *Adam Wayne* as security, we are held and firmly bound

unto THE STATE OF LOUISIANA, in the sum of *One Hundred*

DOLLARS; and for the true and final payment thereof, we bind ourselves, our heirs,

administrators and assigns.

Signed and dated on this *19th* day of *January* A. D., 18*92*

THE CONDITION OF THE ABOVE OBLIGATION IS SUCH,

That Whereas, A **MARRIAGE** is about to take place between the above bound

Jesse Bridges and Miss *Pink Young*

and if there shall not exist any legal impediments why the marriage should not take place,

then the above obligation to be void; else to remain in full force and virtue, according

to law.

Signed and acknowledged before me, this *19th* day of *January* A. D., 18*92*

IN THE PRESENCE OF

Jas M. Smith

Clerk District Court, &c.

his
Jesse + Bridges
mark

Adam Wayne

Jesse Fuller and Lula Bridges – Marriage Application

Know all Men by these Presents,

That we *Jesse Fuller* as principal

and *James D. Cauley* as security, we are held and firmly bound

unto THE STATE OF LOUISIANA, in the sum of *One Hundred*

DOLLARS; and for the true and final payment thereof, we bind ourselves, our heirs,

administrators and assigns.

Signed and dated on this *12th* day of *February* A. D., 18*92*

THE CONDITION OF THE ABOVE OBLIGATION IS SUCH,

That Whereas, A **MARRIAGE** is about to take place between the above bound

Jesse Fuller and Mrs *Lula Bridges*

and if there shall not exist any legal impediments why the marriage should not take place,

then the above obligation to be void; else to remain in full force and virtue, according

to law.

Signed and acknowledged before me, this *12th* day of *February* A. D., 18*92*

IN THE PRESENCE OF

Jas M Smith

Clerk District Court, &c.

his
Jesse + Fuller
mark

J D Cauley

Joe Frank Bilberry and Emma Roberts – Marriage License

STATE OF LOUISIANA, Clerk's Office, Fourth District Court.
PARISH OF UNION.

To any ordained Minister of the Gospel, or to any Justice of the Peace, legally authorized, according to law, to celebrate MARRIAGES within the same place,--GREETING:

You Are Hereby Authorized and fully empowered to unite in the Bonds of Matrimony, and Holy Wedlock, Mr. *Jos F Bilberry*

and Miss *Emma Roberts* agreeable to law, and the usual forms and ceremonies of the State of Louisiana, in the presence of at least three male witnesses, residing within the said parish, and that you certify the same, signed by the parties and the witnesses, with your official signature, and the due return hereof make to this office within thirty days from this date.

Given under my hand and seal of office, on this the *1st*

day of *Sept* A. D., 1900

Edw Everitt
CLERK DISTRICT COURT, ETC

STATE OF LOUISIANA,
PARISH OF UNION.

I Do Hereby Certify, That I have, on this day, in pursuance of the foregoing License, celebrated and solemnized a MARRIAGE between

Mr. *Jos F Bilberry* and Miss *Emma Roberts*

agreeable to the laws and customs of the State of Louisiana. In faith whereof, I have, together with the parties, and in the presence of the undersigned witnesses, signed the present, on this the *8* day of *Sept* A. D., 1900

WITNESSES:

Surely McGee
James McGee
John Bersh

Jos F Billberry
Emma Roberts
R W Thomas

A true record. This *13th* day of *June* 190 5

John Bishop (Robertson) Robinson and Frances Bilberry – Marriage Application
Frances Bilberry is the sister of E. B. Bilberry

John Bishop (Robertson) Robinson and Frances Bilberry – Marriage License
Frances Bilberry is the sister of E. B. Bilberry

THE STATE OF LOUISIANA,
Parish of Union.

TO ANY AUTHORIZED MINISTER OF THE GOSPEL, OR ANY JUSTICE OF THE PEACE,

IN AND FOR THE PARISH OF UNION, GREETING :—

You are hereby authorized to celebrate the Rites of Matrimony between *John B Robertson*

and *Miss Frances Bilberry* of your Parish, and

that you perform said act according to the laws and usages of the State of Louisiana, and make return hereof to

the office of the Clerk, of the *12th* District Court, in and for said Parish, according to law,

Given under my hand and seal of office, on this the *4th* day of *Dec* A. D. 185

C L Barton Clerk.

STATE OF LOUISIANA,
PARISH OF UNION.

I, *S Puckett J. P.*

do hereby certify, that in pursuance of the above license, I did proceed to celebrate the Rites of Matrimony,

between *John B Robertson* and *Miss Frances Bilberry*

the parties named in said license, on the date hereof, according to the laws and usages of the State of Louisiana.

In testimony whereof, I have hereunto signed my name, and caused the said parties to sign their names, in

the presence of the subscribing witnesses, on this the *7* day of *December* A. D. 185 *2*

attest

E. B. Bilberry

J B Bilberry

John B Robertson

Frances Bilberry

S Puckett J. P.

198

John Clark and Cinda Bilberry – Marriage Application

Know all Men by these presents, That we,

[handwritten signatures] as principal and
[handwritten signatures] as security, are held and firmly bound unto THE
STATE OF LOUISIANA, in the sum of *[Five hundred]*
[$500] Dollars, and for the true and final payment
thereof, we bind ourselves, our heirs, administrators and assigns.

Signed and dated on this *4th* day of *[January]* 187*1*

The Conditon of the above Obligation is such, That Whereas,
A Marriage is about to take place between the above bound
Jno Clark and M *Cinda Bilberry*
and if there shall not exist any legal impediments why the Marriage should not take
place, then the above Obligation to be void, else to remain in full force and virtue
according to law. Signed and acknowledged before me, this *4th*
day of *[January]* A. D. 187*1*

IN THE PRESENCE OF

[handwritten signatures]

J. (John) Henry Bilberry and Bessie Rowler – Marriage Application

That we _J. Henry Bilberry_ as principal

and _Francis F. Malone_ as security, we are held and firmly bound

unto THE STATE OF LOUISIANA, in the sum of _One Hundred_

DOLLARS; and for the due and final payment thereof, we bind ourselves, our heirs,

administrators and assign

Signed and dated on this _21st_ day of _May_ A. D., 189

THE CONDITION OF THE ABOVE OBLIGATION IS SUCH,

That Whereas, A MARRIAGE is about to take place between the above bound

J. Henry Bilberry and MISS _E. Bessie Rowler_

and if there shall not exist any legal impediments why the marriage should not take place,

then the above obligation to be void; else to remain in full force and virtue, according

to law.

Signed and acknowledged before me, this _21st_ day of _May_ A. D., 1895

IN THE PRESENCE OF

Ollie Everitt

Clerk District Court, &c.

J. H. Bilberry

F. F. Malone

Jordan B. Bilberry and Mattie Carson – Marriage License

STATE OF LOUISIANA,
PARISH OF UNION, }   Clerk's Office, Third District Court,

To any ordained Minister of the Gospel, or to any Justice of the Peace, legally authorized according to law, to celebrate **MARRIAGES** *within the same place,—GREETING:—*

You are hereby authorized and fully empowered to unite in the Bonds of Matrimony, and Holy Wedlock, Mr. *Jordan B. Bilberry* and M*iss Mattie Carson* agreeable to Law and the usual forms and ceremonies of the State of Louisiana, in the presence of at least three male witnesses, residing within the said Parish; and that you certify the same, signed by the parties and the witnesses, with your official signature, and the due return hereof make to this office within thirty days from this date.

Given under my Hand and Seal of Office, on this the _____ 8th _____ day of *September* A. D., 18 91

W. W. Heard
Clerk District Court, &c.

STATE OF LOUISIANA,
PARISH OF UNION. }

I do hereby Certify, That I have, on this day, in pursuance of the foregoing License, celebrated and solemnized a **MARRIAGE** between Mr. *Jordan B. Bilberry* and M*iss Mattie Carson* agreeable to the Laws and Customs of the State of Louisiana. In faith whereof, I have, together with the parties, and in the presence of the undersigned witnesses, signed the present, on this the _____ 10th _____ day of *September* A. D., 18 91

WITNESSES:

J. E. Munsea   *Jordan B. Bilberry*
R. J. Rodgers   *Mattie Carson*
W. L. Munser   *Rev. T. N. Rodgers*

A true record.   This _____ 14th _____ day of *Sept* 18 91

Jas M Smith
Clerk District Court &c

Ladell Bilberry and Maggie Washington – Marriage License

STATE OF LOUISIANA
PARISH OF UNION

Know All Men by These Presents:

THAT WE, *Ladelle Billberry* as Principal, and

as Security, acknowledge to owe to the Governor of the State of Louisiana, or his successor or successors in office, the sum of ONE HUNDRED DOLLARS, the payment of which we hereby bind ourselves, our heirs and administrators, in solido.

Given under our hands at *Forlle* this *28th* day of *Jan* A. D. 19*24*

The Condition of the above Obligation is Such,

That, whereas, the above bounden *Ladelle Billberry*

has this day obtained a license from the Clerk of the District Court of the PARISH OF UNION, STATE OF LOUISIANA, to marry with

Maggie Watson

Now, if at the time said license was granted, there existed no legal impediments or obstacles to the celebration of said marriage, then, and in such case, this obligation to be null and void; otherwise to remain in full force and virtue in law.

Ladell Billberry
Willie Bilberry

Name of Man *Ladelle Billbury*	Name of Woman *Maggie Watson*
Age *21* Residence *Conway, La*	Age *19* Residence *Conway, La*
Mother *Emma Billberry*	Mother *Sarah Watson*
Residence *Conway, Billbury*	Residence *Dead*
Father *Frank Billbury*	Father *Gene Watson*
Residence *Conway, La*	Residence *Dead*
Former Wife *None* Dead / Living	Former Husband *None* Dead / Living
Relationship of contracting parties *None*	

MARRIAGE LICENSE

STATE OF LOUISIANA
PARISH OF UNION

Clerk's Office, Fourth District Court

To any Ordained Minister of the Gospel, or any Justice of the Peace; or any Person Legally Authorized According to Law, to Celebrate Marriages Within the Same Place—GREETING:

YOU ARE HEREBY AUTHORIZED AND FULLY EMPOWERED TO UNITE IN THE BONDS OF
MATRIMONY AND HOLY WEDLOCK

Mr. *Ladelle Billbury* and M *Maggie Watson* agreeable to Law and the usual forms and ceremonies in the State of Louisiana in the presence of at least three male witnesses, residing within the said Parish, and that you certify the same, signed by the parties and witnesses, with your official signature, and due return hereof make to this office within thirty days from this date.

Given under my hand and seal of office on this the *28*

day of *Jan* A. D. 19*24*   *W B Dawkins* Clerk District Court.

STATE OF LOUISIANA, PARISH OF UNION

I DO HEREBY CERTIFY, That I have, on this day, in the pursuance of the foregoing License, celebrated and solemnized
A MARRIAGE BETWEEN

Mr. *Ladell Billberry* and M *Maggie Watson* agreeable to the Laws and customs of the State of Louisiana.

IN FAITH WHEREOF, I have, together with the parties, and in the presence of the undersigned witnesses, signed these presents on

this the *28* day of *Jan.* A. D. 19*24*

Witnesses:
Mose Simmons
Lee Polunite
A B Ewing

Ladelle Billberry
Maggie Washington
Clare I. G. Cornfeed

Filed and Recorded in the office of Clerk of Court, Parish of Union, State of Louisiana, this *11*

day of *Feby.* A. D. 19*24*

O. T. Gretaher Clerk

Ladell Bilberry and Corinne (Corene) McGough – Marriage License

STATE OF LOUISIANA,
Parish of Union.

Know All Men by These Presents:

THAT WE _Ladell Bilberry_ as Principal, and
J. D. Reeves as Security, acknowledge to owe to the Governor of the State of Louisiana, or his successor or successors in office, the sum of ONE HUNDRED DOLLARS, the payment of which we hereby bind ourselves, our heirs and administrators, in solido.

Given under our hands at _Farmerville La_ this _3_ day of _October_, A. D. 19_36_

The Condition of the above Obligation is such,

That, whereas, the above bounden _Ladell Bilberry_ has this day obtained a license from the Clerk of the District Court of the PARISH OF UNION, STATE OF LOUISIANA, to marry with _Corinne McGough_

Now, if at the time said license was granted, there existed no legal impediments or obstacles to the celebration of said marriage, then, and in such case, this obligation to be null and void; otherwise to remain in full force and virtue in law.

Ladell Bilberry
J. D. Reeves

Name of Man _Ladell Bilberry_	Name of Woman _Corinne McGough_
Age _34_ Occupation _Farmer_ Residence _Marion La_	Age _22_ Occupation _Farmer_ Residence _Oakland La_
Mother _Emma Bilberry_	Mother _Cornelia McGough_
Residence _Marion La_	Residence _Oakland La_
Father _Frank Bilberry_	Father _George McGough_
Residence _Marion La_	Residence _Dead_
Former Wife _Maggie Washington Bilberry_ Dead	Former Husband _No_ Dead Living
Relationship of contracting parties _None_	

MARRIAGE LICENSE

STATE OF LOUISIANA,
Parish of Union.

CLERK'S OFFICE, THIRD DISTRICT COURT

To any Ordained Minister of the Gospel, or any Justice of the Peace, or any Person Legally Authorized According to Law, to Celebrate Marriages Within the Same Place—GREETING:

YOU ARE HEREBY AUTHORIZED AND FULLY EMPOWERED TO UNITE IN THE BONDS OF MATRIMONY AND HOLY WEDLOCK

Mr. _Ladell Bilberry_ and M _Corinne McGough_ agreeable to Law and the usual forms and ceremonies in the State of Louisiana in the presence of at least three male witnesses, residing within the said Parish, and that you certify the same, signed by the parties and witnesses, with your official signature, and due return hereof make to this office within thirty days from this date.

Given under my hand and seal of office on this the _3rd_ day of _October_ A. D. 19_36_

H. N. Atkinson Dy
Clerk District Court.

STATE OF LOUISIANA, PARISH OF UNION

I DO HEREBY CERTIFY, That I have, on this day, in the pursuance of the foregoing License, celebrated and solemnized A MARRIAGE BETWEEN

Mr. _Ladell Bilberry_ and M _Corinne McGough_ agreeable to the Laws and customs of the State of Louisiana.

IN FAITH WHEREOF, I have, together with the parties, and in the presence of the undersigned witnesses, signed these presents

on this the _21_ day of _Oct April_ A. D. 19_36_

Witnesses: _Ladell Bilberry_, _Corrine McGough_

Filed and Recorded in the office of Clerk of Court, Parish of Union, State of Louisiana, this _25th_ day of _Oct Dec_, A. D. 19_36_

P. Rabun, Dy Clerk.

Lawrence Bilberry and Lou Killgore – Marriage License
Lawrence Bilberry is the half-brother of Frank Bilberry

STATE OF LOUISIANA,
PARISH OF UNION.

Clerk's Office, Fourth District Court.

To any ordained Minister of the Gospel, or to any Justice of the Peace, legally authorized, according to law, to celebrate MARRIAGES within the same place,--GREETING:

You Are Hereby Authorized and fully empowered to unite in the Bonds of Matrimony, and Holy Wedlock, Mr. *Laurence Bilberry* and Miss *Lou Killgore* agreeable to law and the usual forms and ceremonies of the State of Louisiana, in the presence of at least three male witnesses, residing within the said parish; and that you certify the same, signed by the parties and the witnesses, with your official signature, and the due return hereof make to this office within thirty days from this date.

Given under my hand and seal of office, on this the *27* day of *Feby* A. D. 190*9* *E R Ramsey*
CLERK DISTRICT COURT, ETC.

STATE OF LOUISIANA,
PARISH OF UNION.

I Do Hereby Certify, That I have, on this day, in pursuance of the foregoing License, celebrated and solemnized a *MARRIAGE* between Mr. *Laurence Bilberry* and Miss *Lou Killgore* agreeable to the laws and customs of the State of Louisiana. In faith whereof, I have, together with the parties, and in the presence of the undersigned witnesses, signed the present, on this the *28th* day of *Feby* A. D. 190*9*

WITNESSES:

J P Allison

J S Burch

C J Goodwin

Laurence Bilberry
Lou *her mark* Killgore
J D Conley M.D.

A true record. This *13* day of *July* 190*9*
E R Ramsey
CLERK DISTRICT COURT, ETC.

L. A. (Lee) Burgay and E. Bernice Bilberry – Marriage License

STATE OF LOUISIANA,
PARISH OF UNION. } *Clerk's Office, Fourth District Court.*

To any ordained Minister of the Gospel, or to any Justice of the Peace, legally authorized, according to law, to celebrate MARRIAGES within the same place,--GREETING:

You Are Hereby Authorized and fully empowered to unite in the Bonds of Matrimony, and Holy Wedlock, Mr. *L. A. Burgay* and Mrs *E. Bernice Bilberry* agreeable to law and the usual forms and ceremonies of the State of Louisiana, in the presence of at least three male witnesses, residing within the said parish; and that you certify the same, signed by the parties and the witnesses, with your official signature, and the due return hereof make to this office within thirty days from this date.

Given under my hand and seal of office, on this the *31* day of *Aug* A. D., 190*0*

Baughman Jr
Clerk District Court, Etc.

STATE OF LOUISIANA,
PARISH OF UNION. }

I Do Hereby Certify, That I have, on this day, in pursuance of the foregoing License, celebrated and solemnized a **MARRIAGE** between Mr. *L A Burgay* and M *E Bernice Bilberry* agreeable to the laws and customs of the State of Louisiana. In faith whereof, I have, together with the parties, and in the presence of the undersigned witnesses, signed the present, on this the *5* day of *Sept* A. D., 190*0*

L. A. Burgay
Mrs Bessie Bilberry

WITNESSES:
Geo M Moon
W J Dugworr
L J Moon

W A Smith M G

A true record. This *8th* day of *Sept* 190*0*

205

**Lorenzo Ellis and Bellzora (aka Georgia Ann/Aunt Pus) Bilberry – Marriage License
Branch Nelson was a witness. Branch married Georgia Ann's sister Hannah Bilberry
(Hiram Ewing was the Minister of the Gospel)**

Mason (Holland) Hollings and Anna Bilberry – Marriage License
Anna Bilberry is the sister of Frank Bilberry

STATE OF LOUISIANA,
PARISH OF UNION.
    Clerk's Office, Fourth District Court.

To any ordained Minister of the Gospel, or to any Justice of the Peace, legally authorized, according to law, to celebrate MARRIAGES within the same place,--GREETING:

You Are Hereby Authorized and fully empowered to unite in the Bonds of Matrimony, and Holy Wedlock, Mr. *Mason Hollings* and Miss *Anna Bilberry* _____ agreeable to law and the usual forms and ceremonies of the State of Louisiana, in the presence of at least three male witnesses, residing within the said parish; and that you certify the same, signed by the parties and the witnesses, with your official signature, and the due return hereof make to this office within thirty days from this date.

    Given under my hand and seal of office, on this the __16th__

day of ____Dec____ A. D., 190_4_

C. L. Ramsey Hy
CLERK DISTRICT COURT, ETC.

STATE OF LOUISIANA,
PARISH OF UNION.

    I Do Hereby Certify, That I have, on this day, in pursuance of the foregoing License, celebrated and solemnized a MARRIAGE between

Mr. *Mason Hollings* and Miss *Anna Bilberry*

agreeable to the laws and customs of the State of Louisiana. In faith whereof, I have together with the parties, and in the presence of the undersigned witnesses, signed the present, on this the __18__ day of ____Dec____ A. D., 190_4_

Mason Hollings
Anna Bilberry
R. A. Gibson
Justice of the Peace

WITNESSES:

J. C. Andrews
John Munn

A true record. This __24__ day of ____June____ 190_5_

_____
CLERK DISTRICT COURT, ETC.

207

Mason (Hollis) Holland and Mandy Andrews – Marriage Application

That we _Mason Hollins_ as principal

and _Britton Andrews_ as security, we are held and firmly bound

unto THE STATE OF LOUISIANA, in the sum of _$100 00_

DOLLARS; and for the true and final payment thereof, we bind ourselves, our heirs,

administrators and assigns.

Signed and dated on this _30 th_ day of _June_ A. D., 1900

THE CONDITION OF THE ABOVE OBLIGATION IS SUCH,

That Whereas, A **MARRIAGE** is about to take place between the above bound

Mason Hollis and Miss _Mandy Andrews_

and if there shall not exist any legal impediments why the marriage should not take place,

then the above obligation to be void; else to remain in full force and virtue, according

to law.

Signed and acknowledged before me, this _30 th_ day of _June_ A. D., 1900

IN THE PRESENCE OF

J. G. Turnbee

_Dj_   *Clerk District Court, &c.*

Mason Hollins

Britton Andrews

208

Prartus Billberry and Dora Gibson – Marriage License
Prartus Billberry is the son of Jack and Frances Billberry

STATE OF LOUISIANA,
PARISH OF UNION.

Clerk's Office, Fourth District Court.

To any ordained Minister of the Gospel, or to any Justice of the Peace, legally authorized, according to law, to celebrate MARRIAGES within the same place,--GREETING:

You Are Hereby Authorized and fully empowered to unite in the Bonds of Matrimony, and Holy Wedlock, Mr. *Prartus Billberry* and Miss *Dora Gibson* agreeable to law and the usual forms and ceremonies of the State of Louisiana, in the presence of at least three male witnesses, residing within the said parish; and that you certify the same, signed by the parties and the witnesses, with your official signature, and the due return hereof make to this office within thirty days from this date.

Given under my hand and seal of office, on this the _14_ day of _Feby_ A. D. 190_6_

E. L. Ramsyon
CLERK DISTRICT COURT, ETC.

STATE OF LOUISIANA,
PARISH OF UNION.

I Do Hereby Certify, That I have, on this day, in pursuance of the foregoing License, celebrated and solemnized a MARRIAGE between

Mr. *Prartus Billberry* and Miss *Dora Gibson* agreeable to the laws and customs of the State of Louisiana. In faith whereof, I have, together with the parties, and in the presence of the undersigned witnesses, signed the present, on this the _15_ day of _Feby_ A. D. 190_6_

WITNESSES:
Henry Staple
Lee McHenry
J. M. Honeycutt

Prartus his X mark Billberry
Dora Gibson
J D Cauley M.D.

A true record. This _1_ day of _May_ 190_8_

Emmet J Leesy
CLERK DISTRICT COURT, ETC.

Robert Bridges, Jr., and Josie Smith – Marriage License
E. B. Bilberry Performed the Ceremony as Justice of the Peace

STATE OF LOUISIANA, }

PARISH OF UNION, }

Clerk's Office, Third District Court.

To any ordained *Minister of the Gospel*, or to any *Justice of the Peace*, legally authorized *according to law*, to celebrate **MARRIAGES** within the same place,—GREETING:—

You are hereby authorized and fully empowered to unite in the Bonds of Matrimony, and Holy Wedlock, Mr. *Robert Bridges Jr* and Miss *Josie Smith* agreeable to Law and the usual forms and ceremonies of the State of Louisiana, in the presence of at least three male witnesses, residing within the said Parish; and that you certify the same, signed by the parties and the witnesses, with your official signature, and the due return thereof make to this office within thirty days from this date.

Given under my Hand and Seal of Office, on this the _____ 9th _____ day of *December* A. D., 1892

Jas M Smith

Clerk District Court, &c.

STATE OF LOUISIANA, }

PARISH OF UNION. }

I do hereby Certify, That I have, on this day, in pursuance of the foregoing License, celebrated and solemnized a **MARRIAGE** between Mr. *Robert Bridges Jr* and M *Josie Smith* agreeable to the Laws and Customs of the State of Louisiana. In faith whereof, I have, together with the parties, and in the presence of the undersigned witnesses, signed the present, on this the _____ 10 _____ day of *Dec* A. D., 1892

WITNESSES:

J. H. Bilberry

J. D. Cauley

Robert Bridges Sr

Robert Bridges

Josie Smith

E B Bilberry
Justice of the Peace

A true record. This _____ 13th _____ day of *Dec* _____ 1892

Jas M Smith

Clerk District Court, &c.

Sam Tucker and Amy Bilberry – Marriage License

STATE OF LOUISIANA,
PARISH OF UNION, }   Clerk's Office Third District Court.

To any ordained Minister of the Gospel, or to any Justice of the Peace, legally authorized according to law, to celebrate **MARRIAGES** within the same place,—GREETING:—

You are hereby authorized and fully empowered to unite in the Bonds of Matrimony, and Holy Wedlock, Mr. *Sam Tucker* and M__ *Amy Bilberry* _____ agreeable to Law and the usual forms and ceremonies of the State of Louisiana, in the presence of at least three male witnesses, residing within the said Parish; and that you certify the same, signed by the parties and the witnesses, with your official signature, and the due return thereof make to this office within thirty days from this date.

Given under my Hand and Seal of Office, on this the ____6____ day of *Feburary* A. D., 188*8*

W. W. Heard Dy
CLERK DISTRICT COURT, &c.

STATE OF LOUISIANA,
PARISH OF UNION. }

I do hereby certify, That I have, on this day, in pursuance of the foregoing License, celebrated and solemnized a **MARRIAGE** between Mr. *Sam Tucker* and M__ *Amy Bilberry* ____ agreeable to the Laws and Customs of the State of Louisiana. In faith whereof, I have, together with the parties, and in the presence of the undersigned witnesses, signed the present, on this the ____9____ day of *Feburary* A. D., 188*8*

WITNESSES :

Thomas Wagner
Napoleon Davis
Lewis Tolion

S. R. Nolen O.M.G
Sam Tucker
Amy Bilberry

A true record. This *23rd* day of *Feb'y* 1888

Jno. M. Smith
CLERK DISTRICT COURT, &c.

Thomas Birch (Burch) and Ann Cook – Marriage License
Thomas Birch (Burch) and Ann Cook are the parents of Liza Roberts

STATE OF LOUISIANA,
PARISH OF UNION.   Clerk's Office, Eleventh District Court.

To any ordained Minister of the Gospel, or to any Justice of the Peace, legally authorized according to law, to celebrate **MARRIAGES** within the same place,—GREETING:—

You are hereby authorized And fully empowered to unite in the Bonds of Matrimony, and Holy Wedlock, Mr. *Thomas Birch* with *Ann Cook* agreeable to Law

and the usual forms and ceremonies of the State of Louisiana, in the presence of at least three male witnesses, residing within the said Parish; and that you certify the same, signed by the parties and the witnesses, with your official signature, and the due return hereof make to this office within thirty days from date.

Given under my Hand and Seal of Office, on this the ____ 10th ____ day of September A. D. 1881

Jas. M. Smith
CLERK DISTRICT COURT.

STATE OF LOUISIANA,
PARISH OF UNION.

I do hereby certify, That I have, on this day, in pursuance of the foregoing License, celebrated and solemnized a **MARRIAGE** between Mr. *Thomas Birch* with *Ann Cook* agreeable to the Laws and Customs of the State of Louisiana. In faith whereof, I have, together with the parties, and in the presence of the undersigned witnesses, signed the present, on this the 11 day of Sept A. D. 1881

WITNESSES:

John his x mark Bragg   Hiram Ewing
Elisha Smith   Thomas his x mark Birch
Doc x mark Taylor   Ann her x mark Birch
                               A true record
                               Jas M Smith Clk Ct

Will Bohannon and Mary (Mamie) Armstrong – Marriage License
Mary (Mamie) Armstrong is the daughter of
Norsis Armstrong and sister of Lawrence Bilberry

PARISH OF UNION. } Clerk s Office, Fourth District Court.

To any ordained Minister of the Gospel, or to any Justice of the Peace, legally authorized, according to law, to celebrate MARRIAGES within the ame place,--GREETING:

You Are Hereby Authorized and f ly empowered to unite in the Bonds of Matrimony, and Holy Wedlock, Mr. _Wi Bohannan_ and Miss _Mary Armstrong_ _____agreeable to law and the usual forms and ceremonies of the State of Louisiana, in the presence of at least three male witnesses residing within the sa parish; and that you certify the same, signed by the parties and the witnesses, with our official signature, and the due return hereof make to this office within thirty days from this date.

Given under my hand and seal of office on this the _11_ _____ day of _Mar_ _____ A. D. 190 7

E F Ballard y
CLERK DISTRICT COURT, ETC.

STATE OF LOUISIANA, }
PARISH OF UNION. }

I Do Hereby Certify, That I have this day, in pursuance of the foregoing License, celebrated and solemnized a MARRIAGE between

Mr. _Will Bohanan_ and Miss _Mary Armstrong_

agreeable to the laws and customs of the State of Louisiana. In faith whereof, I have, together with the parties, and in the presence of the undersigned witnesses, signed the present, on this the _14_ day of _March_ A. D. 190 7

WITNESSES:

Geny G
Bill Georg

Will Bohannan
Mary Armstrong
_Rev Jas ___ __ _

A true record. This _8th_ day of _July_ 190 7

E F Ballard y
CLERK DISTRICT COURT, ETC.

William (Bill) Bridges and Sarah Montgomery – Marriage Application
William (Bill) Bridges is the brother of Delia Bridges;
Son of Robert and Matilda Bridges

That we *William Bridges* as principal

and *Haywood Creech* as security, we are held and firmly bound

unto THE STATE OF LOUISIANA, in the sum of *One Hundred*

DOLLARS; and for the true and final payment thereof, we bind ourselves, our heirs, administrators and

assigns.

Signed and dated on this *15* day of *January* A.D.

THE CONDITION OF THE ABOVE OBLIGATION IS SUCH,

That Whereas, A MARRIAGE is about to take place between the above named

William Bridges and MISS *Sarah Montgomery*

and if there shall not exist any legal impediments why the marriage should not take place, then the above

obligation to be void; else to remain in full force and virtue, according to law.

Signed and acknowledged before me, this *15* day of *January* A.D.

IN THE PRESENCE OF

W W Hen d Dy *his*
Antk D Ora *William + Bridges*
mark

his
Haywood X Creech
mark

214

Willie Bilberry and Lettie Warren-Archie – Marriage License
Willie Bilberry is the son of Frank and Emma Roberts

STATE OF LOUISIANA,
Parish of Union.

Know All Men by These Presents:

THAT WE, *Willie Bilberry* as Principal, and
as Security, acknowledge to owe to the Governor of the State of Louisiana, or his successor or successors in office, the sum of ONE HUNDRED DOLLARS, the payment of which we hereby bind ourselves, our heirs and administrators, in solido.

Given under our hands at *Farmerville La* this *20* day of *Jan* A. D. 19*36*

The Condition of the above Obligation is such,

That, whereas, the above bounden *Willie Bilberry*

has this day obtained a license from the Clerk of the District Court of the PARISH OF UNION, STATE OF LOUISIANA, to marry with *Lettie Warren Archie*

Now, if at the time said license was granted, there existed no legal impediments or obstacles to the celebration of said marriage, then, and in such case, this obligation to be null and void; otherwise to remain in full force and virtue in law.

Willie Bilberry
Zate Doffax

Name of Man *Willie Bilberry*	Name of Woman *Lettie Warren Archie*
Age *34* Residence *Marion La R I*	Age *33* Residence *Oakland La*
Mother *Emma Bilberry*	Mother *Lizzie Warren*
Residence *Marion La R I*	Residence *Oakland La*
Father *Frank Bilberry*	Father *Jap Warren*
Residence *Marion La R I*	Residence *Oakland La*
Former Wife *Andrew Bilberry* Dead	Former Husband *Henry Archie* Divorced Dead
Relationship of contracting parties *None*	

MARRIAGE LICENSE

STATE OF LOUISIANA,
Parish of Union.

CLERK'S OFFICE, THIRD DISTRICT COURT

To any Ordained Minister of the Gospel, or any Justice of the Peace, or any Person Legally Authorized According to Law, to Celebrate Marriages Within the Same Place—GREETING:

YOU ARE HEREBY AUTHORIZED AND FULLY EMPOWERED TO UNITE IN THE BONDS OF **MATRIMONY AND HOLY WEDLOCK**

Mr. *Willie Bilberry* and M *Lettie Warren Archie* agreeable to Law and the usual forms and ceremonies in the State of Louisiana in the presence of at least three male witnesses, residing within the said Parish, and that you certify the same signed by the parties and witnesses, with your official signature, and due return hereof make to this office within thirty days from this date.

Given under my hand and seal of office on this the *20* day of *Jan* A. D. 19*36*

H N Albritton Dy
Clerk District Court

STATE OF LOUISIANA, PARISH OF UNION

I DO HEREBY CERTIFY, That I have, on this day, in the pursuance of the foregoing License, celebrated and solemnized A MARRIAGE BETWEEN

Mr. *Willie Bilberry* and M *Lettie Warren Archie* agreeable to the Laws and customs of the State of Louisiana.

IN FAITH WHEREOF, I have, together with the parties, and in the presence of the undersigned witnesses, signed these presents on this the *20* day of *January* A. D. 19*36*.

Witnesses:
Link Warren
Ether Warren

Willie Bilberry
Lettie Archie
J H Brown, Pastor

Filed and Recorded in the office of Clerk of Court, Parish of Union, State of Louisiana, this *9* day of *June*, A. D. 19*36*.

J C Raburn Clerk.

215

Appendix C

Some Land Patents of Union Parish, Louisiana

Land patents are legal documents that documented the transfer of land ownership from the federal government to individuals. Land patent records generally include the information recorded when ownership was transferred. The map shown below shows some slaveholders who had land patents in Union Parish, Louisiana Sections 3, 14, 28 and 33.

Note 1: Frank Bilberry purchased land on October 17, 1918, from Otis Tugwell in the SE quarter of the NE quarter and the East one-half of the SE one-quarter of **Section 28** in Township 22 North, Range 1 East, Louisiana; Missionary Baptist Church at Meridian, containing 120 acres.

The names listed in **bold letters** are former slaves or slave descendants, who had land patents that are documented by the federal government. The amount of acres in land that each person had is listed in **parenthesis**. Churches and cemeteries where African-Americans worshiped and were buried are shown in **bold italicized letters**.

Note 2: Each number on this map represents a section of approximately one square mile. There are numerous other land patent owners in each section of this map that are not listed. This map is only for illustrating some of the names of slaveholders, former slaves and slave descendants of my great grandfather, Frank Bilberry, who are names were mentioned in this book. The names listed on the map below are as follows:

NAME OF PATENT OWNER	DATE OF PATENT
Britton Honeycutt	Land Patent 1862
Britton Honeycutt	Land Patent 1852
Dennis Andrews	Land Patent 1913
John Honeycutt, Sr.	Land Patent 1837

Lawrence Bilberry	Land Patent 1913
Samuel Morgan	Land Patent 1892
Sandy Wayne, Jr.	Land Patent 1908
Sandy Wayne, Sr.	Land Patent 1902

Source: *Family Maps of Union Parish, Louisiana, Deluxe Edition: With Homesteads, Roads, Waterways, Towns, Cemeteries, Railroads, and More; by Gregory A. Boyd, J. D.; Arphax Publishing Co. 2210 Research Park Blvd., Norman, Oklahoma, USA*

	A	B	C	D	E	F
1	Section 31	Section 32 Britten Honneycut (120)	Section 33 Lawrence Bilberry (Black) (40), Dennis Andrews (Black) (40),*Antioch AME*	Section 34	Section 35	Section 36
2	Section 6	Section 5	Section 4 Elza Bilberry (40)	Section 3 Elza Bilberry (40), John B. Robinson (240), *Antioch Cemetery (Black)*	Section 2	Section 1
3	Section 7	Section 8	Section 9 Britten Honeycutt (40), John B. Robinson (160)	Section 10 John Robinson (420), Mcduel Bilberry (120)	Section 11 Mcduel Bilberry (80), Jacob G. Bilberry (80), Elza B. Bilberry (40)	Section 12
4	Section 18 CONWAY	Section 17 TUGWELL CITY	Section 16	Section 15 John B. Robinson (80), *Meridian Bapt. Church(W) (betw sec.14 &15)*	Section 14 *Center Branch Baptist Church (Black)*	Section 13
5	Section 19 John Honeycutt (40)	Section 20 John Honeycutt (160)	Section 21	Section 22	State Hwy Route 348 Section 23	Section 24
6	Section 30 Joseph Tugwell (240)	Section 29	Section 28 Samuel Morgan (Black) (40), Britten Honeycutt (40), John Honeycu (80)	Section 27	Section 26 *Sweet Lilly Prim. Baptist Church & Cem. & Zion Watts Church*	Section 25
7	State Hwy Route 549 Section 31	Section 32	Section 33 John H. Patterson (80)	Section 34	Section 35	Section 36

Britton Honeycutt – Land Patent in 1862 – Ward Six

Graduation *Examined*
No. 22574 } **THE UNITED STATES OF AMERICA,**

To all to whom these presents shall come, Greeting:

Whereas *Brittain Honeycutt of Union Parish Louisiana*

has deposited in the GENERAL LAND OFFICE of the United States, a Certificate of the REGISTER OF THE LAND OFFICE at *Monroe* whereby it appears that full payment has been made by the said

Brittain Honeycutt according to the provisions of the Act of Congress of the 24th of April, 1820, entitled "An act making further provision for the sale of the Public Lands," for *the Lot on the South half of the South East quarter of the South West quarter of the South West quarter of Section Thirty Two in Township Twenty Three North of Range One East in the district of lands subject to sale at Monroe Louisiana Containing One Hundred and Twenty Acres and Thirty Seven hundredths of an Acre*

according to the official plat of the Survey of the said Lands, returned to the General Land Office by the SURVEYOR GENERAL, which said tract has been purchased by the said *Brittian Honeycutt*

NOW KNOW YE, That the **United States of America**, in consideration of the premises, and in conformity with the several acts of Congress in such case made and provided, HAVE GIVEN AND GRANTED, and by these presents DO GIVE AND GRANT, unto the said *Brittian Honeycutt*

and to *his* heirs, the said tract above described: To have and to hold the same, together with all the rights, privileges, immunities, and appurtenances, of whatsoever nature, thereunto belonging, unto the said *Brittian Honeycutt*

and to *his* heirs and assigns forever.

In testimony Whereof, I, *Abraham Lincoln* PRESIDENT OF THE UNITED STATES OF AMERICA, have caused these letters to be made PATENT, and the SEAL of the GENERAL LAND OFFICE to be hereunto affixed.

GIVEN under my hand, at the CITY OF WASHINGTON, the *Fifteenth* day of *May* in the year of our Lord one thousand eight hundred and *Sixty two* and of the INDEPENDENCE OF THE UNITED STATES the *Eighty Sixth*

BY THE PRESIDENT: *Abraham Lincoln*

By *W O Stoddard* Secretary.

J A Granger Recorder of the General Land Office.

Britton Honeycutt – Land Patent 1852

THE UNITED STATES OF AMERICA,

CERTIFICATE
No. *11101*

To all to whom these Presents shall come, Greeting:

WHEREAS *Britten Honeycutt of Union Parish, Louisiana,*

has deposited in the GENERAL LAND OFFICE of the United States, a Certificate of the REGISTER OF THE LAND OFFICE at *Monroe,* whereby it appears that full payment has been made by the said *Britten Honeycutt,*

according to the provisions of the Act of Congress of the 24th of April, 1820 entitled "An act making further provision for the sale of the Public Lands," for *the South East quarter of the North East quarter, of section twenty eight, in Township twenty two, North, of Range one, East, in the District of Lands subject to sale at Monroe, Louisiana, containing thirty nine acres, and ninety five hundredths of an acre,*

according to the official plat of the survey of the said Lands, returned to the General Land Office by the SURVEYOR GENERAL, which said tract ha s been purchased by the said *Britten Honeycutt,*

NOW KNOW YE, *That the* **United States of America,** in consideration of the Premises, and in conformity with the several acts of Congress; in such case made and provided, HAVE GIVEN AND GRANTED, and by these presents DO GIVE AND GRANT, unto the said *Britten Honeycutt,*

and to *his* heirs, the said tract above described : TO HAVE AND TO HOLD the same, together with all the rights, privileges, immunities, and appurtenances of whatsoever nature, thereunto belonging, unto the said *Britten Honeycutt,* and to *his* heirs and assigns forever.

In Testimony Whereof, I, *Millard Fillmore* PRESIDENT OF THE UNITED STATES OF AMERICA, have caused these Letters to be made PATENT, and the SEAL of the GENERAL LAND OFFICE to be hereunto affixed.

Given under my hand, at the **CITY OF WASHINGTON,** the *first* day of *September* in the Year of our Lord one thousand eight hundred and *fifty two* and of the Independence of the United States the Seventy *seventh*

BY THE PRESIDENT: *Millard Fillmore*

By *Alex. McCormick* a/s Sec'y.

E. S. Terry RECORDER of the General Land Office.

Dennis Andrews – Land Patent 1913

Baton Rouge 01805

4—1000-R.

The United States of America,

To all to whom these presents shall come, Greeting:

WHEREAS, a Certificate of the Register of the Land Office at **Baton Rouge, Louisiana,** has been deposited in the General Land Office, whereby it appears that, pursuant to the Act of Congress of May 20, 1862, "To Secure Homesteads to Actual Settlers on the Public Domain," and the acts supplemental thereto, the claim of

Dennis Andrews

has been established and duly consummated, in conformity to law, for the **southwest quarter of the southwest quarter of Section thirty-three in Township twenty-three north of Range one east of the Louisiana Meridian, Louisiana, containing forty and twenty-one-hundredths acres,**

according to the Official Plat of the Survey of the said Land, returned to the GENERAL LAND OFFICE by the Surveyor-General:

NOW KNOW YE, That there is, therefore, granted by the UNITED STATES unto the said claimant the tract of Land above described; TO HAVE AND TO HOLD the said tract of Land, with the appurtenances thereof, unto the said claimant and to the heirs and assigns of the said claimant forever.

IN TESTIMONY WHEREOF, I, **Woodrow Wilson**

President of the United States of America, have caused these letters to be made Patent, and the seal of the General Land Office to be hereunto affixed.

GIVEN under my hand, at the City of Washington, the **TWENTY-SIXTH**

(SEAL)

day of **MAY** in the year of our Lord one thousand nine hundred and **THIRTEEN** and of the Independence of the United States the one hundred and **THIRTY-SEVENTH.**

By the President: *Woodrow Wilson*

By *M. P. LeRoy* Secretary,

John O'Connell
Acting Recorder of the General Land Office.

RECORD OF PATENTS: Patent Number **337344**

6—2116

221

John Honeycutt, Sr. – Land Patent 1837

`156`

THE UNITED STATES OF AMERICA.

CERTIFICATE
No. 2897

To all to whom these Presents shall come, Greeting:

WHEREAS *John Honeycutt Senior, of Ouachita, Louisiana,*

ha *s* deposited in the **GENERAL LAND OFFICE** of the United States, a Certificate of the REGISTER OF THE LAND

OFFICE at *Ouachita*   whereby it appears that full payment has been made by the said

John Honeycutt, Senior,

                                                  according to the provisions of

the Act of Congress of the 24th of April, 1820, entitled "An Act making further provision for the sale of the Public Lands," for

the East half of the South East quarter, of Section twenty eight, in Township twenty two, of Range one East, in the District of lands subject to sale at Ouachita, Louisiana, containing seventy nine acres, and ninety hundredths of an acre,

according to the official plat of the survey of the said Lands, returned to the General Land Office by the **SURVEYOR GENERAL**, which said tract   has   been purchased by the said *John Honeycutt, Senior,*

                              NOW KNOW YE, That the

United States of America, in consideration of the Premises, and in conformity with the several acts of Congress, in such case made and provided, HAVE GIVEN AND GRANTED, and by these presents DO GIVE AND GRANT, unto the said *John Honeycutt, Senior,*

and to *his* heirs, the said tract above described: **TO HAVE AND TO HOLD** the same, together with all the rights, privileges, immunities, and appurtenances of whatsoever nature, thereunto belonging, unto the said *John Honeycutt, Senior,*

                              and to *his* heirs and assigns forever.

In Testimony Whereof, I, *Martin Van Buren*

PRESIDENT OF THE UNITED STATES OF AMERICA, have caused these Letters to be made PATENT, and the SEAL of the GENERAL LAND OFFICE to be hereunto affixed.

GIVEN under my hand, at the CITY OF WASHINGTON, the *twentieth* day of *June* in the Year of our Lord one thousand eight hundred and *thirty seven* and of the INDEPENDENCE OF THE UNITED STATES the *sixty first*

[L.S.]

BY THE PRESIDENT: *Martin Van Buren*

              By *A Van Buren* Sec'y.

Hudson M Garland RECORDER of the General Land Office.

222

Lawrence Bilberry – Land Patent 1913

Baton Rouge 02594

4—1000-R.

The United States of America,

To all to whom these presents shall come, Greeting:

WHEREAS, a Certificate of the Register of the Land Office at **Baton Rouge, Louisiana,** has been deposited in the General Land Office, whereby it appears that, pursuant to the Act of Congress of May 20, 1862, "To Secure Homesteads to Actual Settlers on the Public Domain," and the acts supplemental thereto, the claim of **Lawrence Billberry** has been established and duly consummated, in conformity to law, for the **northeast quarter of the southwest quarter of Section thirty-three in Township twenty-three north of Range one east of the Louisiana Meridian, Louisiana, containing forty and twenty-one-hundredths acres,**

according to the Official Plat of the Survey of the said Land, returned to the GENERAL LAND OFFICE by the Surveyor-General:

NOW KNOW YE, That there is, therefore, granted by the UNITED STATES unto the said claimant the tract of Land above described; TO HAVE AND TO HOLD the said tract of Land, with the appurtenances thereof, unto the said claimant and to the heirs and assigns of the said claimant forever.

IN TESTIMONY WHEREOF, I, **Woodrow Wilson** President of the United States of America, have caused these letters to be made Patent, and the seal of the General Land Office to be hereunto affixed.

GIVEN under my hand, at the City of Washington, the **TWENTY-SIXTH**

(SEAL)

day of **MAY** in the year of our Lord one thousand nine hundred and **THIRTEEN** and of the Independence of the United States the one hundred and **THIRTY-SEVENTH.**

By the President: *Woodrow Wilson*

By *M. P. LeRoy* Secretary,

John O'Connell Acting Recorder of the General Land Office.

RECORD OF PATENTS: Patent Number **337346**
6—2115

223

Samuel Morgan – Land Patent 1892

288

The United States of America,

TO ALL TO WHOM THESE PRESENTS SHALL COME, GREETING:

Homestead Certificate No. 3536

Application 8530

Whereas there has been deposited in the GENERAL LAND OFFICE of the United States a CERTIFICATE of the Register of the Land Office at *New Orleans Louisiana*, whereby it appears that, pursuant to the Act of Congress approved 20th May, 1862, "To secure Homesteads to actual settlers on the public domain," and the acts supplemental thereto, the claim of *Samuel Morgan* has been established and duly consummated in conformity to law for the *North East quarter of the North East quarter of Section twenty-eight in Township twenty-two North of Range one East of Louisiana Meridian in Louisiana containing containing thirty-nine acres and ninety-five hundredths of an acre*

according to the Official Plat of the Survey of the said Land returned to the GENERAL LAND OFFICE by the SURVEYOR GENERAL.

Now know ye, That there is therefore granted by the UNITED STATES unto the said *Samuel Morgan* the tract of Land above described: TO HAVE AND TO HOLD the said tract of Land, with the appurtenances thereof, unto the said *Samuel Morgan* and to *his* heirs and assigns forever.

In testimony whereof I, *Benjamin Harrison* President of the United States of America, have caused these letters to be made Patent, and the Seal of the General Land Office to be hereunto affixed.

Given under my hand, at the City of Washington, the *first* day of *March*, in the year of Our Lord one thousand eight hundred and *ninety-two*, and of the Independence of the United States the one hundred and *sixteenth.*

By the President: *Benjamin Harrison*

By *M. McKean* Sec'y.

J. R. Conwell Recorder of the General Land Office.

Ad interim.

[L.S.]

Sandy Wayne, Jr. – Land Patent 1908

(RECORD OF PATENTS.)

4-404-tyr.

The United States of America,

To all to whom these presents shall come, Greeting:

Homestead Certificate No. **13482.**

Application **25430.**

           WHEREAS, There has been deposited in the GENERAL LAND OFFICE of the United States a Certificate of the Register of the Land Office at **New Orleans, Louisiana,** whereby it appears that, pursuant to the Act of Congress approved 20th May, 1862, "To secure Homesteads to Actual Settlers on the Public Domain," and the acts supplemental thereto, the claim of **SANDY WAYNE, Junier,**
has been established and duly consummated, in conformity to law, for the east half of the southwest quarter of Section six in Township twenty-two north of Range two east of the Louisiana Meridian, Louisiana, containing eighty and twelve-hundredths acres,

           according to the Official Plat of the Survey of the said Land, returned to the GENERAL LAND OFFICE by the Surveyor General:

           NOW KNOW YE, That there is, therefore, granted by the UNITED STATES unto the said **Sandy Wayne, Junier,**
the tract of Land above described; TO HAVE AND TO HOLD the said tract of Land, with the appurtenances thereof, unto the said **Sandy Wayne, Junier,**

and to **his** heirs and assigns forever.

           IN TESTIMONY WHEREOF, I, **Theodore Roosevelt** , President of the United States of America, have caused these letters to be made Patent, and the seal of the General Land Office to be hereunto affixed.

(SEAL)   GIVEN under my hand, at the City of Washington, the _____twenty-ninth_____ day of ___October___, in the year of our Lord one thousand nine hundred and ___eight___, and of the Independence of the United States the one hundred and ___thirty-third.___

         By the President: *Theodore Roosevelt.*

         By _____, Secretary.

         Recorder of the General Land Office.

Charles Lee Bilberry

Sandy Wayne, Sr. – Land Patent 1902

The United States of America,

To all to whom these Presents shall come, Greeting:

Homestead Certificate No. 8879
Application 14031

Whereas, There has been deposited in the General Land Office of the United States a Certificate of the Register of the Land Office at *New Orleans Louisiana*, whereby it appears that, pursuant to the Act of Congress approved 20th May, 1862, "To secure Homesteads to actual Settlers on the Public Domain," and the acts supplemental thereto, the claim of *Sandy Wayne* has been established and duly consummated, in conformity to law, for the *East half of the South West quarter and the West half of the South East quarter of Section thirty-two in Township twenty-three North of Range two East of Louisiana Meridian in Louisiana, containing one hundred and sixty acres and twenty hundredths of an acre*

according to the Official Plat of the Survey of the said Land, returned to the General Land Office by the Surveyor General.

Now know ye that there is, therefore, granted by the United States unto the said *Sandy Wayne* the tract of Land above described: TO HAVE AND TO HOLD the said tract of Land with the appurtenances thereof, unto the said *Sandy Wayne* and to *his* heirs and assigns forever; and there is reserved from the lands hereby granted, a right of way thereon for ditches or canals constructed by the authority of the United States.

In testimony whereof, I *Theodore Roosevelt*, PRESIDENT OF THE UNITED STATES OF AMERICA, have caused these letters to be made Patent, and the Seal of the General Land Office to be hereunto affixed.

[SEAL]

Given under my hand, at the City of Washington, the *twelfth* day of *February*, in the year of our Lord one thousand *nine* hundred and *two*, and of the Independence of the United States the one hundred and *twenty sixth*.

By the President, *T. Roosevelt*
By *F. M. McKean*, Secretary.
C. N. Bruce, Recorder of the General Land Office.

Appendix D

Family Obituary Collection

These are seemingly simple, but valuable records, which contain a surprising amount of information about family members. They are the final report on the life of those who have found their final resting place.

ANNOUCEMENTS OF FINAL INTERMENT	
NAMES	**DATES OF LIFE AND DEATH**
Adell Bilberry	March 14, 1927—April 28,1997
Barbara Neal Bilberry	October 23, 1934—July 19, 2009
Bessie Benson	May 19,1893—October 30, 1990
Carl Burch	June 1912—1982/Services on November 6, 1982
Charlie (Bud) Bilberry, Sr.	March 25, 1907—November 5, 1979
Corene McGough- Bilberry	November 17, 1915—October 31, 1984
Edd Bilberry	February 12, 1912—July 25, 1985
Eddie Bilberry, Sr.	March 20, 1913—March 31, 1997
Elder Ladell Bilberry, Sr.	August 4, 1902—November 3, 1970
Ella Holland-Lowe	September 29, 1905—June 15, 2000
Emma Bilberry	August 26, 1882—September 12, 1972
Etta Nelson	August 19, 1879—December 22, 1962
Flossie Mae Holland-Jones	July 22, 1922—April 24 or 26, 2001
Gordie Bilberry-Burch	October 12, 1893—July 30, 1983
Jacob Garret (J. G.) Bilberry	Died in camp near Alexandria – April 2, 1863
Jessie Bernard Bilberry, Sr. (Reverend)	July 20, 1904—February 24, 1961
Jewel L. Bilberry	March 12, 1902—November 29, 1981
Joe B. Dixon-Bilberry	November 25, 1906—June 25, 1989
John Davis Holland	December 20, 1925—April 28, 1990

Lou Emma Holland-Furlough-Glossom	October 9, 1915—May 1, 1982
Luemmer Horn	December 5, 1924—March 16, 1989
Mary Evylene Arbertha Thurmond	November 22, 1916—October 31, 2003
Odessa Elliott-Burch	August 12, 1917—January 29, 1990
Sarah Alabama Montgomery-Ellis	March 15, 1911—July 1986

Adell Bilberry's Obituary, son of Ladell Bilberry (exterior cover)

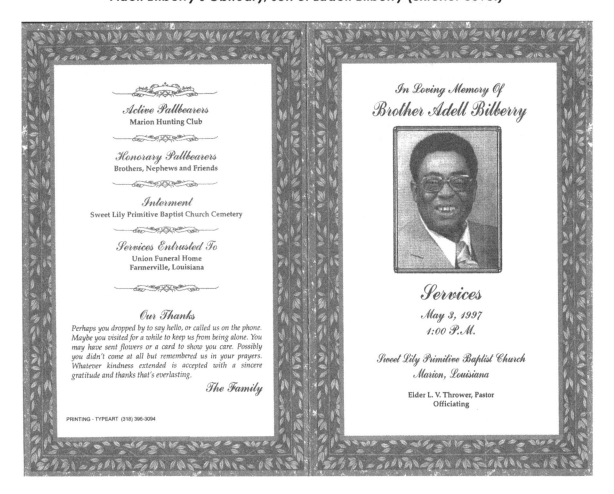

Active Pallbearers
Marion Hunting Club

Honorary Pallbearers
Brothers, Nephews and Friends

Interment
Sweet Lily Primitive Baptist Church Cemetery

Services Entrusted To
Union Funeral Home
Farmerville, Louisiana

Our Thanks
Perhaps you dropped by to say hello, or called us on the phone. Maybe you visited for a while to keep us from being alone. You may have sent flowers or a card to show you care. Possibly you didn't come at all but remembered us in your prayers. Whatever kindness extended is accepted with a sincere gratitude and thanks that's everlasting.

The Family

PRINTING - TYPEART (318) 396-3094

In Loving Memory Of
Brother Adell Bilberry

Services
May 3, 1997
1:00 P.M.

Sweet Lily Primitive Baptist Church
Marion, Louisiana

Elder L. V. Thrower, Pastor
Officiating

Adell Bilberry's Obituary, son of Ladell Bilberry (interior cover)

Obituary
of
Brother Adell Bilberry

March 14, 1927　　　　April 28, 1997
Sunrise　　　　　　　　Sunset

On Monday morning, April 28, 1997, God called Brother Adell Bilberry to His heavenly home. . . a home not made with hands.

Brother Adell Bilberry was born to the late Ladell Bilberry, Sr. and Sister Maggie Washington Bilberry on March 14, 1927.

Brother Adell Bilberry united with Sweet Lily Primitive Baptist Church at an early age and was a faithful member until the clarion call of God called him home.

He is survived by his wife, Mrs. Barbara Bilberry; three children: Peggy Travis and Mr. Charles Bilberry of Las Vegas, Nevada; Mrs. Fonda Deleon of San Celemente, California; grandson Jared Bilberry; five brothers: Mr. Johnny Bilberry of Farmerville, Louisiana; Mr. Clarence Bilberry, Kansas City Missouri; Mr. Herbert Bilberry and Mr. Ladell Bilberry of Kansas City, Kansas; Mr. Richard Bilberry of Topeka, Kansas; four sisters: Miss Loreace Watley, Mrs. Loeace Walker, Miss Emma Payne of Kansas City, Kansas; Mrs. Clara Jones of Kansas City, Missouri; one uncle, Elder Jethro Horn of Farmerville, Louisiana; and a host of nieces, nephews, relatives and friends.

Order of Service

Processional

Song...*Amazing Grace*

Scripture ....Brother Ladell Bilberry, Jr.

Prayer.......................Brother Ladell Bilberry, Jr.

Words of Comfort........Rev. Jesse B. Bilberry, Pastor
Mount Pilgrim Baptist Church
Baton Rouge, Louisiana

As A Father....................Rev. Charles L. Bilberry
Associate Minister
Greater New Jerusalem
Missionary Baptist Church
Las Vegas, Nevada

Acknowledgements ....Sister Barbara Nell Gatson

Obituary (Read Silently)

Solo.................................Sister Maxine McGaskey

Eulogy...................................Elder L. V. Thrower

Parting View

Recessional

Usher Service.................Zion Watts Baptist Church
Center Branch Baptist Church
and Others

The Family will receive guests at the
Fellowship Hall following the interment.

Barbara Neal Bilberry's Obituary (exterior cover)

In Loving Memory

of

Barbara Neal Bilberry

Sunrise
October 23, 1934

Sunset
July 19, 2009

Celebration Services Held At:

Palm Mortuary Northwest
6701 North Jones Blvd.
Las Vegas, NV 89131

Friday, July 24, 2009
11:00 a.m.

Bishop James M. Rogers, Sr.
Greater New Jerusalem Missionary Baptist Church
Officiating

Barbara Neal Bilberry's Obituary (interior cover)

Obituary

Mrs. Barbara N. Bilberry was born on October 23, 1934 between the union of Charlie Brown and Willie Mae Brown in Farmerville, Louisiana. Both parents and four brothers preceded her in death. Barbara accepted Christ at an early age by uniting with the Millard Hill Baptist Church in Farmerville, Louisiana. She later united with the Sweet Lily Primitive Baptist Church. Barbara moved to Las Vegas, Nevada in 1997 where she united with the Greater New Jerusalem Missionary Baptist Church. She worked as a nursing assistant for eleven years.

Barbara was united in marriage to Adell Bilberry for forty-six years. Her husband preceded her in death. She leaves to cherish her memories; daughters, Peggie Joyce Travis (husband Melvin) of Las Vegas and Fonda Deleon (husband Shano) of Montecito, California; son, Charles Lee Bilberry (wife Taryn) and grandson, Jared Bilberry of Las Vegas. She also leaves a host of cousins and friends.

Barbara was a woman that was loved by all.
She will be missed by many.

Order of Service

Musical Prelude

Processional

Selection..Winds Beneath My Wings
By Organist

Scripture Reading:

Old Testament..Elder Robert Patterson

New Testament...Elder Bessie Evans

Prayer...Minister Annie Ferrell

Tributes:

As A Friend.. Louise Perry

As a Mother..Peggie J. Travis

As A Mother...Dr. Charles L. Bilberry

Expressions (2 minutes please)

Obituary...Read Silent/Soft Music

Memorial Tribute Video...................................... Palm Mortuary

Solo...Sharon Smith

Eulogy...Bishop James M. Rogers, Sr.
Greater New Jerusalem
Missionary Baptist Church

Final Viewing...Palm Mortuary in Charge

Recessional

Usher Service...Greater New Jerusalem
Missionary Baptist Church

* Repast will be at Palm Mortuary in the hospitality room.

Bessie Benson's Obituary, mother of Georgia Willie Mae Bilberry (exterior cover)

ACTIVE PALLBEARERS
(Grandson & Great Grandson)

Woodie Benson Sr.   James E. Henderson Sr.
Cardell Benson   Donald Bilberry
James E. Henderson, Jr.   Alphonso D. Henderson

HONORARY PALLBEARERS

Robert Benson   Eddie Wayne Bilberry
Jerry Clark   Hersey Lamont Ross
Dewayne Henderson   Willie J. Benson

FLOWER BEARERS

Granddaughters & Nieces

INTERMENT

Sweet Lily Primitive Baptist
Marion, La.

Under the direction of
Union Funeral Home

Acknowledgement

The family of Sister Bessie Benson wishes to thank you for your many acts of kindness during our hour of bereavement.

Thank you,

In Loving Memory

of

Sister Bessie H. Benson

Saturday, November 3, 1990
1:00 P.M.

Sweet Lily Primitive Baptist Church
Marion, Louisiana

Elder L.V. Thrower, Pastor

Bessie Benson's Obituary, mother of Georgia Willie Mae Bilberry (interior cover)

1893   1990

Let not your heart be troubled; you believe also in me.
In my father's house are many mansions,
If it were not so, I would have told you,
I go to prepare a place for you.

On Oct. 30, 1990, the death angel came to the bed of sister Bessie and bore the spirit of sister Bessie away to a land that is free from pain and sorrow. Her journey here was long and hard. Rest now Sister Bessie for the battle has been fought and the victory won.

Sister Bessie was born May 19, 1893. One of seven children born to the late Willis Henderson and Tilda Raburn Henderson. With love for God and Jesus Christ, she was baptized, and remained a member of the Sweet Lily Primitive Baptist Church until her death.

Sister Bessie was married to the late brother Robert Benson and to this union six children were born. 3 sons- Woodie, Francis, and Jack Benson and 1 daughter- Robbie Benson preceeded her in death.

Sister Bessie leaves to mourn her passing, 2 loving and devoted daughters; Mrs. Willie Mae Bilberry, Monroe, La. and Mrs. Madie Davis of Marion, La.; a loving and devoted daughter-in-law Mrs. Morean Benson of Marion, La.; one sister-in-law Rebecca Finley of Farmerville, La., and one son-in-law Eddie Bilberry of Monroe, La. She also leaves to mourn 19 grandchildren (5 preceeded her in death); 32 great grandchildren (5 preceeded her in death); 3 great great grandchildren and a host of nieces, nephews, cousins, friends and other relatives.

We commended the family to the love and compassion of our kind heavenly father.

Wait on the Lord, be of good courage and he shall strengthen thine heart.   Psalm 27:14

"When I must leave you"

When I must leave you for a little while
Please do not grieve and shed wild tears
And hug your sorrow to you through the years,
But start out bravely with a gallant smile;
And for my sake, and in my name
Live on and do all things the same
Feed not your loneliness on empty days,
But fill each waking hour in useful ways.
Reach out your hand in comfort and in cheer
And I in turn will comfort you, and hold you near
And never, never be afraid to die
For I am waiting for you in the sky.

ORDER OF SERVICE

Processional

Hymn ....

Scriptures

Old and New Testament ....Rev. Jesse Charles

Prayer .... Rev. Willie Mack

Solo .... Bro. James Henderson, Jr.

Expression

As a Christian.................... Deacon George Tate

As a neighbor.................... Bro. Lorenza Burch

Acknowledgement .... Sis Magree Bold

Celebration of life ....Obituary ... Sis. Joan Radford

Solo ....Sis. Shirley Tate

Eulogy........................... Elder L.V. Thrower

Viewing the remains

Mistress of Ceremony .... Sis. Magree Bolds

Carl Burch's Obituary, son of Angeline Bilberry-Douglas (exterior cover)

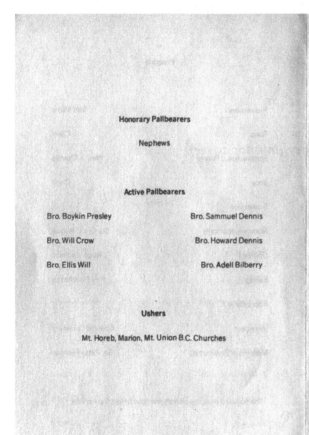

Honorary Pallbearers

Nephews

Active Pallbearers

Bro. Boykin Presley   Bro. Sammuel Dennis

Bro. Will Crow   Bro. Howard Dennis

Bro. Ellis Will   Bro. Adell Bilberry

Ushers

Mt. Horeb, Marion, Mt. Union B.C. Churches

1912   1982

Funeral Service

of

Brother Carl Burch

to be held at the

Mt. Horeb Baptist Church

Marion, La.

**Saturday,
November 6, 1982
2:00 P.M.**

Rev. Jessie Charles, Pastor

Carl Burch's Obituary, son of Angeline Bilberry-Douglas

Carl Burch's Obituary (interior cover)

Obituary

Brother Carl Burch was born June 1912 to the late Bro. Tommie Burch and Sister Angeline Douglas.

He accepted Christ at an early age at the Centerbranch B.C.

He leaves to mourn his passing three daughters, Edwiner Sondue, Robie Riley, Oakland, Calif., and Shirley Dennis, Monroe; three sons, T.L. Burch, Oakland, Calif., Huey Lee and Chester Burch of Washington, D.C.; three brothers, Ezell Burch, Grady Douglas and J.D. Douglas, all of Marion; four sisters, Georgia Ann Page, Annie Ree Maine, Elisa Cooper, all of Farmerville, and Dorthy Douglas of Marion; eighteen grandchildren, eight great-grandchildren; and a host of relatives and friends.

Program

Processional	Soft Music
Song	Choir
Scripture and Prayer	Rev. J. Charles
Song	Choir
Expression	
Acknowledgements	Sis. Ora L. Wayne
Obituary	Read in silence
Eulogy	Rev. H. Johnson
Recessional	
Interment	Concord Cemetery
Mistress of Ceremonies	Sis. Patsy Pearson

The body will be in the church one hour before the service.

Charlie (Bud) Bilberry, Sr.'s Obituary; Husband of Dellie Dixson-Bilberry Obituary (exterior cover)
Correction: Obituary Birth Year is 1907

Pallbearers, Honorary Pallbearers and Custodian of Flowers

THE USHER BOARD
OF
CANAAN BAPTIST CHURCH

———

Interment

LOVEDALE CEMETERY
5175 E. Bristol Road, Flint, Michigan

———

Services By
GREENE HOME FOR FUNERALS
2210 Detroit Street, Flint, Michigan
Phone CE 2-7469

In Memoriam of

Brother Charlie Bilberry, Sr.
Born March 25, 1927 - Expired Nov. 5, 1979

Services Held

11:00 A.M. Saturday, November 10, 1979

Canaan Baptist Church
910 E. Gillespie Street, Flint, Michigan

Reverend William Duncan, Officiating

**Charlie (Bud) Bilberry, Sr.'s; Husband of Dellie Dixson-Bilberry Obituary
(interior cover)**

Psalms 84:10

"For a day in thy courts is better than a thousand. I had rather be a doorkeeper in the house of my God than to dwell in the tents of wickedness."

Memorial Services

Processional .... Prelude
Selection .... Mass Choir
Scripture .... Rev. Alfred Robbs
Prayer .... Rev. H. B. Dixon
Selection .... Mass Choir
Remarks: (3 minutes each)
   Brother A. J. Gray
   Trustee Eddie Collins
Solo .... Sis. Mariah Brooks
Acknowledgments, Resolutions
  and the
   Obituary .... Sis. Mary Richardson
Selection .... Mass Choir
Eulogy .... Rev. William Duncan
     Pastor, Canaan Baptist Church
Recessional .... Postlude

Corene McGough-Bilberry's Obituary, wife of Ladell Bilberry, Sr. (exterior cover)

ACKNOWLEDGEMENT

It is such a comfort to know that in dire times of need we have loyal friend who share our concern. We say "Thank You."

—The Family

PALLBEARERS

Seab Horn, Jr.	Herbert Billberry, Jr.
Jethro Horn	Eddie Horn
Charles Davis, Jr.	Frankie Horn

HONORARY PALLBEARERS

Adelle Billberry	Herbert Billberry
Johnny Billberry	LaDille Billberry, Jr.
Clarence Billberry	Richard Billberry

A Service of Mrs. J. W. Jones Memorial Chapel
Kansas City, Kansas

A Service of Union Parrish Funeral Home
Farmerville, Louisiana

In Loving Memory of

CORENE BILLBERRY

SUNDAY, NOVEMBER 4, 1984 — 2:00 P.M.

SWEET LILY PRIMITIVE BAPTIST CHURCH
Marion, Louisiana

Officiating
ELDER LAVELL THROW

Interment
SWEET LILY CEMETERY
Marion, Louisiana

Corene McGough-Bilberry's Obituary, wife of Ladell Bilberry, Sr. (interior cover)

OBITUARY

Servant of God well done;
 Rest from thy loved employ;
The battle fought, the victory won;
 Enter thy Master's joy.

The pains of death are past;
 Labor and sorrow cease;
And life's long warfare closed at last;
 Her soul is found in peace.

Mother Corene Billberry was born in Truxno, Louisiana, on November 17, 1915, to the late George and Cornelius McGough. She departed October 31, 1984, at the age of 68.

She wsa married to the late Elder LaDelle Billberry, Sr., in 1936. To this union ten children were born. Two preceded her in death.

Mother Billberry joined Sweet Lily Primitive Baptist Church after she married, where she was a faithful member. She later moved to Kansas City, Kansas, and joined the Zion Travelers Missionary Baptist Church. She was a faithful member. Mother Billberry was a Sunday School teacher, member of Mother Board and sang in the choir.

Surviving are seven sons: Clarence Billberry, K.S., Mo.; Herbert Billberry and LaDelle Billberry, Jr., K.C., Kansas; Adell Billberry and Clyde Billberry, Marion, La.; and Johnny Billberry and Richard Billberry, Farmerville, La.; five daughters: Mrs. LoEast Watkins, Ms. Loreace Watley and Mrs. Emma Payne, all of K.C., Kansas; Mrs. Clare Davis Nabors, Houston, Texas, and Mrs. Lou Emma Horn, Provencal, La.; 66 grandchildren; 56 great-grandchildren; one great-great-granddaughter; one sister: Mrs. Thelma Warren of Farmerville, La.; one brother-in-law: Mr. Eddie Billberry, Monroe, La.; and a host of nieces, nephews, other relatives and friends.

THE SERVICE

PROCESSIONAL

SCRIPTURE .... Minister

PRAYER

SONG

ACKNOWLEDGEMENTS
AND CONDOLENCES

SONG

REMARKS

OBITUARY .... Read Silently

EULOGY

RECESSIONAL

———— •••• ————

"Christianity does not exempt one from death; it only insures triumph over death. Moses died, Paul died, and all must die. There is no other way of entrance into our heavenly Father's house. Soon all will be over with all that are here. There is not far from us that hidden certainty of death. There are some of us within a hands-breath of the grave and yet it is not apparent to those around us, because we were shocked when we heard that Mother Billberry had passed away. Although we knew Mother Bilberry was not well, determination kept her real condition hidden from us; but our Lord knew and in His own time relieved Mother Billberry of all her earthly woes."

Edd Bilberry, Sr.'s Obituary (exterior cover)

PALLBEARERS

Edd Bilberry, Jr.

Paul Bilberry

George Bilberry

Willis Andrews

Eddie Butler

David Goldsby

Donald Kendrix

Jessie B. Andrews

IN LOVING MEMORY

of

BRO. EDD BILBERRY, SR.

Services at

ANTIOCH A.M.E. CHURCH
TRUXNO, LOUISIANA

WEDNESDAY, JULY 31, 1985

11 A. M.

REV. C. L. TRAYLOR, OFFICIATING

REV. M. H. HILL, PASTOR

Charles Lee Bilberry

Edd Bilberry, Sr.'s Obituary (interior cover)

OBITUARY

The Lord is my light and my salvation;
whom shall I fear? The Lord is the
strength of my life; of whom shall I
be afraid?
                    --Psalms 27:1

Bro. Edd Bilberry, Sr. was born February 12, 1912, in Truxno, Louisiana. He was the son of Lawrence Bilberry and Lue Kilgore Bilberry. He departed this life Thursday, July 25, 1985.

He united with Antioch A. M. E. Church and remained a member until death.

He was united in holy matrimony to Mae Bell Warren on August 11, 1945. To this union, five children were born, three preceded him in death.

Survivors include: Mae Bell Bilberry, wife; one daughter, Billie Tinsley; one son, Edd Bilberry, Jr.; one stepson, Jessie B. Andrews; two sisters, Dorsey McElroy and Willie Mae Wayne; two brothers, Paul Bilberry and George Bilberry; one grandson, John E. Tinsley, II; two granddaughters, Katrina & Katicia Bilberry and other relatives and friends.

PROGRAM

Processional

Song

Scripture   Rev. C. L. Traylor

Prayer

Acknowledgements & Condolences
                              Sis. Mary Morgan

Obituary   Sis. Mary Morgan

Song

Eulogy   Rev. C. L. Traylor

Recessional

Eddie Bilberry, Sr.'s Obituary, husband of Georgia Willie Mae Bilberry (exterior cover)

IN LOVING MEMORY

OF

BROTHER EDDIE BILBERRY, SR.

Saturday, April 5, 1997
1:00 p.m.

Mount Olivet Baptist Church
500 Swayze Street
Monroe, Louisiana 71201

Rev. Oliver W. Billups, Jr.
Officiating

Eddie Bilberry, Sr.'s Obituary, husband of Georgia Willie Mae Bilberry (interior cover)

Let not your heart be troubled: ye believe in God, believe also in me.   John 14:1

OBITUARY

Brother Eddie Bilberry, Sr. departed this life on March 31, 1997, 4:30 a.m.- St. Francis Medical Center. He was born March 20, 1913 in Marion LA., to the late Frank and Emma Bilberry.

He was an honorable discharged Veteran of World War II.

Brother Bilberry confessed Christ at an early age uniting with the Sweet Lily Baptist Church, Marion, LA. He later united with the Mount Olivet B. C. of Monroe, LA. on April 25, 1986.

He was employed at the Holiday Inn and retired from the same.

He leaves to cherish his memory, his devoted wife of fifty two (52) years, Mrs. Willie Mae Bilberry. Four children were born to this union: one daughter: Eddye L. Washington (William) Saginaw, MI; Three sons: John W. Bilberry (Sherrell) Norfolk,VA, Eddie W. Bilberry, Jr., and Donald R. Bilberry, Monroe, LA. Seven grandchildren and two great-grandchildren. He was preceded in death by one sister, four brothers and one grandson.

ORDER OF SERVICE

Processional................................"Jesu, Joy of Man's Desiring"
(J. S. Bach)

Selection..Choir

Scriptures.......Old and New Testament-Rev. James E. Jackson
Pastor, Pleasant Green B. C.

Lord's Prayer..Sis. Barbara Taylor

Selection..Choir

Expressions...Sis. Eunice Washington

Words of Comfort.................................Rev. Jesse B. Bilberry
Pastor, Mount Pilgrim B. C., Baton Rouge, LA

Acknowledgments and Condolences

Obituary.........................Read Silently....................Soft Music

Hymn................................"Father I Stretch My Hands To Thee"

Eulogy..Pastor Oliver W. Billups, Jr.

Parting View

Recessional

Song and Usher Service...Mount Olivet

Elder Ladell Bilberry's Obituary, son of Frank Bilberry (exterior cover)

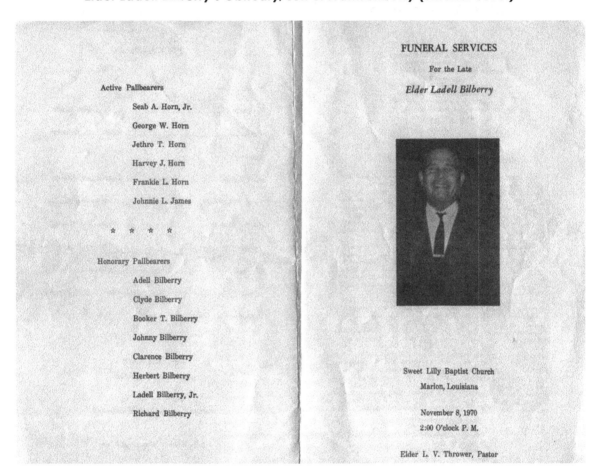

Active Pallbearers

Seab A. Horn, Jr.

George W. Horn

Jethro T. Horn

Harvey J. Horn

Frankie L. Horn

Johnnie L. James

☆   ☆   ☆   ☆

Honorary Pallbearers

Adell Bilberry

Clyde Bilberry

Booker T. Bilberry

Johnny Bilberry

Clarence Bilberry

Herbert Bilberry

Ladell Bilberry, Jr.

Richard Bilberry

FUNERAL SERVICES

For the Late

Elder Ladell Bilberry

Sweet Lilly Baptist Church

Marion, Louisiana

November 8, 1970

2:00 O'clock P. M.

Elder L. V. Thrower, Pastor

**Elder Ladell Bilberry's Obituary, son of Frank Bilberry and
Emma Bilberry (interior cover)
Note: Eddie Thompson is stated in the obituary as the uncle of Ladell Bilberry**

Like a ship that's left its mooring
And sails bravely to sea.
So Someone dear has sailed away
In calm serenity.
But there is promise of greater joy
Than earth could have in store.
For God has planned a richer life
Beyond the unseen shore.

OBITUARY
of
Elder Ladell Bilberry

August 4, 1902 . . . . . . November 3, 1970

☆

On Tuesday evening, Nov. 3, at 5:30 p.m. God called Elder Ladelle Bilberry, Sr. to his Heavenly home, where there's always day and never night; always joy, never sorrow; always howdy and never goodbye. Elder Bilberry was the son of Mr. and Mrs. Frank Bilberry. He was born Aug. 4, 1902. He was married to Miss Maggie Washington in 1922. To this union seven (7) children were born. She preceeded him in death in1936. In 1937, he married Miss Corene McGough. To this union nine (9) children were born.

Elder Bilberry was a hard working man and provided a good living for his family. He strived to live an upright Christian life before his children and to rear them in the fear and admiration of the Lord. He joined Sweet Lilly Baptist Church at an early age. He was called to the ministry in 1936. He pastored Antioch Baptist Church for seventeen (17) years. He also pastored Cross Roads Baptist Church, and New Bethel Baptist Church for a period of years. He leaves his estrange wife. He leaves to morn his mother, Mrs. Emmer Bilberry, five daughters, Mrs. Luemmer B. Horn of Provencal, La.; Mrs. Sarah Lee James of West Monroe, La.; and Mrs. Clara Davis of Kansas City, Kansas. He leaves Mrs. Loeast Richard, Mrs. Loreac Watley, and Miss Emmer Jean Bilberry of Kansas City, Kansas. Eight sons (8) to mourn, Mr. Adelle Bilberry and Mr. Clyde Bilberry of Marion, La.; Mr. Johny Bilberry and Mr. Booker T. Bilberry of Farmerville, La.; Mr. Clarence Bilberry, Mr. Herbert Bilberry and Mr. Richard Bilberry of Kansas City, Kansas; P.F.C. Ladelle Bilberry, Jr., U. S. Army, Ft. Beaux, Ala.; forty-eight (48) grandchildren, ten (10) great-grandchildren, two brothers, Mr. Eddie Bilberry of Monroe, La.; Mr. Charlie Bilberry of Flint, Mich. Five (5) son-in-laws. Seven (7) daughter-in-laws. One uncle, Eddie Thompson, and a host of nieces, nephews, relatives and friends.

Daddy, we will lay you
to rest where the wild
flowers bloom and
the birds sing so
sweetly in the spring.

PROGRAM

Processional—

Scripture .... Rev. Maltel

Prayer .... Elder L. R. Thrower

Hymn—

As A Friend .... Deacon Louis Nabors

As A Friend .... Deacon John Evans

As A Christian .... Deacon J. C. Benson

Acknowledgements .... Mrs. Ora Wayne

Obituary .... Mrs. Odessa Burch

Eulogy .... Rev. L. V. Thrower

Recessional:

Miss Orine Bright
Mistress of Ceremonies

Interment — Sweet Lilly Cemetery

Union Funeral Home in Charge

Ella Holland-Lowe's Obituary (exterior cover)
Daughter of Anna Bilberry-Holland and Mason Holland

Sunrise
September 29, 1905

Sunset
June 15, 2000

I'm Gone Home
Y'all
Sister Ella Lee Holland Lowe
"Granny"

~ Services ~
Saturday, June 24, 2000
11:00 A. M.

Mount Union Missionary Baptist Church
Oakland Highway
Marion, Louisiana
Reverend Freddie Lee Smith, Pastor

Ella Holland-Lowe's Obituary (interior cover)
Daughter of Anna Bilberry-Holland and Mason Holland

OBITUARY

" I have fought a good fight, I have finished my course, I have kept the faith:" II Timothy 4:7. "The Lord is my shepherd; I shall not want." Psalm 23:1. "In my father's house are many mansions: if it were not so, I would have told you. I go to prepare a place for you. And if I go and prepare a place for you, I will come again, and receive you unto myself; that where I am, there ye may be also." John 14:2-3.

These are only a few scriptures that our Grandmother loved and often recited. She loved the Lord and He heard her cry because on June 15, 2000, our Grandmother picked up her cross, put it on her shoulder and went home to be with our Lord and Savior, Jesus Christ.

Sister Ella Lee Holland Lowe was born September 29, 1905 to the late Mason and Anna Bilberry Holland. She confessed Christ at an early age and united with the Saint Paul Baptist Church and later united with Marion Baptist Church. Everyone who loved and knew Sister Lowe called her "Granny".

Granny was united in holy matrimony to the late James "Ranktum" Lowe. To this union were born four daughters: EverLee Lowe Rowland, Mae Etta Lowe Williams, LouBerta Lowe Fields and Geneva Lowe, and one son, Willie Vell Lowe. All preceded her in death. Granny had five brothers: Johnny Holland, Willis Holland, Columbus Holland, James Holland and Floyd Holland; four sisters: Mittie Pearl Holland, Ollie Bell Holland, Lou Emma Furlough Glosson and Lottie Mae James, who also preceded her in death.

Granny leaves to cling to her cherished memories two sisters: Flossie Jones of Monroe, LA and Clara Waters of Toledo, OH, nineteen grandchildren, forty three great grandchildren, twenty great-great grandchildren and a host of nieces, nephews, cousins and friends.

Emma Bilberry's Obituary, Wife of Frank Bilberry exterior cover

ACTIVE PALLBEARERS

Adell Bilberry
Charles Bilberry, Jr.
Jesse B. Bilberry, Jr.
Johnny B. Bilberry
Johnny Bilberry
Ralph W. Bilberry

HONORARY PALLBEARERS

Clyde Bilberry   Joe F. Bilberry
Booker T. Bilberry   Charles L. Bilberry
Clarence Bilberry   Edward L. Bilberry
Herbert Bilberry   Johnny D. Bilberry
Ladell Bilberry, Jr.   Eddie Bilberry
Richard Bilberry   Donald Ray Bilverry

FLOWER BEARERS

Sweet Lillie
Centerbranch Church

USHERS

Centerbranch
Zion Watts
Sweet Lillie

Interment - Sweet Lillie Cemetery

UNION FUNERAL HOME

in Charge

OBSEQUIES

for the late

Mrs. Emma Roberts Bilberry

to be held at
Sweet Lillie Primitive Baptist Church
Marion, Louisiana
September 16, 1972
2:00 P.M.
Elder L. V. Thrower, Pastor

Emma Roberts' Obituary, wife of Frank Bilberry (interior cover)

OBITUARY

The lights are out
In the mansion of clay,
For the curtains are drawn
For the dweller's away.
She silently slipped
O'er the threshold by night
To make her abode
In the city of light.

On Tuesday afternoon, September 12, 1972, God called Sister Emma Roberts Bilberry to her Heavenly home where there's always a day and never night; always joy and never sorrow.

Sister Bilberry was the daughter of Will and Eliza Roberts. She was born August 26, 1882. She grew up to be what all parents hope their daughters to be; kind, thoughtful, always thinking of others and willing to give of herself whenever she was needed.

She joined Sweet Lillie Church and supported the Church to the best of her ability for years.

At this hour of sorrow, we all mourn her passing, but we must all realize that we are born to die, and it is appointed for all.

We all feel so blessed to have had Sister Emma with us for for so long. This is one of the things that will help us to overcome in the lonely months ahead.

During the last few days there has been many recollections of memory of how Sister Emma has helped each one and re-membrances of things she has said and done for years.

She is survived by two children, Charles Bilberry Sr. of Flint, Michigan; Eddie Bilberry of Monroe, Louisiana; Two brothers, Clinton Roberts of Blythe, California and Charlie Roberts of East Chicago, Indiana; 33 grandchildren, 70 great grandchildren and 15 great great grandchildren.

Processional

Song .... "Near the Cross"

Scripture and Prayer .... Elder L. Thrower

Song .... "Amazing Grace"

Expressions:

As A Neighbor .... Sis. Minnie Howard

As A Christian .... Deacon A. Finley
Deacon Louis Nabors

As A Friend .... Deacon J. C. Benson
Deacon John Evans

Obituary

Acknowledgements

Song .... "When I've Walked the Last Mile"
Sis. Betty A. Maine

Funeral Oration .... Elder Dennis McGaskey

Recessional

Mistress of Ceremonies .... Sis. Ora L. Wayne

Etta Nelson's Obituary,
Daughter of Branch Nelson and Hannah Bilberry-Nelson (exterior cover)

THE FUNERAL RITES

To The

SACRED MEMORY OF THE *ceaster wyant*
LATE *mothers sister*

MOTHER ETTA ELLIS

AUGUST 19TH 1879
DEPARTED
THIS LIFE DECEMBER 22, 1962

SERVICES

DECEMBER 30, 1962
2:00 P. M.
BENTON TEMPLE CHURCH OF GOD IN CHRIST AT
622 E. Washington
Stuttgart   Arkansas

HONORED IN LIFE
TRIUMPHANT IN DEATH
BLESSED IN ETERNITY

-o-o-o-o-o-

RELERFORD AND SON FUNERAL HOME IN CHARGE

Etta Nelson's Obituary,
Daughter of Branch Nelson and Hannah Bilberry-Nelson (interior cover)

OBITUARY

Of the late Etta Nelson. She was born in
Conway, State of Louisanna. In the year
of 1879, August 19th to the Parents, of
Mr. and Mrs. Bryant and Hamna Nelson, who
Proceeded her in death.

She confessed Christ at an early age, &
was married to Mr. James C. Ellis, who
Proceeded her in death.

She moved to the State of Arkansas in 1912
and to this union 8 Children were born.

She was united to the Church of God In
Christ in the year of 1948 under the lea-
dership of the late Rev. Thomas Miller
she Served in the Church of God In Christ
at Forrest City Later moved to Compton
Califorinia and Served under the late Rev.
Conley. Later came back to Arkansas and
Served in The Benton Temple Church of God
In Christ where She remained until death.

She departed this Life December 22, 1962

She leaves to Mourn her loss 3 Sons.
 Loyce Ellis Chicago, Ill.
 Refus Ellis, Stuttgart, Arkansas
 Willie Ellis of Compton, California
3 Daughters
 Hannah Hatcher, Brooklyn, New York.
 Carrie Thornton, Monroe, La.
 Judy Dotson, Forrest City, Arkansas.

25 Grandchildren and 23 Great Grandchildren
and a Host of Relatives and friends to mourn
her passing.

PROGRAM

Processional
Invocation .... Eld. J. D. Alexander
Scripture Reading........ Eld. A. B. Holmes
Cong. Song............... Sis. Senra Taylor
Remarks...................Eld. G. H. Gennie
Solo.....................Sis. Ester Pendelton
Resolutions: Churches, Madison Ark. and
                         Forrest City, Ark.
Song by the Chours ....Precious Memories
Remarks:
Condolence and Telegrams:..Sis. Daisy Brown
Solo .... Sis. Fannie Lollis
Eulogy.................... Eld. C. L. Benton

PALLBEARS
HONORARY
    Mrs. Mary Lindsey
    Mrs. Essie M. Offord
    Mrs. Loddia Wafford
    Mrs. Lillian Montegomery
    Mrs. Gustane Griffin

ACTIVE

    Mr. George Johnson
    Mr. B. N. Montgomery
    Mr. Eddie Robberson
    Mr. Foster Stigger
    Mr. L. Higgins

Flossie Mae Holland-Jones' Obituary,
Daughter of Anna Bilberry-Holland and Mason Holland (exterior cover)

HOMEGOING
CELEBRATION OF
Sis. Flossie Mae Jones
SUNRISE   *SUNSET*
7/22/22 ═══ *4/26/01*

Springhill Baptist Church
3517 Church Street
Monroe, La 71203
Pastor, Jimmie Spears
May 4, 2001

Scripture: For we know that if our earthly
house of this tabernacle were dissolved, we
have a building of God, an house not made
with hands, eternal in the heavens.
            2 Corinthians 5:1

Flossie Mae Holland-Jones' Obituary (interior cover)
Daughter of Anna Bilberry-Holland and Mason Holland (interior cover)

OBITUARY

Sis. Flossie Jones was born July 22, 1922, to the late John and Anna Bilberry Holland. She departed this life Thursday, April 24, 2001. She confessed Christ at an early age and later became a member of the Springhill Baptist Church under the leadership of the late Rev. D. L. McCall. She remained a member until her death. Flossie united in Holy Matrimony with the late Ovall Jones. To this union one child was born, the late Earssie Lean Candley Ward. She was also preceded in death by five sisters and five brothers: (sisters) Mittie Pearl Holland, Ollie Bell Holland, Lou Emma Furlough, Ella Lowe, Glosson and Lottie Mae James (brothers) Johnny Holland, Willis Holland, Columbus Holland, James Holland, and Floyd Hollands.

Flossie leaves to cherish six grandchildren whom she reared as her own: Roy Candley (Victorville, Ca), Marie Bigsby and husband Ralph (West Monroe, La), Calvin Ward and wife Pam (Lake Charles, La), Sylvester Ward and wife Pat (Monroe, La), Sharon King and husband Otis (Monroe, La), and Ricky Candley (Monroe, La), a sister, Clara Waters (Toledo, OH), 28 great grandchildren, 17 great great grandchildren, and a host of nieces, nephews, cousins and friends.

Scripture: I have fought a good fight, I have finished my course, I have kept the faith.
2 Timothy 4:7

PROGRAM

PROCESSIONAL
Song.............................Brittany Ward
Scriptures.................Evangelist Smith
Prayer........................Rev. JE Jackson
Song...............................James Diarse
Expressions....................................
Obituary......Soft Music/Read Silently
Solo...................Bro. Malcom Williams
Eulogy.........Bishop Richard L. Brown

FUNERAL DIRECTOR IN CHARGE

M.C.........Sis. E'Terica Rucks
Song Service............
Usher Service......City Wide

ACTIVE PALLBEARERS

Roy Candley — Otis King
Calvin Ward — Gene Ward
Sylvester Ward — Greg Sims

HONORARY PALLBEARERS

Ivan Ward — Montreal Ward
Greg Ward — Ivan L. Jones
Donald Gibson — Sylvester Webster

Internment
City Cemetary

Dinner Will Be Served
Powell Rec. Center

Funeral Direction
Smith Funeral Home
907 Winnsboro Road
Monroe, La 71202

Gordie Bilberry-Burch's Obituary (exterior cover)

In Appreciation

Each lovely card
Each comforting word
Each visit to our grieved abode
Each lovely flower
Each gracious prayer--
To all who now our burden share
Accept our thanks and gratitude
And may we say as well
Your kindness meant far more to us
Than words can ever tell.

The Family

October 12, 1893   *July 30, 1983*

In Loving Memory of

Mrs. Gordie Burch

Mother of Blooming Grove Baptist Church

Give her of the fruit of her hands; and let her
own works praise her in the gates. Proverbs 30:31

Blooming Grove Baptist Church
Farmerville, Louisiana
Rev. Henry E. Island, Pastor
Thursday, August 4, 1983 - 4:00 P.M.

Gordie Bilberry-Burch's Obituary (interior cover)

OBITUARY

I have fought a good fight
I have finished my course
I have kept the faith

Henceforth, there is laid up for me a crown of righteousness which the Lord, the righteous Judge shall give me at that day. And, not for me only, but unto all them, also, that love His appearing.

Sister Gordie Etta Burch (fondly known and called "Aunt Gordie") was born October 12, 1893 in Marion, Louisiana to Mr. John (Jack) Bilberry and Mrs. Francis Morgan Bilberry. She departed this life July 30, 1983 at 6:35 p.m., in Union General Hospital.

She was married to Mr. John Burch, who preceded her in death.

She united with the Center Branch Baptist Church in 1907, where she served as a faithful member. After moving to Farmerville, Louisiana she united with the Blooming Grove Baptist Church in 1921. Here she served as an usher, Treasurer of the Southside Home Mission, Chairperson of the Cooking Department and Mother of the Church.

Survivors are a daughter, Mrs. Vera P. Cleveland, Farmerville, Louisiana; a grandson, Eric R. Cleveland; three great-grandsons, all of Houston, Texas; a dear great-great niece, Paula Rita Harrison, Harvey, Illinois; a host of nieces, nephews, other relatives and friends.

REST NOW

No more sorrow will be yours,
No more burdens will you bear,
No more heartaches will you endure,
Weighted down with endless care,
Rest, Now!

While here on earth you did your best,
A friend to all you tried to be.
This day, you have no regrets
This day from sorrow you are free.
Rest, Now!

No more will you fret and worry
About what a day might bring,
You have gone to that city,
Where God's holy angels sing,
Rest, Now!

Jacob Garret (J. G.) Bilberry – Obituary; son of McDuel Bilberry and brother of

E. B. Bilberry
Source: Meridian Baptist Church Minutes

57

Bro. J. G. Bilberry's Obituary.

Whereas, it has pleased an over-ruling providence to remove from us by an untimely death a beloved brother Jacob G Bilberry – who departed this life away from home and friends in camps near Alexandria La, April 2nd 1865 and whereas we deem it proper to give an expression of feelings for departed worth, therefore Resolved that in the death of Bro Bilberry the church loses a zealous and worthy member, and society a good and obliging citizen and that in the work of God an honest man, At the call of his country he repaired to the tented field, there to sicken and die, perhaps neglected in his last sickness. He lived a quiet, orderly christian life, and we have the assurance that he died the Christians death and is now enjoying the Christians reward; therefore let us not mourn as without hope.

Resolved that we sympathize and condole sincerely with his bereaved widow and orphans in this severe bereavement, and recommend them to the tender mercies of him who heareth the young ravens when they cry –

Resolved that these preamble and resolutions be recorded in the church book and a copy be furnished his bereaved family, —

J. G. Robinson
W. D. M. Britton } Committee

Jesse Bernard Bilberry, Sr.'s (exterior cover)

ACTIVE PALLBEARERS
Farmerville Lodge No. 203

HONORARY PALLBEARERS
Bus Drivers and Teachers, Eastside High School

FLOWER BEARERS
Ushers

MISTRESS OF CEREMONIES
Mrs. Vada Kemp

Funeral Services

For the Late

Reverend Jesse Bernard Bilberry, Sr.

To Be Held At The

Eastside High School Gymnasium

Farmerville, Louisiana

February 26, 1961

1:00 O'clock P.M.

Jesse Bernard Bilberry, Sr.'s Obituary (interior cover)

OBITUARY

Of

REV. JESSE BERNARD BILBERRY, SR.

July 20, 1904 · · · · · February 24, 1961

The Lord is my shepherd; I shall not want. He maketh me to lie down in green pastures; he leadeth me beside the still waters. He restoreth my soul: he leadeth me in the paths of righteousness for his name's sake. Yea, though I walk through the valley of the shadow of death, I will fear no evil: for thou art with me; thy rod and thy staff they comfort me.

Thou preparest a table before me in the presence of mine enemies; thou anointest my head with oil; my cup runneth over.

Surely goodness and mercy shall follow me all the days of my life; and I will dwell in the house of the Lord forever.

On Friday morning, February 24, at 6:30 A.M., God called Reverend Jesse Bernard Bilberry, Sr. to his heavenly home where it's always day and never night; always joy and never sorrow; always howdy and never good-bye. Reverend Bilberry was the son of Mr. and Mrs. Frank Bilberry. He was born July 20, 1904. He was married to Miss Joe B. Dixon, September 13, 1928. To this union ten children were born: six sons and four daughters. He joined the Sweet Lily Baptist Church at an early age, and later became a member of the Millard Hill Baptist Church; was called to the ministry in 1936, and for a period of years pastored Sweet Lily and Antioch Baptist Churches; was pastor of Mt. Calm and Olive Branch Baptist Churches until death; was a teacher and principal in the public schools of Union Parish for more than thirty years.

He leaves to morn, his wife, Mrs. Joe B. Bilberry, Farmerville, La; six sons, Jesse Bernard Bilberry, Jr., St. Joseph, La., Johnny B. Bilberry, Shreveport, La., Ralph J. Bilberry, Southern University, Joe Frederick Bilberry, Charles Lane Bilberry, and Edward La Don Bilberry, Farmerville, La.; four daughters, Mrs. Frankie L. Lewis, Dayton, Ohio, Mrs. Lelia R. Mack, Baton Rouge, La., Miss Barbra J. Bilberry, Southern University, and Miss Elaine Bilberry, Farmerville, La.; his mother, Mrs. Emmer R. Bilberry, Farmerville, La.; three grandchildren, three brothers, Ladell Bilberry, Marion, La., Charlie Bilberry, Flint, Michigan, and Eddy Bilberry, Monroe, La.; two daughter-in-law two son-in-law and a host of sisters and brother-in-law , nieces, nephews, other relatives and friends.

PROGRAM

Processional—

Music .... God Walks Beside Thee
Eastside High School Choir

Invocation .... Rev. B. J. Washington
Pastor, Blooming Grove Baptist Church

Music .... Bro. Mose Thompson

Expressions .... Rev. W. M. Rutland, Dec. J. R. Smith
Bro. Mose Thompson

Acknowledgements .... Mrs. Rutha M. Fields

Obituary .... Mrs. Earlie Hodge

Solo .... Eastside High School

Eulogy .... Rev. P. Rayfied Brown, III
Pastor, Calvary Missionary Baptist Church, Monroe, La.

Funeral Directors in Charge—

Recessional—

Interment in Farmerville Cemetery

Union Funeral Home in Charge

Jewell L. Bilberry's Obituary (exterior copy)
Son of William Henry Bilberry

OBSEQUIES

for the late

Deacon Jewel L. Bilberry

"And God shall wipe away all tears from their eyes; and there shall be no more death, neither sorrow, nor crying, neither shall there be any more pain: for former things are passed away."
Revelation 21:4

HONORARY PALLBEARERS
Deacons

ACTIVE PALLBEARERS
Grandsons

FLOWERBEARERS
Ushers & Stars

INTERMENT
Farmerville Cemetery
Under the direction of Union Funeral Home

NOTE OF THANKS
The members of the family wish to express their sincere appreciation for the prayers, cards, florals and every act of kindness extended during the illness and death of their loved one.

Center Branch Baptist Church

Marion, Louisiana

Rev. Henry J. Johnson, Pastor

Saturday, December 5, 1981

2:30 P.M.

Jewell L. Bilberry's Obituary (interior cover)
Son of William Henry Bilberry

OBITUARY

"For I am now ready to be offered and the time of my departure is at hand. I have fought a good fight, I have kept the faith, Hence forth there is laid up for me a crown of righteousness, which the Lord, the righteous judge, shall give me at that day, and not to me only, but unto all them also that love his appearing."

II Timothy 4:6-8

Brother Jewel L. Bilberry was born March 12, 1902 to the union of the late William Henry Bilberry and Mrs. Georgia Holley Bilberry.

He departed this life Sunday morning, November 29, 1981, at the Veteran Administration Hospital, Shreveport, La. after a brief illness.

He united with the Center Branch Baptist Church at an early age. He served as treasurer of the Building Fund, assistant Superintendent of the Sunday School and a deacon until his death.

He served his country in the U.S. Armed Forces. He was a member of the American Legion, Hendrix Payne Post 539, Prince Hall Masonic Lodge Number where he served as secretary until death and the order of the Eastern Star, Budding Rose Chapter 86.

His survivors are three daughter, Mrs. Moreen Benson, Marion, La., Mrs. Lillie Mae Walter, West Monroe, La., Mrs. Kathleen W. Isabel, Los Angelles, Ca. one son, Mr. Lavell Lewis, Farmerville, La., seven grand children, thirteen great grand children, one brother Mr. Thomas Marlow, Compton, Ca., one aunt Mrs. Gordia B. Burch, Farmerville, La. and a host of neices, nephews, relatives and friends.

Sun set and Evening Star
And one clear call for me
And may there be no mourning at the bar.
When I put out to sea.

ORDER OF SERVICES

Processional		
Music		
Scripture		
Prayer		
Song.	"Near The Cross"	Choir
Expressions		Dea. Arnet Douglas
		Dea. Roosevelt Taylor
		Bro. Albert Payne
Acknowledgements		Sis. Katie Douglas
Obituary	(Read Silently)	Soft Music
Solo		Sis. Rose M. Thomas
Eulogy		Rev. H.J. Johnson
Recessional		
Mistress of Services		Sis. Odessa Burch

Joe B. Dixson-Bilberry's Obituary (exterior cover)

Obsequies
for the late
Mrs. Joe B. Dixson Bilberry
1906 - 1989

to be held

FRIDAY, JUNE 30, 1989 - 7:00 P.M.

MT. PILGRIM MISSIONARY BAPTIST CHURCH

9700 Scenic Highway   Baton Rouge, Louisiana

Reverend Jesse B. Bilberry, Jr., Pastor

and

SATURDAY, JULY 1, 1989 - 12:00 NOON

GUMSPRING MISSIONARY BAPTIST CHURCH

Farmerville, Louisiana

Reverend R. L. Belton, Officiating

Joe B. Dixson-Bilberry's Obituary (interior cover)

The Obituary

"For I am now ready to be offered and the time of my departure is at hand. I have fought a good fight, I have finished my course, I have kept the faith: Henceforth there is laid up for me a crown of righteousness, which the Lord, the righteous judge, shall give me at that day: and not to me only, but unto all them also that love his appearing. II Timothy 4:6-8

Mrs. Joe B. Dixson Bilberry, the daughter of the late Joe Dixson and Lelia Payne Dixson, was born November 25, 1906, in Farmerville, Louisiana. On Sunday evening, June 25, 1989, the dear Lord, at his own appointed time called our beloved mother to a land of peace and joy.

She was called and baptized at a very early age and became a member of the Gumspring Baptist Church. She was a Deaconess and a member of the Gumspring Women's Mission. She remained faithful until she moved to Baton Rouge, Louisiana, where she united with the Mt. Pilgrim Baptist Church and remained faithful until her home going.

She leaves to cherish sweet memories her devoted children—four daughters, Frankie Lewis of Chesapeake, Virginia; Lelia Mack, Barbra Hall and Elaine Bilberry of Baton Rouge; five sons, Reverend Jesse B. Bilberry, Jr. of Baton Rouge; Colonel Ralph W. Bilberry of Atlanta, Georgia; Joe F. and Charles Lane Bilberry, both of Dayton, Ohio; and Edward Bilberry of Pasadena, California; a sister, Mrs. Dellie Dixson Bilberry of Flint, Michigan; an uncle and an aunt, Abe and Pearl Payne of Vivian; two brothers-in-law, Eddie Bilberry and Jethro Horn; four sisters-in-law, Mrs. Nannie Dixson, Mrs. Willie Mae Bilberry, Mrs. Lettie Bilberry and Mrs. Clara "Chris" Dixson; six daughters-in-law, Mesdames Verta, Bernadette, Valerie, Barbara, Gail and Lee; two sons-in-law, Robert and Ralph; thirteen grandchildren, three great grandchildren, many nieces, nephews and other relatives and friends.

She was preceded in death by her husband, Reverend Jesse Bernard Bilberry, Sr. and a son, Johnny Bernard Bilberry, Sr.

John Davis Holland's Obituary (exterior cover), son of Anna Bilberry

SERVICE OF DELIVERANCE
FOR
MR. JOHN DAVIS HOLLAND

TO BE HELD AT
POWELL CHURCH OF GOD AND CHRIST
601 Plum Street
Monroe, Louisiana

1:00 P.M.
May 8, 1990

John Davis Holland's Obituary (interior cover), son of Anna Bilberry

OBITUARY

Mr. John Davis Holland was born December 20, 1925 and departed this life on April 28, 1990 after a lengthy illness. He was born to the late Mason and Anna Holland in Marion, Louisiana. For most of his adult life, he resided in Monroe, Louisiana and was a member of the Powell Church of God in Christ under the leadership of Elder Billy Caldwell.

He leaves to cherish his memory, six children: Jackie Kennedy of Oakland, California, JoAnn Galbert, Shirley Ross, Robert Smith, Herman Smith and Chuckie Swayze, all of Monroe; three sisters, Mrs. Ella Lowe of Marion, Louisiana, Mrs. Clara Waters of Toledo, Ohio, and Mrs. Flossie James of Monroe, Louisiana; Two aunts, Mrs. Mittie Pearl Fields of Farmerville, Louisiana and Mrs. Dollie Mayfield of Seattle, Washington; Fifteen grandchildren, nine great grand-children and a host of nieces, nephews, relatives and friends.

"Brother, we love you, but God loves you best.
He looked over His garden and saw an empty space.
He chose a beautiful flower like you to fill
   the void
because He only takes the best."

Your family

Lou Emma Holland-Furlough-Glossom's Obituary (exterior cover)
Daughter of Anna Bilberry-Holland and Mason Holland

Active Pallbearers

Bro. L. Dismuke
Bro. Cletis Charles
Bro. Freddie Hill

Bro. F. Pryor
Bro. A. Pryor
Bro. Artis Pryor

Honorary Pallbearers
Deacons of the Pleasant
Hill Baptist Church

Ushers
Pleasant Hill B.C.
Fellowship B. Church
Sweet Union B. Church

Flowerbearers
Pleasant Hill Baptist
Church Choir

Acknowledgement
The family gratefully acknowledges with sincere appreciation
the many acts of kindness & comforting expressions of sympathy
shown during the illness and passing of our loved one.

Funeral Services
for
Sister Lou Emma Holland Furlough Glosson

to be held at the
Pleasant Hill Baptist Church
Spearsville, Louisiana
Friday, May 7, 1982
1:00 P.M.
Rev. James F. Mason,
pastor

Lou Emma Holland-Furlough-Glossom's Obituary (interior cover)
Daughter of Anna Bilberry-Holland and Mason Holland

Obituary

The death angel came for the bright spirit of Sis. Lou Emma Holland Furlough Glosson May 1, 1982 at E.A. Conway Hospital, Monroe, La.

She was born Oct. 9, 1915 to Mr. & Mrs. Mason Holland. She united with the Marion Baptist Church at an early age. Then she later joined Countyline & Pleasant Hill Baptist Church.

She married Brother Garfield Furlough. To this union eight children were born.

Later she united with Brother Willie Glosson, to this union three children were born.

Survivors include her husband, Bro. Willie Glosson; six sons, Rosevelt Furlough & Jacob Furlough, both of Houston, Tex., Theous Furlough of Farmerville, Benjamin Furlough of Germany, Dan Ira & Willie Lavell Glosson, both of Detroit, Mich.; four daughters, Flossie Lee Dismuke of Chicago, Ill, Gloria Dismuke & Earline Matthews, both of Spearsville, Jearline Rivers of Detroit, Mich., and Lou Ann Scott of El Dorado, Ark.; four step daughters, Gloria Wines, Benji Dean Dismuke, Dorothy Jean Beard, and Carrie Hinson; three step-sons, John L. Glosson, Marvin Glosson, and Bobbie Lee Glosson; three sisters, Ella Lowe, Flossie Mae Jones and Clara Mae Waters; one brother, John Davis; 44 grandchildren, 15 great grandchildren and a host of nieces, nephews, relatives and friends.

The sun is set
The day is Gone
For our loved one
Has been called home.
Rest in peace
In Christ dear mother and wife
For we shall soon meet
On the other side
"Praise the Lord"

Program

Processional	Minister L.F. Bibby
Scripture & Prayer	Guide Me Over
	Thy Great Jehovah
Song	Choir
Tributes	Bro. Mickey Dismuke
As a friend & neighbor	Ms. Henry Terry
Obituary	Soft music
Acknowledgements	Sis. M. Pryor
Solo	Sis. Georgia Williams
Eulogy	Rev. J.F. Mason
Recessional	
Interment	Pleasant Hill Cemetery
	Laran, La.
Mistress of Services	Sis. Mary D. Charles
Union Funeral Home in charge	

267

Luemmer Horn's Obituary (exterior cover)

IN LOVING MEMORY

of

SISTER LUEMMER B. HORN

1924   1989

WEDNESDAY, MARCH 22, 1989

12:00 NOON

ANTIOCH PRIMITIVE BAPTIST CHURCH
Provencal, Louisiana

ELDER L.V. THROWER, PASTOR

Choose you this day whom ye will serve
as for me and my house; we will serve the Lord.

Joshua 24:15

Luemmer Horn's Obituary (interior cover)

PROGRAMME

PROCESSIONAL------------(All Stand)

HYMN--------------------"What A Friend We
Have In Jesus"

SCRIPTURES-------------Elder Larry Smith
Elder Dennis McGaskey

PRAYER-----------------Elder Nathaniel
McGaskey

HYMN-------------------"Amazing Grace"

REMARKS----------------Bro. Jacob Nabors
Bro. Louis Nabors, Sr.

RESOLUTIONS------------Antioch Baptist Church

SPECIAL TRIBUTE--------The Children

HYMN-------------------"Jesus Keep Me Near
The Cross"

ACKNOWLEDGEMENTS AND OBITUARY---
Sis. Maxine McGaskey

SOLO-------------------"Precious Lord"
Bro. Louis Nabors, Jr.

SERMON-----------------Elder L.V. Thrower

REVIEWAL:

RECESSIONAL:

INTERMENT--------------Antioch Cemetery

OBITUARY

Mrs. Luemmer B. Horn crossed over into Glory on March 16, 1989 at 5:00 p.m. She was born on Dec. 5, 1924 to the late Elder Ladell and Maggie Bilberry.

At an early age, she united with the Primitive Baptist Church where she remained an active member until death.

Our beloved united in marriage to Seab A. Horn on Dec. 5, 1937. To this union they were blessed with fourteen (14) children.

She leaves to mourn her passing her devoted and loving husband, Deacon Seab A. Horn, Sr. of Provencal, LA.; four (4) daughters, Mrs. Maggie L. Payton and Mrs. Lola Garner of Natchitoches, LA., Mrs. Hazel Brown of Shreveport, LA. and Mrs. Deborah Reliford of Provencal, LA., seven sons, Mr. Seab A. Horn, Jr., Mr. Jethro Horn, Mr. Frankie L. Horn and Mr. Willie Paul Horn of Kansas City, Kansas, Mr. George Horn of Del City, Oklahoma, Mr. Harvey Horn of Elliot City, MD. and Mr. Eddie Paul Horn of Provencal, LA.; three (3) children preceded her in death. She also played a major role in the rearing of Booker T., Robert and Shirley Bilberry.

Bereaved brothers are; Mr. Adell Bilberry and Mr. Clyde Bilberry of Marion, LA., Mr. Johnny Bilberry of Farmerville, LA., Mr. Clarence Bilberry of Kansas City, Missouri, Mr. Richard Bilberry, Mr. Ladell Bilberry, Jr. and Mr. Herbert Bilberry of Kansas City, Kansas. Four (4) sisters; Ms. Loreace Watley, Mrs. Loeast Watkins and Ms. Emma Payne of Kansas City, Kansas, Mrs. Clara Jones of Kansas City, Missouri; two (2) brothers-in-law, six sisters-in-law; three (3) aunts, one (1) uncle; thirty four (34) grandchildren, ten (10) great grandchildren; a host of many neices, nephews, cousins and friends whom she loved as if they were her own. Many shared the gentleness of her love and share in this memory.

Mrs. Luemmer B. Horn was a Retired Assistant Teacher for the Natchitoches Parish School Board for seventeen years.

Mary Evylene Arbertha Thurmond's Obituary (exterior cover)
Daughter of Mattie Bilberry and Grand Daughter of Jack and Francis Bilberry

Mary Evylene Arbertha Thurmond

Enjoy Your Life In Eternity

Sunrise
November 22, 1916

Sunset
October 31, 2003

Services

Tuesday · November 4, 2003 · 11:00 a.m.

St. John Missionary Baptist Church

5700 North Kelley Avenue
Oklahoma City, Oklahoma

Dr. M. L. Jemison · Officiating

Mary Evylene Arbertha Thurmond's Obituary (interior cover)
Daughter of Mattie Bilberry and Grand Daughter of Jack and Francis Bilberry

Mary Evylene Arbertha Thurmond

YOU LIVED YOUR LIFE WELL!

"The Lord Is My Shepherd I Shall Not Want." - *Psalms 23*

Birth Celebration	November 22, 1916
	By Loving Parents
	Simon & Mattie Bilberry Arbertha
	In Roland, Arkansas
Education	Boley, Oklahoma Public Schools
Married	Clarence Thurmond
Favorite Things to Do	Cooking, Shopping & Traveling
Descriptive Characteristics	Big Hearted (Sharing, Loving, Caring and most of all, Giving)
Favorite Flower	Yellow Rose
Favorite Church	St. John Baptist Church Deaconess II
Favorite Bible Chapter	Psalms 23
Favorite Organization	OKC Federation of Colored Women's Club President & Treasurer
Favorite Employment	Head Start
Volunteer	Neighbor for Neighbor, Homeroom Mother & Head Start
Apples of Her Eye	Charline Woods, Lucy Thurmond Livingston, Clarence Thurmond & Carrie Lee Thurmond Kennedy
Second Generation Apples	Mary Shells, Lewis W. Livingston, Lori J. Livingston, Edwan Thurmond, Eddie Shells, Angel Shells, Charline Harris, Freddie Shells, Derrick Ware, Brandon Thurmond, Johnathan Kennedy & Ryan Kennedy
Other Fruit of The Tree	Many Nephews, Nieces & Great Grandchildren

She was one of four children, and was preceded in death by her sister, Carrie Arbertha Hinton; her brother, Simon Arbertha; and her loving husband, Clarence.

A brother, Sherman Arbertha of California, her children, grandchildren, great grand-children, and many nephews and nieces survive her. She leaves to celebrate a host of other relatives and friends.

Odessa Elliott-Burch's Obituary (exterior cover)

1917   1990

𝔥𝔬𝔪𝔢𝔠𝔬𝔪𝔦𝔫𝔤 𝔖𝔢𝔯𝔳𝔦𝔠𝔢𝔰

of

𝔖𝔦𝔰𝔱𝔢𝔯 𝔒𝔡𝔢𝔰𝔰𝔞 𝔈. 𝔅𝔲𝔯𝔠𝔥

𝔖𝔞𝔱𝔲𝔯𝔡𝔞𝔶, 𝔉𝔢𝔟𝔯𝔲𝔞𝔯𝔶 3, 1990
11:00 𝔞.𝔪.

𝔷𝔦𝔬𝔫 𝔥𝔦𝔩𝔩 𝔅𝔞𝔭𝔱𝔦𝔰𝔱 𝔠𝔥𝔲𝔯𝔠𝔥
𝔉𝔞𝔯𝔪𝔢𝔯𝔳𝔦𝔩𝔩𝔢, 𝔏𝔬𝔲𝔦𝔰𝔦𝔞𝔫𝔞

𝔯𝔢𝔳. 𝔗𝔬𝔪𝔪𝔦𝔢 𝔠𝔞𝔯𝔯, 𝔭𝔞𝔰𝔱𝔬𝔯
𝔯𝔢𝔳. 𝔍𝔢𝔰𝔰𝔦𝔢 𝔠𝔥𝔞𝔯𝔩𝔢𝔰, 𝔒𝔣𝔣𝔦𝔠𝔦𝔞𝔱𝔦𝔫𝔤

𝔗𝔥𝔞𝔫𝔨 𝔜𝔬𝔲

Note: Perhaps you sent a lovely card, or sat quietly in a chair, perhaps you sent a floral piece, if so we saw it there. Perhaps you spoke the kindest words as any friend could say, perhaps you were not there at all, just thought of us that day, whatever you did to console our hearts, we thank you so much whatever the part.

Thanks
The Family

Odessa Elliott-Burch's Obituary (interior cover)

1917   1990

Servant of God well done;
Rest from thy loved employ;
The battle fought, the victory won;
Enter thy master's joy.

The pains of death are past;
Labor and sorrow cease;
And life's long warfare closed at last;
Her soul is found in peace.

OBITUARY

A busy life came to a close January 29, 1990 when Sister Odessa Burch was called to her heavenly home.

Sister Odessa was born August 12, 1917 to the late Bro. John Elliott and Sis. Lavada Jane Henry Elliott. Being from a Christian home, she was baptized and fellowshipped in the New Hopewell Baptist Church and remained until death. After she married the late Edward Burch, she served at Center Branch B.C. in many activities, and later at Zion Watt B.C. serving as Sunday School and Bible instructor, mission president, Treasurer for Benevolent Fund and chairlady for Church Beautification.

Sis. Burch was educated in the school of Union Parish and received her B.S. Degree from Grambling State University in Elementary Education. She did further studies at the University of Arkansas at Little Rock. She retired in 1971, having taught for 30 years.

She leaves to cherish her memory: two daughters, Mrs. Johnette Mack of Marion, La. and Mrs. Linda B. Evans of Lafayette, La.; three grandchildren, LaLoni, Angelica and Jennifer Evans of Lafayette; two brothers, Elihue Elliott of Detroit, Michigan, J.P. Elliott of Kansas City and Bruce Elliott, Bernice, La.; one sister, Mrs. Gordie George, Bernice, La.; and a multitude of nieces, nephews, relatives and friends.

Sister Odessa E. Burch

1917   1990

Rest, Now!

No more sorrow will be yours,
No more burdens will you bear,
No more heartaches will you endure,
Weighted down with endless care,
Rest, Now!

While here on earth you did your best,
A friend to all you tried to be.
This day, you have no regrets.
This day from sorrow you are free.
Rest, Now!

No more will you fret and worry
About what a day might bring,
You have gone to that city,
Where God's holy angels sing.
Rest, Now!

Sarah Alabama Montgomery-Ellis' Obituary (exterior cover)

ACTIVE PALLBEARERS

Bro. James King

Bro. John King

Bro. Lacey Montgomery

Bro. Ardell Smith

Bro. Ruby Douglas

Bro. Adell Bilberry

HONORARY PALLBEARERS

Deacons of Sweet Lilly

FLOWER BEARERS

Ushers

INTERMENT

Meredian Cemetery

UNION FUNERAL HOME IN CHARGE

NOTE OF THANKS

The family of Sarah Ellis wishes to thank you for all your prayers, cards, calls, flowers, food and support during our time of bereavement. May God richly bless all of you.

THE FAMILY

In Loving Memory

of

Sis. Sarah Montgomery Ellis

to be held at

Sweet Lilly Primitive Baptist Church

Marion, La.

July 25, 1986

2:00 P.M.

ELDER L. V. THROWER, PASTOR

Sarah Alabama Montgomery-Ellis' Obituary (interior cover)
Sarah was named after her father George's sister, Sarah Montgomery-Morgan.
Sarah Montgomery was the wife of Sam Morgan.
Source: 1880 U.S. Census, Union Parish Ward Six

OBITUARY

There can be no real and abiding happiness without sacrifice. Our greatest joys do not result from our efforts toward self-gratification, but from a loving and spontaneous service to others' lives. Joy comes not to him who seeks it for himself, but to him who seeks it for others.

Such was the life of sister Sarah Montgomery Ellis. She was born March 15, 1911 to the late Brother George Montgomery and Sister Minnie Ann Roberts Montgomery. She was the baby of eleven (11) children. Her mother passed away six (6) months after she was born and she was reared by her grandmother Eliza Jane and grandfather Will Roberts with the help of her uncles Lee, Genie, C.C., Charlie Roberts, and aunt Emmer Bilberry.

Her life was a strong reflection of the Christian home. She joined the church at eleven (11) years of age under the pastorate of Elder Rich Thrower.

In 1942, she was united in holy matrimony to Mr. Johnny Ellis. Having no children of her own, Sister Ellis devoted many of her energies to caring for children of others. She worked in many capacities in the church. She served as church treasurer, chairperson of cemetery fund, and enjoyed cooking food for not only her church, but all the churches in the area.

She leaves to cherish her memories a loving and devoted husband, Mr. Johnny Ellis of Marion, La.; one sister, Mrs. Berdie Maine, Marion, La.; two (2) brothers, Mr. James Montgomery of Farmerville, La. and Mr. Rodell Montgomery, Marion, La.; a host of nieces, nephews, adopted sisters and brothers and other relatives and friends.

When I must leave you for a little while, please do not grieve and shed wild tears and hug your sorrow through the years. But start out bravely with a gallant smile, and for my sake and in my name, live on and do all things the same.

Never, Never be afraid to die, for I am waiting for you in the sky.

PROGRAM

Processional	
Song	
Scripture and Prayer	Rev. Jessie Charles
Song	
Expressions	Dea. Johnny Bilberry
	Sis. Virginia Davenport
Acknowledgements	Sis. Genelle Watley
Obituary	Sis. Katie Douglas
Song	
Funeral Oration	Elder L.V. Thrower
Recessional	

Mistress of Ceremony - Sis. Lue Emma Horn

Appendix E

Meridian Missionary Baptist Church Minutes: Some Slaves (servants) and Members of the Church

The Missionary Baptist Church of Christ at Meridian was constituted into a "Regular Missionary Baptist Church" on October 1, 1956. The proceedings of the second annual session of the Union Parish, Louisiana Missionary Baptist Association held in 1948, indicates that this was the fourth oldest church in the association; the oldest being formed in 1840. The church held its last church service on August 6, 1972. Cordell Allen was the pastor.

John Earl Ellis of Marion, Louisiana mentioned to me during our interview on August 2, 2010, that the people of the community had built a new church. Meridian Baptist Church was now open again. When, I drove toward the town of Marion, Louisiana, I noticed a sign advertising the church at the intersection of Highway 33 and Highway 348. The church is not only a place where you can worship God, but it was a vital source of information for reconstructing your family tree. Meridian Baptist Church laid dormant for over thirty years. I must say that I was happy to see that the church was worshipping again and continuing its history.

Noted Slaves Members of the Meridian Missionary Baptist Church

MINUTES OF NEW MEMBERS			
SLAVE NAMES	DATES	SERVANTS OF OWNER(S)	PAGE NO.
James and Hannah	January 1857	Sister M. A. Masterson	9
Frank	November 1856	Brother W. D. Cooper Lane	8
Thomas	April 1865	J. M. Lane	55
Thomas	October 1856	Bradley Estate and Milly, a servant of E. B. Bilberry; both were baptized	
Caesar	September 1858	Mr. McColby and Dinah, servant of Mr. H. Carver	13
Lucinda	September 1860	Brother C. M. Cooper; Margaret, servant of brother J. G. Bilberry	32

Source: Meridian Missionary Baptist Church Minutes, Louisiana Tech University

Letter of Dismissal

September 1865-**Thomas** former servant of J. M. Lane (Meridian Baptist Church Minutes, pg. 59)

November 1858-**Milly**, servant of E. Bilberry (Meridian Missionary Baptist Church Minutes, pg. 24)

September 1890—**Lonnie Russell (Black)** – joined the Primitive Baptist Church. He was excluded from the fellowship of the church (Meridian Missionary Baptist Church Minutes, pg. 202)

Bilberry names in the Meridian Missionary Baptist Church are listed below

Minutes October 1856 – October 1935	
NAMES	**PAGE NUMBER(S)**
Bilberry, E.	24
Bilberry, E.B.	8
Bilberry, Fannie (Vestal)	410
Bilberry, Fannie	91 & 191
Bilberry, J.G.	23, 32, 38, 55-57-57, & 86
Bilberry, J.T.	100
Bilberry, Jack	202
Bilberry, Jacob G.	57
Bilberry, Mack	202, 278, 372, 410, 412
Bilberry, Mark	91
Bilberry, Mrs. Jacob G.	57
Bilberry, Nannie	88
Bilberry, S.C.	62
Bilberry, Sarah	23 & 86
Bilberry, Synthia	246

Appendix F

Miscellaneous Documents of Family and Extended Family Members

Adell (Abe) Billberry World War I – (Draft) Registration Card

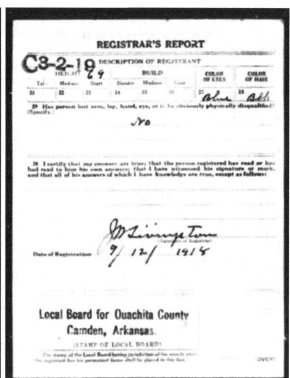

Dollie Thompson-Mayfield Social Security Application

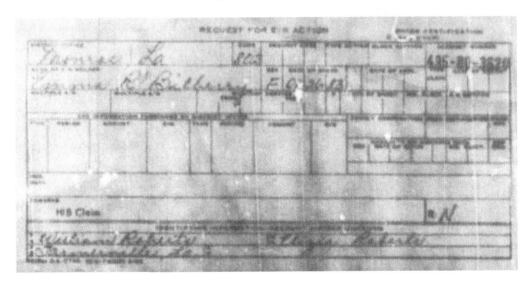

Emma Bilberry Social Security Application

Laura (Archie) Bilberry Social Security Application

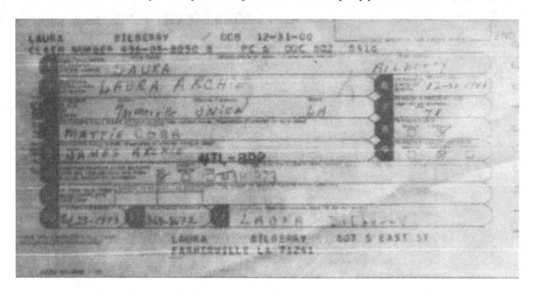

Succession of Lorenzo (Rance) Ellis

P.D.NO. 1522
SUCCESSION OF RANCE ELLIS, DECD.
PETITION, AFFID. & JUDGMENT RECOGNIZING AND PLACING HEIRS IN POSSESSION:Filed Nov.23,1928.

TO THE HONORABLE THE THIRD JUDICIAL DISTRICT COURT IN AND FOR THE PARISH OF UNION,STATE OF LOUISIANA:

The petition of Georgia Ann Ellis, widow of Rance Ellis, deceased, and L.G. Ellis, J.P. Ellis, Hannah Ellis Burch, Jesse Ellis, Lorenzo Ellis, Jr., Hettie Lee Andrews, Elsie Mae Jackson, Etta Ellis, Octavia Ellis Benson, Otis Ellis, Johnnie Ellis and Claud Ellis all of lawful age and residents of Union Parish, Louisiana, and Earl Ellis, aged 18 years and a resident of Union Parish, Louisiana, with respect, shows:

1

That Rance Ellis departed this life in Union Parish, Louisiana, in which he had his domicile, during the month of July, in the year 1927.

2.

That petitioner, Georgia Ann Ellis, is the surviving widow of said decedent, and that all other petitioners herein are the sole heirs at law of said decedent, being his sole children and grand-children, as hereinafter shown.

3.

That all of your petitioners herein, except his said widow, and except petitioners, L.G. Ellis and J.P.Ellis, together with George Ellis, deceased, are the sole children of said decedent, having been born of his marriage with petitioner, Georgia Ann Ellis; that said George Ellis died about 20 years ago, leaving as his sole heirs, petitioners L.G.Ellis and J.P.Ellis, his sole children, born of his marriage with Annie Mae Ellis, deceased,

4.

That he died intestate, leaving both real and personal property within the jurisdiction of this Court, all of which was acquired by him during his marriage to petitioner, Georgia Ann Ellis, which belonged to the community of acquets and gains which existed between him and his said surviving spouse.

5.

That said decedent left no debts; that petitioners accept the succession of said decedent, Rance Ellis, purely, simply and unconditionally; and that they desire to be recognized and put in possession.

6.

That said estate is exempt from the payment of the inheritance tax, being worth less than $2,000.00 and as having always born its just proportion of taxation; that they desire that F.W.Murphy Sheriff and Tax Collector of Union Parish be ordered to show cause why said succession should not be decreed exempt from payment of the inheritance tax.

WHEREFORE, petitioners pray that petitioner, Georgia Ann Ellis, widow of said Rance Ellis be recognized as the surviving spouse in community of the deceased, entitled, as such, to the ownership of one undivided half of all the property, both real and personal, left by the deceased, and to the usufruct of the other undivided half; and all other petitioners herein pray to be recognized as the sole heirs of their said father and grand-father, entitled as such, to the ownership of one undivided half of all the property, both real and personal, left by said deceased, subject to the usufruct in favor of said Georgia Ann Ellis.

And that a rule issue to F.W.Murphy Sheriff ordering him to show cause why said estate should not be relieved from the payment of the inheritance tax, and for general relief.

G.H.Holloway, Attorney for Petitioners.

State of Louisiana,
Parish of Union.

G.H.Holloway, being first duly sworn, dealared: That he is the attorney for the above-named petitioners; that he has read said petition and that all facts therein set forth and contained are true and correct to the best of his knowledge and belief.

G.H.Holloway

Tutor and Under Tutor of the minor heirs of Hannah Bilberry-Nelson; wife of Branch Nelson; sister of Georgia Bellzora Bilberry-Ellis—Page 1

State of Louisiana, Parish of Union.--- In Re tutorship of the minor heirs of Hannah Nelson Decd.

Personally came and appeared before me the undersigned authority Sandy Goldsby who swear that he will wall and faithfully discharge and perform all the duties incumbent on him as under-tutor of the minor heirs of Hannah Nelson decd.

Sandy Goldsby

Sworn to and subscribed before me at Farmerville, La. on this the 20th day of January,1906.
J. W. Elder,
Notary Public.

STATE OF LOUISIANA | FOURTH DISTRICT COURT.
PARISH OF UNION

This shall certify to all whom it may concern, That on the 20 day of Jany. A. D. 1906 an application was made to the Honorable Judge of the said District court in and for Union parish La. by Branch Nelson praying that he might be appointed tutor to the minor heis of Hannah Nelson Decd.

Now know ye, that he has been and he is hereby appointed tutor to the said minors, and that he has fulfilled all the requisites of the law. Witness our hand and seal of said court, on this the 20 day of Jany. A. D. 1906.
Edw. Everett,
Clerk District Court.

STATE OF LOUISIANA | FOURTH DISTRICT COURT.
PARISH OF UNION

This shall certify to all whom it may concern, That on the 20 day of Jany, A. D. 1906 an application was made to the Honorable Judge of the said District Court, in and for Union parish La. by Branch Nelson praying that Sandy Goldsby might be appointed under tutor to the minor heirs of Hannah Nelson Decd.

Now know ye, that Sandy Goldsby has been and he is hereby appointed under-tutor to the said minors and that -- has fulfilled all the requisites of the law. Witness our hand and seal of said court, on this the 20 day of Jany. A. D. 1906.
Edw. Everett,
Clerk District Court.

PROCES VERBAL FAMILY MEETING, PETITION TO HOMOLOGATE & ORDER: Filed 23 day of Jany,A.D.1906

To the Hon. Judge of Fourth Dist. court, Union parish, State of Louisiana.
Your petitioner J. B. Nelson, tutor of the minor heirs of Hannah Nelson decd. represents unto your Hon. court that a family meeting composed of the nearest of kin of the minor heirs of Hannah Nelson decd. was duly convoked and held before J. W. Elder Notary Public on the 20th. day of January 1906 and made the recommendations contained in the attached proces verbal, which is made a part hereof.

Wherefore he prays that same be approved and homologated and made the judgment of this court and that he be authorized to make an execute deeds in accordance therewith and for other necessary orders.
Price Roberts & Elder
Attorneys for petitioner.

The foregoing petition togather with the recommendation of the family meeting being considered and the law being in favor hereof, it is hereby ordered, adjudged and decreed that the proceedings of the family meeting held on the 20th day of January 1906 before J. W. Elder, Notary Public of Union parish in the interest of the minor heirs of Hannah Nelson decd. are hereby approved, homologated and made the judgment of the court and he with the instructions of said family meeting.

Thus done read and signed on this the 23 day of January. 1906. at Farmerville, La.
R. B. Dawkins
Judge of Fourth District court of
Louisiana.

State of Louisiana — Parish of Union.
I do solemnly swear that I will faithfully and impartially discharge and perform all the duties incumbent on me as a member, and will give my advice touching the interest of the minor heirs of Hannah Nelson decd, according to the matters and things set forth in the application for a family meeting, and give any other advice I might deem necessary to the interest of said minors according to the best of my ability and understanding. So help me God.

Attest : G. E. Murphy
        Chas. B. Roberts
Sworn to and subscribed before me
at Farmerville, La. on this the
20th. day of January 1906.

J. W. Elder, Notary Public.

his
Rance (X) Ellis
mark
Hiram (X) Montgomery
his mark
Jack (X) Bilberry
his mark
Sam (X) Morgan
his mark
Henry Bilberry.

Fourth District court, Union parish, State of Louisiana.
Be it remembered that on this the 20 day of January 1906 pursuant to an order issued out of the Hon. Fourth Dist. court in and for Union parish, State of Louisiana, said order bearing even date herewith and to me directed, authorizing and commanding me to convoke a family meeting in the interest of the minor heirs of Hannah Nelson decd. Said family meeting to give their advice touching the interest of the said minors as to whether it is their best interest to sell the timber of said land at a private sale for the purpose of effecting a partition said land composing the estate of the minor heirs of Hannah Nelson decd. Said minors owning an undivided 4/14 interest in said real property, and to give any other advice touching the interest of said minors.

Now therefore I, J. W. Elder, Notary Public duly qualified and acting within and for Union parish, State of Louisiana, having caused to appear before me Rance Ellis, Hiram Montgomery, Jack Bilberry, Henry Bilberry and Sam Morgan all being the nearest relatives of said minors residing within the circle prescribed by law in such cases, and all of whom waive the three days notice prescribed by law and said members af after taking the oath subscribed to the oath at the beginning hereof proceeded at my office in the town of Farmerville, La. in Union parish to deliberate on the subject matter herein set forth and after mature consideration and deliberation said members unanimously recommended that all

Tutor and Under Tutor of the minor heirs of Hannah Bilberry-Nelson; wife of Branch Nelson; sister of Georgia Bellzora Bilberry-Ellis—Page 2

the merchanable pine, oak, cypress and gum timber on the real property as shown by the inventory taken this day before me, said Notary be sold for the purpose of effecting a partition between the minor heirs and majors and the tutor J. B. Nelson and for the further reason that now seems to be a good time for the selling of timber; the timber to bring a minimum price of $ 176:90 the amount of the inventoried value, the minors 4/14 of this amount to be used by their tutor for the purpose of giving the minor children a reasonable education and to care for and feed them and any reasonable expenses for their sustainance The major heirs and J. B. Nelson desiring a parition of the timber on the following land to wit: SE¼ of SW¼ & that part of SW¼ of SW¼ lying east and south of a certain branch & N½ of SW¼ sec. 9 & N½ of NW¼ sec. 16- Twp-22,1-East, said sale to be made at a private sale & the tutor is authorized & empowered to make and sign a deed to said timber for said minors.

In testimony whereof I have caused the members to sign hereto as well as the undertutor who was present during the deliberations and signs this proces verbal approving same and all sign in the presence of --- and ---- two good and lawful witnesses called for the purpose on this the day and date above written.

Attest:
R. L. Davis
Chas. B. Roberts

I hereby approve tha above.
 Sandy Goldsby, Undertutor.
J. W. Elder, Notary Public.

his
Rance (X) Ellis
mark
his
Hiram (X) Montgomery
mark
Jack Bilberry
Sam Morgan
 (X) his mark
Henry Bilberry

Succession of Hannah Bilberry-Nelson; wife of Branch Nelson; sister of Georgia Bellzora Bilberry-Ellis—Page 3

Notary Public, in and for said parish and state, directing, authorizing and commanding me to take an inventory and cause an appraisement to be made of all the property, real and personal, rights and credits, belonging to and composing the estate of minor heirs Hannah Nelson deceased, situated in Union parish, La. It being community property existing between deceased and his surviving spouse.

Now therefore I, J. W. Elder, Notary Public, duly qualified and acting within and for the said parish of Union and state of Louisiana, and being aided and assisted by Henry Bilberry and Sam Morgan two good and lawful male citizens residing in said parish and state, who after being duly appointed and sworn by me as appraisers proceeded at my office at the town of Farmerville, La. in the presence of J. M. Wallace and Chas. B. Roberts, two legal witnesses called for the purpose, to take said inventory and appraisement as hereinafter stated to wit:

REAL PROPERTY:
SE¼ of SW¼ & that part of SW¼ of SW¼ lying east and south of a certain branch & N½ of SW¼ sec. 9 & N½ of NW¼ sec. 16, twp. 22. 1 east. containing two hundred and thirty five acres more or less.
Land and improvements appraised at $ 411:50. Entire interest
Timber on above land appraised at $ 176:00 Entire interest.
Entire interest appraised at $ 587:50 Land and timber.
Minors interest being 4/14 of whole amounts to $ 167:14

PERSONAL PROPERTY:

10 milk cows	$ 70:00
3 mules	300:00 (three hundred)
10 hogs	20:00
House hold & kitchen furniture	75:00
Wagon	15:00
Farm tools	4:00

Entire interest personal property appraised at $ 584:00 (five hundred eighty four)
and minors interest being 4/22 of whole amounts to $ 166:85

Now therefore I, said J. W. Elder Notary, being aided and assisted as aforesaid, do make the following recapitulation to wit:

Total amount of real property brought forward $ 167:14

Total amount of personal property brought forward $ 166:85

Total amount of inventory $ 333:99
Three hundred & thirty three & 99/100 dollars.
Having completed the taking of said inventory and appraisement as aforesaid, we this day close this our proces verbal of same.
In testimony whereof I have caused said appraisers to sign their names hereto, on the day and date above written, in the presence of the aforesaid witnesses, who also sign with said appraisers and me, said J. W. Elder, Notary, and I have affixed my seal of office hereto authenticating this inventory.

Attest: J. M. Wallace   Henry Billberry
        Chas B. Roberts,   his
                                  Sam (X) Morgan
                                        mark
J. W. Elder.

ABSTRACT OF INVTY: Filed Jany. 20/ 06.
State of Louisiana, Parish of Union.
I, the undersigned legal authority, do hereby certify that the amount of the property belonging to and composing the estate of the minor heirs of Hannah Nelson decd. as shown by the inventory now on file in my office is the sum of one thousand one hundred seventy one and 50/100 dollars of which five hundred and eighty seven and 50/100 dollars is real property and five hundred and eighty four dollars is personal property. the personal property being described as follows to wit: SE¼ of SW¼ and that part of SW¼ of SW¼ lying east and south of a certain branch and N½ of SW¼ sec. 9 and N½ of NW¼ sec. 16 Twp. 22-R-1-East This property being all community property belonging to the deceased and her surviving spouse J. B. Nelson and the minors owning an undivided 4/14 interest.
Witness my hand and seal this the 20 day of January 1906.
                                  Edw. Everett,
                                  Clerk of court etc.

CERTIFICATE & ORDER APPOINTING TUTOR & UNDER TUTOR: Filed Jany. 20/ 06
Clerks office Fourth, District court,
Union parish.
State of Louisiana, Parish of Union, Fourth Dist. court.
I, E. L. Ramsey Dy. clerk of court do hereby certify that the abstract of inventory in the above entitled tutorship has been recorded in the mortgage records of Union parish La. as the law requires.
                                  E. L. Ramsey Dy. clerk of court.
The above and foregoing certificate and the application filed this day & the law considered it is hereby ordered that J. B. Nelson be appointed natural tutor to the said minors and that Sandy Goldsby be appointed under-tutor to said minors.
Witness my hand and seal of office this the 20th day of Jany. A. D. 1906
                                  Edw. Everett, clerk of court &c.

State of Louisiana, Parish of Union--- In Re minor heirs of estate of Hannah Nelson decd.

Personally came and appeared before me the undersigned authority J. B. Nelson, a resident of this parish, who having been by me duly sworn deposes and says that he will well and faithfully discharge and perform all the duties incumbent on him an tutor to the minor heirs of Hannah Nelson decd. So help him God.
                                  J. B. Nelson
Sworn to and subscribed before me at Farmerville, La. on this the 20th. day of January,1906
                                  J. W. Elder, Notary Public.

Succession of E. B. (Elza) Bilberry, Jr., son of E. B. Bilberry, Sr., and Mary Jane Honeycutt-Bilberry

Succession of E. B. Bilberry Jr.

To the Honorable the Judge of the 3rd District Court of La. holding session in and for Union Parish:—

The petition of J. Fletcher Sampler a resident of Union Parish, La., with respect would represent unto your Honl Court that E. B. Bilberry Jr., departed this life in your said parish on or about the 20th day of August 1897. leaving a small estate in your said Parish consisting of personal property also leaving debts due by him which are unpaid. Petitioner represents that he is a privileged creditor of said estate to the amount of about Three Hundred and Thirty five & 10/100 Dollars, That he has called upon the relatives of said deceased and requested them to apply to be appointed Administrator of said Estate and open same by due course of law. and they refuse to do so. He avers that said Estate should be opened by an administration and in due course of law— That some of the relatives have been disposing of some of said property without right or authority, and it is now necessary that said estate be administered upon in order to protect the creditors— Petitioner avers that he is the largest creditor and has the right, to be appointed administrator of said Estate; Wherefore petitioner prays, that this his application be advertised according to law and as the law requires, that there be an order appointing and commanding W. H. Heard a Notary Public in & for Union Parish to take an Inventory of said Estate, within ten days, and finally that he be appointed and qualified as the Administrator of said Estate and that Letters of Administration issue to him and that he be permitted to enter upon the discharge of said duties. He prays for orders that may become necessary in the premises and for general relief—

Everett & Everett.
Attys. for Petitioner

Land Deed
Horton Armstrong, Mamie Armstrong-Bohannon and Edna Armstrong-Ward Deed Land to Lawrence Bilberry

```
: : : : : : : : : : : : : :
No. 15575
Horton Armstrong et al                    :
To--Deed Land                             :
Lawrence Billberry                        :
: : : : : : : : : : : : : :    State of Louisiana, Parish of Union.
```

Know all men by these presents: That we, Horton Armstrong, whose wife is Laura Armstrong, and Mamie Bohannon, wife of Will Bohannon, all do hereby, by this act and these presents, sell, convey, and deliver unto Lawrence Billberry a resident of Union Parish, Louisiana, whose wife is Lula Billberry, the following described real property situated in Union Parish, Louisiana, to-wit:

All of my undivided interest in and to the East half of the South East quarter of the South West quarter of Section thirty-three, Township Twenty-three North Range 1 East, and the North East quarter of the North West quarter of Section four, township twenty-two North Range 1 East, containing 60 acres, more or less.

Now the consideration for which this sale is made is the sum and price of twenty-five ($25.00) dollars, each, cash in hand paid, the receipt whereof is hereby acknowledged.

To have and to hold the property above described and herein above sold to the person herein above named with full and complete warranty of title and full subrogation of all rights of action of warranty.

Thus done and signed on this the 19 day of Dec. 1923.

Attest: for Horton Armstrong

Norris Harrington
J. A. McMurry

Attest for Mamie Bohannon

Girdie Bohannon
H. E. Buckley
Morry Allem

Attest to Edna Ward

H. E. Dawkins
Billie Andrews

State of Louisiana, Parish of Union.

Before me, came and appeared Norris Harrington, who when sworn deposes that he is one of the attesting witnesses to the foregoing deed and that he saw the parties to the said deed, to-wit: Horton Armstrong, sign the same and that his signature is true and genuine.

Signed and acknowledged and sworn to   Thos. F. Wooten, Notary Public
before me this Dec. 19, 1923.   (seal)

State of Louisiana, Parish of Union

Before me, came and appeared H. E. Buckley, who when sworn deposes and says that he is one of the attesting witnesses to the signature of Mamie Bohannon, and that he saw her sign the same and that her signature is true and genuine and signed at the same time with affiant and his co-witness.

                              H. E. Buckley

Sworn to and subscribed before me on this 2 day of Aug. 1927.

                    R. W. Rhodes, Notary Public (seal)

State of Louisiana, Parish of Union

Before me, came H. E. Dawkins, who when sworn says he saw Edna Armstrong Ward who signed as Edna Ward sign the above deed and that her signature thereto is her true and genuine signature, signed in his and his co-witnesses presence.

                              H. E. Dawkins

Sworn to and subscribed before me this 3rd day of Aug. 1927.

                    Z. C. Rabun, C. D. C. & Notary Public   (seal)

A true and correct record on this the 3rd day of August A. D. 1927 at 9:53 o'clock A. M.

                                   D. C. &c

his
Horton X Armstrong
         mark

Mamie Bohanan
         mark

Edna Ward

Land Deed
Mattie Arbertha (daughter of Jack and Francis Bilberry); Gordie Burch, G. B. Bilberry, Georgia Bilberry and Thomas Gardner Deed Land to E. D. (Ed) Burch; Mattie and Gordie are daughters of Jack and Francis Bilberry; Georgia Bilberry is the wife of Henry Bilberry (Henry Bilberry was the son of Jack and Francis Bilberry); G. B. (Georgia Bellzora) Bilberry was Jack Bilberry's aunt. She married Lorenzo Ellis.

Source: 1900 U.S. Census Ward Six Union Parish; Union Parish Clerk of Courts; Interview with John Earl Ellis – August 2, 2010.

```
No. 55550            :
Mattie Arbertha, et al  :
To-Deed Land         :
E. D. Burch          :
:  :  :  :  :  :  :  :  :  :  :  :  :

Know all men by these presents, that we, Mattie Arbertha, Gordie Burch,  G. B. Bilbery,
Georgia Bilbery and Thomas Gardner, heirs of Francis Bilbery, deceased, for and in
consideration of the sum and price of Fifty Dollars, cash, the receipt of which we and each
of us hereby acknowledge, do by this act and these presents sell, deliver and convey unto
E. D. Burch, a resident of Union parish, Louisiana (once married and  now living with
Odessa Elliott) the following described property located in Union parish, Louisiana, to-wit:

All the undivided interest which we and each of us own in and to the following property:

One strip of land 220 yards wide and 440 yards long on the west side of the SE¼ of NW¼

of Section 22 in Twp. 22 North of Range 1 East, containing 20 acres, more or less, with

all improvements thereon located.

To have and to hold said property unto said E. D. Burch, his heirs and assigns forever.

Done and signed on this the 10 day of Dec, 1939. in the presence of Orine Bright and
Celia Smith and Will Dan McNeelds, the undersigned competent witnesses.

Attest:

        Orine Bright                    Mattie Arbertha
                                        Gordie Burch
        Celia Smith                     G. B. Bilbery
                                        Georgia Bilbery
        Will Dock Fields                Thomas Gardner
                                        E. D. Burch

State of Louisiana, Parish of Union.
```

(William) McDuel Bilberry Family Group Sheet with First Wife Mary Simmons
E. B. Bilberry was born circa 1827 and was deceased circa 1920
Courtesy of Larry Edwards

Name	William McDuel BILBERRY	
Birth	abt 1807	North Carolina
Death	aft 1860	Morehouse Parish, Louisiana
Other spouses: Missouri J. BARRON		
Spouse	**Mary SIMMONS**	
Children		
1 F	**Mahalia BILBERRY**	
Birth	27 Oct 1829	Alabama
Death	15 Oct 1911	Marion, Union Parish, Louisiana
Spouse	Miller Bledsoe EDWARDS	
Marriage	abt 1860–61	
Spouse	Elisha BRASHIER	
2 F	**Frances BILBERRY**	
Birth	14 Nov 1830	
Death	14 Jun 1907	
3 M	**Elza B. BILBERRY**	

(William) McDuel Bilberry Family Group Sheet with Second Wife Mary Simmons
Courtesy of Larry Edwards

Name	William McDuel BILBERRY	
Birth	abt 1807	North Carolina
Death	aft 1860	Morehouse Parish, Louisiana
Other spouses: Mary SIMMONS		
Marriage		Dallas County, Alabama
Spouse	**Missouri J. BARRON**	
Children		
1 M	Henry BILBERRY	
2 M	James M. BILBERRY	
3 F	Nancy A. BILBERRY	
4 F	Georgia Ann BILBERRY	

Notes for William McDuel BILBERRY

Found the purchase of 79.725 acres of land on 2 Sep 1839 in Alabama Land Records.
Found McDuel Bilberry in 1840 U.S. Census for Alabama.

The 1860 U.S. Census for Morehouse Parish, Louisiana, shows a household headed by a McD Bilberry, age 53, born in North Carolina. There were 3 children in the household: Henry, age 11; James M., age 9; Nancy, age 7; and Georgia Ann, age 5. The next household was head by a M. Brazier (Brashier), female, age 30, with 2 children: McDuel and Mary. Assuming this M. was Mahalia Bilberry, daughter of McDuell.

Found in the Louisiana Land Records the purchase of 119.81 acres of land on 1 Sep 1852 by a McDuel Bilberry.

Mahalia Bilberry Family Group Sheet with First Husband Elisha Brashier
Courtesy of Larry Edwards

Name	Elisha BRASHIER	
Birth	1828	Tennessee
Death	14 Dec 1852	Union Parish, Louisiana
Burial		Meridian Cemetery, Union Parish, Louisiana
Spouse	**Mahalia BILBERRY**	
Birth	27 Oct 1829	Alabama
Death	15 Oct 1911	Marion, Union Parish, Louisiana
Burial		Edwards Cemetery, Union Parish, Louisiana
Father	William McDuel BILBERRY (~1807->1860)	
Mother	Mary SIMMONS	
Other spouses: Miller Bledsoe EDWARDS		
Children		
1 F	**Mary Jane BRASHIER**	
Birth	18 Sep 1852	
Death	14 Aug 1887	
Spouse	Jessie BRANTLEY	
2 M	**Mack D. BRASHIER**	
Birth	23 Sep 1850	
Death	8 Mar 1918	

Notes for Elisha BRASHIER

Found Elisha Brashier and Mahalia Brashier in the 1850 U.S. Census for Union Parish, Louisiana. Elisha was 23 years of age and born in Tennessee; Mahalia was 21 and born in Alabama.

Notes for Mahalia BILBERRY

The 1860 U.S. Census for Morehouse Parish shows a household headed by M. Brashier with 2 children, McDuel, age 9, and Mary, age 7. From this listing, I am assuming that Mahalia had 2 children by her late husband, Elisha Brashier or Brasher.

Found land owneship in Patent Map 4, T23-N R1-3. Issued 1853.

Found that Mahalia Bilberry Brashier and Elisha Brashier may have had a daughter, Mary Jane, born 18 June 1852 and died 14 Aug 1887. Buried in Edwards Cemetery. The 1880 U.S. Census for Union Parish shows a household headed by Jesse W. Brantley and wife Mary J., age 28. Mary J. could be Mary Jane Brashier, daughter of Mahalia and Elisha Brashier.

Found in the 1860, 1870, 1880, 1900, and 1910 U.S. Censuses.

Mahalia Bilberry Family Group Sheet with Second Husband Miller Bledsoe Edwards
Courtesy of Larry Edwards

Name	Miller Bledsoe EDWARDS	
Birth	8 Nov 1813	Oglethorpe County, Georgia
Death	5 Mar 1897	Marion, Union Parish, Louisiana
Burial		Edwards Cemetery, Union Parish, Louisiana
Religion	Protestant - Baptist	
Father	Reuben Lemuel EDWARDS (1785-1869)	
Mother	Nancy BLEDSOE (1787-1854)	
Other spouses: Mary Ann WATTERS		
Marriage	abt 1860-61	

Spouse	Mahalia BILBERRY	
Birth	27 Oct 1829	Alabama
Death	15 Oct 1911	Marion, Union Parish, Louisiana
Burial		Edwards Cemetery, Union Parish, Louisiana
Father	William McDuel BILBERRY (~1807->1860)	
Mother	Mary SIMMONS	
Other spouses: Elisha BRASHIER		

Children

1 F	Francis Mahalia EDWARDS	
Birth	8 Feb 1862	Union Parish, Louisiana
Death	Oct 1919	Marion, Union Parish, Louisiana
Spouse	Joseph HUDSON	
Marriage	7 Jan 1882	Union Parish, Louisiana

2 M	Elza (Elzy) Alonzo EDWARDS	
Birth	1 Apr 1863	
Death	15 Aug 1886	Marion, Union Parish, Louisiana
Spouse	Sarah Ann Elizabeth ALBRITTON	
Marriage	25 Nov 1884	Union Parish, Louisiana

3 M	Perry Claiborne EDWARDS	
Birth	9 Apr 1866	
Death	1 Feb 1943	Marion, Union Parish, Louisiana
Spouse	Rosannah (Fannie) BRANTLEY	
Marriage	4 Jan 1888	Union Parish, Louisiana

4 M	Ellenborough (E. B.) EDWARDS	
Birth	22 Dec 1869	
Death	25 Oct 1937	Farmerville, Union Parish, Louisiana
Spouse	Mary S. (Mollie) SCARBOROUGH	
Marriage	23 Jan 1890	Union Parish, Louisiana

Notes for Miller Bledsoe EDWARDS

Miller Edwards moved his family from Talladega County, Alabama between 1845 and 1846.

The 1840 United States Census shows that Miller Edwards lived in Talladega Country, Alabama.
The 1840 U.S. Census shows the following in the household: Males: Under 5, 2; 5-10, 1; 10-15, 1; 15-20, 2; 20-30, 1; 30-40, 1; and 40-50, 1. Females: Under 5, 2; 5-10, 1; 10-15, 1; 15-20, 1; 20-30, 1; and 30-40, 1.

Miller Edwards was also found in the following U.S. Censuses for Union Parish, Louisiana:
1850, 1860, 1870, and 1880.

Marriage record of Miller Edwards and Mary Ann Watters found in marriage records of Perry County, Alabama. 23 Sept 1834; 1 Oct 1834.

Police Jury Session, Union Parish, LA, 2 June 1845: Hands of Miller Edwards used to build road.

Registered Voter List, Union Parish, LA, 6 Sept 1867: Miller Edwards, #1518, page 46.

Notes for Mahalia BILBERRY

The 1860 U.S. Census for Morehouse Parish shows a household headed by M. Brashier with 2 children, McDuel, age 9, and Mary, age 7. From this listing, I am assuming that Mahalia had 2 children by her late husband, Elisha Brashier or Brasher.

Additional Notes for Mahalia Bilberry Family Group Sheet with Second Husband Miller Bledsoe Edwards
Courtesy of Larry Edwards

Name	**Miller Bledsoe EDWARDS**
Spouse	**Mahalia BILBERRY**

Notes for Mahalia BILBERRY (Continued)

Found land owneship in Patent Map 4, T23-N R1-3. Issued 1853.

Found that Mahalia Bilberry Brashier and Elisha Brashier may have had a daughter, Mary Jane, born 18 June 1852 and died 14 Aug 1887. Buried in Edwards Cemetery. The 1880 U.S. Census for Union Parish shows a household headed by Jesse W. Brantley and wife Mary J., age 28. Mary J. could be Mary Jane Brashier, daughter of Mahalia and Elisha Brashier.

Found in the 1860, 1870, 1880, 1900, and 1910 U.S. Censuses.

Appendix G

Extended Family Photo Collection

Raymond Menser; Son of Amanda Bright

Amanda (Mandy) Bright; Daughter of John and Mattie Bright

Mattie Bright; Wife of John Bright

Georgia Bilberry Wife of Henry Bilberry; mother of Jewell Bilberry

Hannah (Pat) Burch Wife of Rodell Burch, Sr.

John Bernard Honeycutt, Son of Austin Honeycutt
Courtesy of Julian Honeycutt

Columbus Billberry (tallest man) delivering ice to an Okmulgee Fish Market in Okmulgee, Oklahoma ; Son of Fred and Rosa Billberry

Sweet and Tommy Burch

Mary Morgan

Letha (Dolly) Burch-Julks with husband Andy Julks
Letha is the sister of Liza Burch-Roberts
Courtesy of Johnnie Campbell, Sr.

John Bishop Robinson
Deacon and Clerk at Meridian Baptist Church, Conway, Louisiana
First wife was Mary A. E. Eckles
Second wife was Frances Bilberry (Frances is the sister of Elzy B. Bilberry)

Emmitt and Johnnie B. Burch

Charley H. Roberts and Mary Havanah Smith-Roberts
Courtesy of Sandra Campbell

Charley H. Roberts on his 40th birthday with his box camera; he was a photographer
Courtesy of Sandra Campbell

Charley H. Robert and Mary Havanah Smith-Roberts' Daughters in their prime
Left to Right: Mary Lee, Robertine, Deanna, Orine
Courtesy of Sandra Campbell

Two Old African American Churches Southwest of Marion, Louisiana
Zion Watts Baptist Church   **Center Branch Missionary Baptist Church**
Courtesy of Benny Archie Courtesy of Benny Archie

299

Elder Ladell Bilberry

Sweet Lilly Primitive Baptist Church former Pastors

Elder Rich Thrower

Elder J. B. Bilberry

Elder L. R. Thrower

Elder Ben Hayes

Adell Montgomery   **Caroline Warren**

Standing: Left to Right is Johnnie M. Montgomery-Nelson – daughter of Adell and Lucile-Loyd Montgomery; and Lizzie Warren – daughter of Mary Lee Warren. Sitting: Mary Lee Warren — granddaughter of Lura Bridges; Lura Bridges is the aunt of Frank Bilberry. Mary turned 90 years old in 2010.

Branch and Hannah Bilberry-Nelson Family
Hannah is the sister of Georgia (Aunt Puss) Bilberry
Branch taught school at Antioch Community School

At the bottom of the picture Left to Right: Rudolph Nelson, and Adell Nelson
Sitting in the middle Left to Right: Jordan Branch Nelson, Hannah Bilberry-Nelson
Standing Left to Right: Etta Nelson, Raymond Nelson, Torre Nelson, Lavonia Nelson, Annie Bell Nelson

Sandy Wayne, Jr. Family
Sitting Left to Right: Georgia Ann Wayne, Moses Wayne, Fannie Wayne-Young, Sandy Wayne, Jr.

Standing in back Left to Right: John Wayne, King Wayne, Thomas Wayne

Glossary of Genealogical Terms

Ancestor – A person you descended from; also known as a progenitor.

Census Record – The census is an official record of the population. The U.S. Federal Census was first taken in 1790, and has been taken every decade thereafter. U.S. Federal Census records are confidential for 72 years, so the latest census records available for public view are from 1930. Census record details may include: name, family members, age, state or country of birth, parents' birth places, year of immigration, address, marriage date and status, occupation, etc.

Certificate – An official document typically issued by the government recording an event. Example: birth certificate.

Certified copy – A copy of a document certified as a true copy of the original by some authority with a seal, signature, or stamp.

Church Record – Religious institutions keep official records about their congregations and important events like christenings, baptisms, marriages, and burials. Details may include: name of person, event type, date, and location, name of church and/or parish, and witnesses.

Circa – Estimated date. Example: circa 1940.

Collection – A compilation of records distinguished by source, record type, or other criteria.

Decade – A period of ten years. The U.S. Census was taken every decade beginning in 1790.

Deceased – A person that has passed away.

Descendant – A person whose descent can be traced to a particular individual or group.

Family Group Sheet – A basic form containing information about a family unit (parents and children); dates and locations of vital events that typically include birth, marriage, and death.

Family Tree – Visualization of ancestry or pedigree.

Genealogy – The study of family history.

Generation – People/offspring, of the same or approximate age group, living at the same time.

Heir – Someone entitled to receive an inheritance. Inheritance may include: property, possessions, titles, etc.

Intestate – The condition of a deceased person's estate if no "Will" was executed.

Land Patent – This is the transfer of property title from government to the first private owner/titleholder of a piece of property.

Land Record – Indicates that a piece of property is owned by a particular person; also, known as a deed. Details may include: name of owner, location, purchase date, sell price and/or period of ownership.

Maternal – Descending from your mother's line.

Newspaper Record – Information about a person or event printed in a local, state, or country-wide publication. This could record an ancestor's personal achievement, participation in a club, activity, or other notable event.

National Archives and Records Administration – is an independent organization located in Washington, D.C. It is responsible for keeping and preserving the nation's records. It houses important historical documents like the Constitution, Declaration of Independence and Bill of Rights as well as many collections of interest to family historians including: military records, immigration records, passenger lists, naturalization records, census records, photographs, and more.

Obituary Record – Record of a person's death. Obituaries typically are written by an immediate family member to commemorate the life of the deceased, and relay information about funeral arrangements to the community. These records are printed in local newspapers and may include: name of the deceased, death date, city/state of residence, family members, notable achievements, date and place of funeral; also known as an 'obit'.

Oral History – Facts, traditions, and stories passed from one generation to the next by word of mouth.

Occupation – Is the type of work that a person does. Example: carpenter; also known as a profession.

Paternal – Descending from your father's line.

Pedigree Chart – A list of ancestors, records of ancestry, family tree in a basic chart that tracks the family's tree (e.g., siblings, parents, uncles, aunts, grandparents, great-grandparents). Each new generation adds another branch to the tree.

Primary Source – A first-hand account of a particular event. Primary sources may include written letters, personal interviews, speeches, diaries, etc.; also known as an original source.

Public Record – Information recorded by local, state, or federal government agencies that is available to the public (e.g., vital records and court records).

Probate Record – A court record that relates to a deceased person's "Estate" or "Will"; this record may be a: will, estate inventory, list of heirs, etc.

Secondary Source – A second-hand account of a particular event; secondary source interpret and summarize information based on primary sources, and other secondary sources, not personal experience. Secondary sources may include: newspaper articles, television, websites, textbooks, etc.

Surname – Also, known as last name or family name.

Veteran – A person who has served on active duty in the armed forces and was discharged or released.

Vital Record – Records of important life events including birth, death, marriage, and divorce. Details may include: name, date of event, parents, and spouse.

Notes Within Chapters

Chapter One: Brief History of Union Parish

1. Some Slaveholders and Their Slaves Union Parish, Louisiana 1839-1865, Harry F. Dill and William Simpson, published by Heritage Books, Inc. 1997
2. Union Parish, Louisiana: Union Parish, Louisiana, Bernice, Louisiana, Spearsville, Louisiana, Marion, Louisiana, Farmerville, Louisiana, and Lille, Louisiana; published by LLC, Memphis, Tennessee, USA in 2010

Chapter Two: My Visit to the Old Home Place

3. Joe Frank Bilberry and Emma Roberts – Marriage License of Union Parish, Louisiana Clerk of Court (see Appendix B); Papa Frank's name was written in the marriage license as Joe F. Bilberry; witnesses for the marriage ceremony were Sumly McGee, James McGee and John Burch
4. Land Purchase, Union Parish, Louisiana Clerk of Court
5. Ladell Bilberry and Maggie Washington – Marriage License of Union Parish, Louisiana Clerk of Court (see Appendix B); witnesses at this marriage were Mose Simmons, Lee Roberts and Abraham Ewing. Willie Bilberry, the uncle of Ladell Bilberry, witness the purchase of the license. Maggie Washington and her parents name were spelled Watson instead of Washington
6. Louisiana Secretary of State, Vital Records (see Appendix A)
7. A Pictorial Handbook and History of the Founders of the Sweet Lilly Primitive Baptist Church, Sarah Ellis and John Earl Ellis; this book was made by the church to document the founding members and officers of the church
8. Ibid., pg. 2
9. Ibid., pg. 2
10. Ladell Bilberry and Corene McGough – Marriage License of Union Parish, Louisiana Clerk of Court (see Appendix B); witnesses at this marriage were Gordie Thomas, Louis G. Roberts and Charlie Roberts; J. D. Reeves witness the purchase of the license
11. This entry was posted in Primitive Baptists, church history. Bookmark the permalink.

Chapter Three: The End of Jim Crow Education: My Educational Journey

12. www.townofmarion.com
13. http://en.wikipedia.org/wiki/Plessy, paraphrased
14. Ibid., 36

Chapter Four: Daddy's Smoking Caught up with Him

No Endnotes

Chapter Five: Researching Family History: Many Branches, Several Leaves and Two Colors

15. Photo and caption – Monroe News Star – Monroe, Louisiana
16. Photo and caption – Las Vegas Review Journal – Las Vegas, Nevada
17. U.S. Census Bureau – Washington D.C. – Population of the United States in 1870 and 1880 – Union Parish, Louisiana
18. Ibid
19. wikipedia.org/wiki/United States Census)
20. U.S. Census Bureau (Washington D.C., Population of the United States in 1900), Union Parish, Louisiana; Frank Bilberry was counted in the household of Alcandor and Ada Ewing on June 1900; three months later Joe Frank Bilberry married Emma Roberts on September 1900
21. Marriage License, Union Parish, Louisiana Clerk of Court (see Appendix B); one of the witnesses was Bill George
22. U.S. Census Bureau ,Washington D.C., Population of the United States in 1900, Union Parish, Louisiana
23. Horton Armstrong, et al. – To Deed Land to Lawrence Billberry. Others mentioned in this deed were Lula Billberry, Mamie Bohannon, Edna Armstrong-Ward, Laura Armstrong, Will Bohannon and Girdie Bohannon. Note: Mamie, Edna and Horton are half-brother and sisters of Lawrence Bilberry
24. Meridian Missionary Baptist Church Minutes in Union Parish, Louisiana, 1856-1976, Louisiana Tech University Library special collection in Ruston, Louisiana (see Appendix E)
25. Edwards Family Group Sheet (see Appendix F)
26. Elizabeth Fox-Genovese – Within the Plantation Household: Black and White Women of the Old South, p. 86
27. Administration of Mary Feazle-Honeycutt's Estate and Alfred Honeycutt Interrogation, Union Parish Clerk of Court
28. Louisiana Secretary of State, Vital Records (see Appendix A); there is a slave name Jordan mentioned in the interrogation transcript of Alfred Honeycutt in the Hunt County, Texas Court on page 61
29. Jordan and Mattie Carson – Marriage License of Union Parish, Louisiana Clerk of Court (see Appendix B); witnesses at this marriage were J. C. Menser, M.L Menser and R.J Rodgers
30. State of Arkansas, State Board of Health, Bureau of Vital Statistics (see Appendix A)

31. U.S. Census Bureau, Washington D.C., Population of the United States in 1870, Union Parish, Louisiana

32. Ouachita Parish Deed – A. J. Morgan to John Honeycutt recorded on Book No. F, Page No. 137

33. Lorenzo Ellis and Belzora Bilberry – Marriage License of Union Parish, Louisiana Clerk of Court (see Appendix B); witnesses at this marriage were Dock McHenry, Elisha Smith and Branch Nelson

34. U.S. Census Bureau – Washington D.C, Population of the United States in 1900 – Union Parish, Louisiana

35. Andrew Billingsley, Black Families in White America, Englewood Cliffs, New Jersey: Prentice-Hall, Inc. 1968, p. 69

36. Vincent Harding, There Is a River: The Black Struggle for Freedom in America, San Diego: Harcourt Brace Jovanovich Publishers, 1981, reprint, Harvest/HBJ, 1992, pp. 260

37. http://wiki.answers.com What was the Freedman's Bureau

38. http://usgwarchives.net/la/lafiles.htm

39. Michael J. Klarman, From Jim Crow to Civil Rights: The Supreme Court and the Struggle for Racial Equality (Oxford University Press, 2004); Shawn Leigh Alexander: "The Afro-American Council and its Challenge of Louisiana's Grandfather Clause" in Chris Green, Rachel Rubin and James Edward Smethurst, eds., Radicalism in the South since Reconstruction (New York: Palgrave Macmillan, 2006)

40. Lerone Bennett, Jr., Before The Mayflower: A History of the Negro in America 1619-1964 (revised edition), pg. 234-235

41. Michael J. Klarman, From Jim Crow to Civil Rights: The Supreme Court and the Struggle for Racial Equality (Oxford University Press, 2004); Shawn Leigh Alexander: "The Afro-American Council and its Challenge of Louisiana's Grandfather Clause" in Chris Green, Rachel Rubin and James Edward Smethurst, eds., Radicalism in the South since Reconstruction (New York: Palgrave Macmillan, 2006)

42. United States Social Security Administration Application (see Appendix F)

43. Isaac and Angeline Douglas Marriage License, Union Parish, Louisiana Clerk of Court (see Appendix B); witnesses at this marriage were R. Cooper and Lee Roberts. Note; Angeline listed Jordan Billberry as her father

44. Ibid., (see Appendix B)

45. Louisiana Secretary of State, Vital Records (see Appendix A)

46. Willie Frank and Lettie Bilberry Marriage License, Union Parish, Louisiana Clerk of Court (See Appendix B); Willie was formerly married to R. D. Andrews; witnesses were Link Warren and Etta Warren

47. Ibid., (see Appendix B)

48. Ibid., (see Appendix B)

49. Ladell and Corene Bilberry Marriage License, Union Parish, Louisiana Clerk of Court (see Appendix B)

50. Family Obituary Collection (see Appendix D)

51. Ibid., (see Appendix D)

52. Family Obituary Collection (see Appendix D)

53. Louisiana Secretary of State, Vital Records (see Appendix A and F)

54. Anderson and Dela (Delia) Thompson Marriage License Application, Union Parish, Louisiana Clerk of Court (See Appendix B);both are listed as Ed Thompson's parents on Ed Thompson's marriage license. Ed Thompson is listed as the uncle of Ladell Bilberry (see Ladell Bilberry's Obituary in Appendix D)
55. Barbra J. Bilberry, phone interview by author, October 2010. Barbra often visited her grandmother Emma Bilberry and would ask her questions about her grandfather, Frank Bilberry's mother and father
56. Louisiana Secretary of State, Vital Records (see Appendix A); Norsis is mentioned as the mother of Lawrence Bilberry and Bridges Bilberry (possibly Britten Honeycutt) is listed as the father. Norsis Armstrong who was married to Fred Armstrong is possibly his mother

CHAPTER SIX: Mama's Death
No Endnotes

CHAPTER SEVEN: What They Knew: Oral History Interviews
No Endnotes

CHAPTER EIGHT: Adell and Johnny Bilberry's – Retirement Party Where is the D'Loutre River? Three Sisters Visit the Old Family Home Site near Marion, Louisiana
No Endnotes

CHAPTER NINE: Remembering Our Heritage

CHAPTER TEN
Short Biographies
More on the Honeycutt's and their Extended Families
No Endnotes

CONCLUSION
57. Andrew Billingsley, Black Families in White America (Englewood Cliffs, New Jersey: Prentice Hall, Inc. 1968), 39

LIST OF CHARTS AND ILLUSTRATIONS

The Illustrations included in this book are from the collections of the author, unless otherwise noted below. Additional copies of documents and credits are as follow:

1. State of Louisiana Map
2. Deed showing Land Purchased by Frank Bilberry in 1918, page 28: Union Parish, Louisiana Clerk of Courts
3. Frank Bilberry's Land Purchase receipt in 1918, page 29: Union Parish Clerk of Courts
4. Marion High School Belated Graduation, page 35: Monroe, Louisiana News-Star
5. Marion High School Belated Graduation, page 36: Las Vegas Review- Journal, Las Vegas, Nevada
6. Alfred Honeycutt's application for administration of Mary Feazle-Honeycutt's Estate, page 55: Union Parish, Louisiana Clerk of Courts
7. Alfred Honeycutt's appointment as administrator of Mary Feazle- Honeycutt's estate, page 56: Union Parish, Louisiana Clerk of Courts
8. Fragment of 1870 U.S. Census, Union Parish Ward Six, Union Cross Road (Oakland, Louisiana), page 66
9. Horton Armstrong, Mamie Armstrong-Bohannon and Edna Armstrong-Ward Deed Land to Lawrence Bilberry, page 297: Union Parish, Louisiana Clerk of Courts
10. Mattie Arbertha, Gordie Burch, G.B Bilberry, Georgia Bilberry and Thomas Gardner Deed Land to E.D Burch, page 298: Union Parish, Louisiana Clerk of Courts

BIBLIOGRAPY

PRIMARY SOURCES

Bureau of the Census 1860 – Union Parish, Louisiana Slave Schedule – Washington, D.C

Bureau of the Census – *The Ninth Census of the United States* – Washington, D.C: Population of the United States in 1870

Bureau of the Census – *The Tenth Census of the United States* – Washington, D.C: Population of the United States in 1880

Bureau of the Census – *The Twelfth Census of the United States* – Washington, D.C.: Population of the United States in 1900

Bureau of the Census – *The Thirteenth Census of the United States* – Washington, D.C.: Population of the United States in 1910

Bureau of Land Management – General Land Office of the United States Register of Land Office at Ouachita, Louisiana in 1837

Bureau of Land Management – General Land Office of the United States Register of Land Office at Monroe, Louisiana in 1852

Bureau of Land Management – General Land Office of the United States Register of Land Office at Monroe, Louisiana in 1862

Bureau of Land Management – General Land Office of the United States Register of Land Office at New Orleans, Louisiana in 1892

Bureau of Land Management – General Land Office of the United States Register of Land Office at New Orleans, Louisiana in 1902

Bureau of Land Management – General Land Office of the United States Register of Land Office at New Orleans, Louisiana in 1908

Bureau of Land Management – General Land Office of the United States Register of Land
Office at Baton Rouge, Louisiana in 1913

Meridian Missionary Baptist Church Minutes – Louisiana Tech University, Prescott Memorial Library – Special Collections, Manuscript and Archives

State of Louisiana – State Board of Health – Bureau of Vital Statistics – *Certificate of Death*

Social Security Administration – *Application For Social Security*

State of Arkansas – State Board of Health – Bureau of Vital Statistics – *Certificate of Death*

State of California – Certification of Vital Records – County of San Joaquin – Stockton, California – *Certificate of Death*

State of Louisiana – Parish of Union – Union Parish Clerk of Court – *Marriage License*

State of Washington – Department of Health Vital Records – Public Health-Seattle and King County Vital Statistics – *Certificate of Death*

INTERVIEWS

Andrews, Willis – Phone Interview by author – December 2010

Bilberry, Jesse Bernard, Jr., – Phone Interview by author – December 2010

Bilberry, Jessie Mae – Interview by author – July 2010

Bilberry, Paul – Interview by author – 1997

Ellis, John Earl – Interview by author – July 2010

Johnson, Lucy Nell – Interview by author – July 2010

Waters, Clara – Interview by author – September 2010

Wayne, Leola – Interview by author – July 2010

JOURNALS AND PUBLICATIONS

Family Search – *Freedman's Bank Records* – Family History Resource File – The Church of Latter Day Saints

Heritage Quest – *1870 U.S. Federal Census* – Generation Archives

Union Primitive Baptist Association of Arkansas and Louisiana – *Minutes of the One Hundred Twenty Second Annual Session at Pine Grove Primitive Baptist Church, Strong, Arkansas* – September 9, 10, 11, 2005

Sweet Lilly Primitive Baptist Church – *Pictorial Handbook and History of the Founders of the Sweet Lilly Baptist Church, Marion, Louisiana*

NEWSPAPERS

Monroe News-Star, Monroe, Louisiana

Las Vegas Review Journal, Las Vegas, Nevada

WEBSITES

Usgwarchives.net/la/union

Familysearch.org

Ancestry.com

BOOKS

Balmer, Randall – Mine Eyes Have Seen the Glory A Journey Into The Evangelical Subculture In America – New York: Oxford University Press, 2000

Bennett, Jr., Lerone – *Before the Mayflower* – Chicago: Johnson Publishing Company, 1983

Billingsley, Andrew – *Black Families in White America* – Englewood Cliffs, New Jersey: Prentice-Hall, 1968

Books, LLC – *Union Parish, Louisiana, Bernice, Louisiana, Spearsville, Louisiana, Marion, Louisiana, Farmerville, Louisiana, Lillie, Louisiana, Downsville, Louisiana, Junction City, Louisiana.* Memphis: Books LLC, 2010

Brown, Jr., Canter and Brown, Barbara Gray – *Family Records of the African American*

Pioneer of Tampa and Hillsborough County – Tampa: University of Tampa Press, 2003

Dill, Harry F. and Simpson, William – *Some Slaveholders and Their Slaves Union Parish Louisiana 1839-1865* – Bowie, Maryland: Heritage Books, Inc., 1997

Gibson, Lyle E. *Black Tie White Tie Chronicle of an American Family 1739-1940* – Kansas City, Kansas: Cushani Publishing, Inc., 2002

Hatcher, Patricia Law – *Producing a Quality Family History* – Salt Lake City: Ancestry, Inc., 1996

Perkins, Spencer and Rice, Chris – *More Than Equals Racial Healing for the Sake of the Gospel* – Downers Grove, Illinois: Intervarsity Press, 2000

Scruggs, Afi-Odelia E. – *Claiming Kin Confronting the History of an African American Family* – New York: St. Martin's Press, 2002

Wiencek, Henry – *The Hairstons An American Family in Black and White* – New York: St. Martin's Griffin, 2000

Yates, Susan and Ioannou, Greg – *Publish Your Family History Preserving Your Heritage in a Book* – Toronto: Dundurn Press, 2010

Last Name Index

Term Index